Working Together in Children's Services

Related titles:

Partnerships for Inclusive Education
A Critical Approach to Collaborative Working
Liz Todd
978–0–415–29844–5 (hbk)
978–0–415–29845–2 (pbk)
978–0–203–96749–2 (ebk)

The New Early Years Professional
Dilemmas and Debates
Edited by Angela D. Nurse
978–1–84312–423–8

Developing Early Years Practice
Linda Miller, Carrie Cable and Jane Devereux
978–1–84312–317–0

IMPROVING THE HUMAN CONDITION:

A Curricular Response to Critical Realities

Prepared by the
ASCD 1978 Yearbook Committee.

James John Jelinek,
Chairperson and Editor.

Association for Supervision and
Curriculum Development,
Suite 1100, 1701 K Street, Northwest,
Washington, D.C. 20006.

Stock Number: 610-78132
Library of Congress Catalog Card Number: 77-94464
ISBN 0-87120-088-0

Contents

Foreword

Elizabeth S. Randolph

Charles A. Lindbergh once observed that the possibility of a nuclear holocaust which would end the world had been plucked from the indefinite future and placed like a burning coal into the hands of his generation. The writers of the ASCD 1978 Yearbook take a long look at some of the burning coals that society, and most specifically those who educate the future citizens of our society, must juggle successfully if we are to survive.

The complexities of issues facing an increasingly interdependent world are examined, and curricular responses to increasingly critical realities are suggested. The issues are future-oriented, but necessitate action now. The role assigned to the schools is to provide training in analytical thinking, to bring the future into what we do in schools. We must "bring future consequences into the personal awareness of the young, and help them to develop their reflective, rational skills for engaging in cogent decisions that go beyond the material gratifications of a free enterprise technology."

What will be the nature of a future-oriented curriculum? Among other things is proposed an interdisciplinary field of study of "consummate importance to man and his young" called Ekistics. The 1970 edition of the *World Book Dictionary* defines *Ekistics* as the study of the ecology of human beings in settlements. It draws concepts and values from the social sciences, the humanities, and the sciences.

In a penetrating discussion of what is needed to understand the global dimensions of citizenship, authors Abramowitz, Leighton, and Viederman quote Abraham Sirkin's key concepts "with which we will have to refurbish our minds" to live comfortably with ourselves and others. Although the entire list is intriguing, two of the concepts hardest or us to accept may be these . . . that we will live increasingly with major uncertainties and that not every problem has a solution.

Is curricular innovation equal to the realities discussed in the chapter on "Justice, Society, and the Individual": the realities of (a) lack of trust in other human beings, (b) increased friction and conflict among vastly multiplied human beings, (c) continuing loss of political integrity, (d) unprecedented increase in criminal behavior, decline in authentic interpersonal relationships between people? The authors take the position that curriculum substance and curriculum implementors both have the capacity to respond to these realities.

What is the role of schooling in a changing society? Authors Engle and Longstreet take the position that "accelerating change, multiplying information, and runaway technological analyses, reflective reasoning, and an increased independence from enculturating processes must take precedence over all other possible functions of schooling."

The distinguished contributors to the 1978 ASCD Yearbook, agreeing that technological and social change is outracing the educational system, apply their individual and collective insights to the critical realities of our day. Educators at every level will appreciate their suggestions for improving the human condition through curricular response to these realities.

We express appreciation to James John Jelinek, who served as chairperson of the committee responsible for this yearbook and also as its editor. We also thank the members of the committee and the writers of the several chapters. Without such a generous gift of professional time and thought, an analysis such as that presented here would not be available to us.

In my opinion, this yearbook is a fitting tribute to the genius and dedication of Robert R. Leeper, who is retiring after 28 years as editor for the association. ASCD is indebted to Dr. Leeper for publications which always have been in the finest traditions of journalism and of ASCD.

ELIZABETH S. RANDOLPH, *President 1977-78*
Association for Supervision and
Curriculum Development

1

Critical Realities
in School and Society

Arthur Hoppe

THE PEOPLE have always expected miracles of their schools. Every other social institution may be wavering in its moral stance, confused in its purposes, selfish in its behavior, immune to its negative effects on the public's welfare, or even coming apart at the seams; but the schools must resist all that. They must be stalwart and stable, committed to the highest ideals, teach all the basics and a great deal more to learners of all ages, attempt to correct all the social ills, and do it all at a modest cost. Granted, that many facets of our lives are vastly more improved than our forefathers might ever have dreamed. Granted, that educators essentially agree that personal and social improvements are the special work of the school. Still, the task does not rest solely with the school. It clearly is shared with such institutions as the home, the church, the media, the various levels and branches of government, business, industry, labor, the professions, and more. It is shared by many individuals and groups who wield such power as to shape the quality of life in the environments they pervade.

Yet, the school's role is unique. Its central function, its charge from society, is the education of its members, particularly the young, in such fashion that they may live in harmony with themselves, with each other, and with their several environments; that they might pursue their various purposes and solve their different problems with maximum regard for the freedom of each individual *and* for the collective welfare of everyone; that they approach life with the maximum possible optimism, so that their growing abilities to improve the human condition will gain power from the inclination to try.

What *are* the critical realities in school and society in these times? How can schools help society, particularly but not exclusively its young

1

members, identify those conditions and problems that are most crucial in human living? And more important, how best help them deal with these matters in such ways as to effect improvement, so that the experience of schooling will make a more and more significant difference?

The writers of this yearbook are firmly convinced that every school community should address these questions, and particularly now. It is more true today than ever that the schools dare not remove themselves from the arena of everyday life. It is a precarious position, at best, to say that art is taught for art's sake or math for math's sake or poetry for the sake of poetry or science for the sake of science or anything for its own sake alone. At worst it could be disastrous. All schooling, all teaching and learning, want a value base. In our society, that base is to be found in the enduring tenets of democracy, in the basic beliefs of the Judaic-Christian traditions, in our persistent concern for the optimum freedom and development of every individual together with the highest possible quality of human living for all groups and for society as a whole. So if art be taught in the schools, this is why; or math or science or history or literature or whatever. It is the *quality* of our living together that is enhanced by the best possible development of each individual. It is the quality of the experience that people have in school that helps them to develop personal meanings and judgments, and preferences for the true and the just, the good and the beautiful. Thus, it is the improvement of the human condition that is the special concern of those who deal with curriculum and instruction.

Until very recent times, and in the view of many professional educators even today, the subject approach to curriculum organization has characterized our schools almost exclusively. Each subject has had its allotted time slot in the school: each taught in its tight little compartment, each disconnected from and unrelated to every other subject. The task of the school seemed to be to ladle out appropriate doses of each subject to students every 50 minutes or so in the school day. Rarely did they have school experiences which required that they relate several subjects to each other, and apply them in concert to practical affairs in their daily lives. That some students have been able to do this, once out of school, attests to an intriguing aspect of human intelligence that schools generally have done very little to enhance. And yet the application of practical intelligence, to use Raup's concept,[1] has been the proclaimed goal of schooling for decades. How can students best be helped to understand the *uses* of knowledge, the *interrelationships* among the disciplines? How can they gain personal meaning, as against rote memory,

[1] R. Bruce Raup *et al. The Improvement of Practical Intelligence.* New York: Harper & Row, Publishers, 1950.

from what they do in school? How can they best learn that *the* reason for their being in school at all is to enable them to deal more and more effectively with the compelling interests and concerns and problems of their daily lives in their homes, in their total communities? The blending of the disciplines in the pursuit of personal needs and community concerns will have to become the common feature of curriculum and instruction in schools where teachers and students together are bent on improving the human condition. If this be their goal, there is no other way to it except to deal directly with *the critical realities* in school and society.

The Critical Realities

What *are* the critical realities? The answers may vary a bit from one observer to another. They are always screened through the observer's personal point of view, each individual's private store of experience, unique perceptions, and more. There may be arguments over definitions and emphases. There may be persistent differences from one community or one region to another, and from one period of time to another. If disputes over such matters arise, the important thing is that they be openly discussed, so that parents and teachers and students may reach some common understanding on items that are designated as critical for them in their own time and in their own world, and so are worthy of higher priority on the attention scale in school.

Change. The obvious and the most pervasive of all the critical realities on the scene today is *change*. Change is affecting every facet of our lives and seems to be accelerating day by day. Change is disturbing, unsettling, even painful to human beings; therefore many people accept change most reluctantly. Changes nourish one another and multiply. Changes have no moral controls except those applied by society. Each time the question is asked, could we do thus and so, the prior question ought to be, *should we*. Some changes seem inconsequential or almost automatic and inevitable: virtually beyond human control. Some are vastly more critical than others in their effects upon society. These latter should be singled out for special concern so that the directions they take will enhance the human condition. It is the responsibility of every person and every organization involved with change to see to it that the direction of the change is toward the greater good of man and his environment. This has not always been the case: and that is precisely the reason why the analysis of proposed or potential changes should come within the regular school curriculum, and why the ways and means of directing the course of change should be learned by every student in school. This is the road to *planning the future*. Young and old will have to examine the conspicuous conditions of our lives and appraise them against the basic values we hold. Needed changes will become clear enough, and the critical requirement of us all then will be the skill and the will to make them happen.

The Economy. The intricate web of activities and behaviors which are labeled "the economy" want special attention in curriculum and instruction. Ours is a "free" economy. People are free to produce goods and services, to sell and to buy as they wish, to profit however much they can from such enterprise, and to reinvest their savings as they choose. The results from this system are not always in the best interests of all concerned. Needed improvements have their base in government, law and justice, in ecology, pollution and conservation, in a firm commitment to human values. One of the most disheartening conditions in the current economy is inflation—"stagflation," as Gunnar Myrdal called it, because of the odd phenomenon of spiraling prices along with growing unemployment.

Although concerted efforts at balance have been made, unemployment percentages are still larger among minority groups and among the young; with the introduction of an unpredicted hazard, we find educated persons even with advanced degrees and leadership skills now out of work. A survey of unemployed persons in four major cities conducted by the United States Department of Labor revealed that 75 percent were still not working even four months after receiving the last of their unemployment benefits. Prices seem to go only one way—up. The increases often seem unrelated to the rise in wages in most sectors. The local public telephone increased in cost by 100 percent. A pound of coffee or meat may go up in price by 20 or 30 cents at a time, not by a few pennies; the proportion applies to most products and most services. At the close of 1975, the Chicago Motor Club estimated that the cost of driving an automobile of intermediate or standard size 10,000 miles would run 22.5 cents or 24.8 cents per mile for the respective cars. A year or two before, it was estimated to be ten or twelve cents per mile. The average wage in most lines of work today seems like the fondest hope of workers of eight or ten years ago; but today it buys no more, and often less in the way of goods and services, than did the average wage of a decade before. About 25 percent of children in the United States live in families whose incomes are rated below the poverty level. Again, the percent *doubles* for children where women are heads of household and for minority families. Housing, illness and hospitalization, taxes, transportation: costs skyrocket, but salaries generally lag behind.

According to Galbraith, our persistent economic attitude has attached irrational importance to production of material goods.[2] This has led to uncontrolled economic expansion, to the worship of profits, to the generation of insatiable desires for *things*. Madison Avenue and the mass media have played their roles efficiently in the sustaining of that attitude. In addition to the artificial overstimulation of human wants, far more attention has been given to production and output than to the human condition of work and workers. There has been comparatively little effort to make work easier or more agreeable or more pleasant for the wage earner, although authorities have long realized the importance of such effort. It seems more and more difficult to identify a dynamic balance between private income and costs, or jobs and workers, or supply and demand. Is the enormous power of Big Labor, expressed in unionism, any better—or any worse—than the unbridled power of Big Management? In February of 1976, a conservative Chicago newspaper screamed fraud in the medical profession, to the tune of $3,000,000 in Medicaid and Medicare kickbacks to physicians. Private industries like Penn Central and Lockheed were able to secure federal subsidies running into millions of dollars. Lockheed was later accused of making multi-million dollar payoffs for business deals abroad.

Multinational corporations pose unique problems. These are companies that operate in at least six countries and have an annual sales volume of at least $100 million. In 1975, there were over 200 multi-national corporations with sales over one billion dollars per year. The potential for political influence, the actual power base, of such vast organizations is almost beyond the ken of ordinary citizens.[3] By their own admission, these economic giants dole out millions in bribery of one form or another: $1.25 million by United Brands in Honduras, nearly $5 million by Gulf Oil, $46 million by an Italian affiliate of EXXON over an eight-year period. Smaller nations, "developing" nations can hardly resist the dangle of jobs and money which the multinationals offer. But what have been the effects on the job market in the United States? What relation to periodic currency crises? To tax recoveries in host nations and to the exhaustion of their natural resources? Do jobs and dollars present mixed blessings to the unwary? Who will answer such questions—in the best interests of the common people of this generation, and the next, and the next?

There have been hopeful signs in such meetings as the North-South Dialogue—formerly the Conference of International Economic Coopera-

[2] John Kenneth Galbraith. *The Affluent Society*. Boston: Houghton Mifflin Company, 1958.

[3] See the January 24 and February 7, 1976 issues of *Saturday Review* for extended discussions of multinational corporations.

tion—the United Nations Conferences on Trade and Development, or the Dartmouth Conferences which have involved the United States and the Soviet Union since 1960 in a continuing series of policy discussions. The best solution will require international discussion. The critical decisions must involve those most affected by the decisions. The interdependence of nations in the economic sphere is one of the clear facts of modern industrial life: it is ignored by any nation only at its peril.

There are those who would argue that people do not discover new values and meanings in prosperous times, but only in times of oppression, of war or other crisis; that at such a time, men must fall back on basic cultural imperatives or rediscover values that had been represented during the good times. I am not sure this is historically correct: crisis evokes meanness as well as creativity; more important, "crisis" is itself a conception, a product of our conceptions, not a Kantian *a priori* proposition. The age of abundance has it grandeurs and miseries which are both like and unlike those of any other age, and the searching of aims and discovery of motives appropriate to our new forms of perils and opportunity, along with the discovery of ways to institutionalize our collective aspirations, seems to me the fundamental economic and metaeconomic task.[4]

This discussion is not meant to deny the positive contributions of a free economy to human life. They are many, and undeniable. But wherever the critical realities of modern economic activity cause human misery at home or abroad, wherever the wanton misuse and depletion of natural resources and human resources restrict the free development of a people, wherever political power that has grown out of economic advantage is exercised to the special benefit of the few for their continued profit: wherever such activities persist in the face of widespread human want and degradation, an entire population may be moved to make such radical changes as might endanger the total system. Strikes and demonstrations are one kind of reaction to such problems; total war is another. This is the compelling reason that urges looking beyond the positive advantages of a free economy and cries out for careful study of the critical issues and the economic realities of our time. As George Counts warned us several decades ago: "Only by achieving a union of economic stability and political liberty can our democracy hope to endure."[5]

Technology and Science. Where will it all end: in a great blazing white mushroom cloud, or in the most peaceful, just, creative, humane kind of life that has ever been known on this planet? Science has raised

[4] David Riesman. *Abundance For What? and Other Essays.* Garden City, New York: Doubleday & Company, Inc., 1964. p. 308. Copyright © by David Riesman. Reprinted by permission.

[5] George S. Counts. *Education and the Promise of America.* New York: Macmillan Publishing Co., Inc., 1945. p. 15.

the question; people must supply the answer. There are living today the largest collection of scientists the world has ever known: 90 percent of the research scientists who ever lived are living today. The strength of their method is attested in every facet of our lives. The application of science to technology has produced the automatic factory—producer of automatic wealth, some say—and has enabled men to walk in space and on the moon. One man with one machine can fairly fill a dump truck with a single bite of earth. We now have "pocket-size" television sets with two-inch screens, and "smart machines" which combine microprocessors (MPU) and memory chips into microcomputers inside such devices as watches, ovens, phones, scales—for automatic management of specific operations. In many secondary school classes in mathematics or physics, nearly every student has an electronic calculator: so popular, so inexpensive, so practically useful have these small miracles of science and technology become. Of course, the computer itself is one of the most wondrous products of our time. A few years ago the earlier computers could accomplish 20 million operations per second; a few years hence computers are slated to handle a billion operations per second. The laser has been a remarkable aid in the testing of metals; it might enable miracles in communication transfer; and it might generate an international race for the death ray. The splitting of the atom gave us the frightful bomb, but it has also provided an enormous source of energy for use in medicine, in transportation, and in supplying nuclear power to large urban areas. There has been much argument about the safety of nuclear power units. One long-experienced engineer with the Government Nuclear Regulatory Commission resigned to draw attention to the need for more certain safety measures in such power facilities. Finally, critical observers of the American scene, notably Dennis Gabor and Herman Kahn,[6] view thermonuclear war as the greatest single threat to the continuation of our life and culture.

Science and technology have provided modern miracles in the medical world, and this despite the bottleneck that rejects two out of every three applicants for medical school, and despite the malpractice suits that have produced individual awards in the millions of dollars while increasing insurance rates for medical doctors at a horrendous rate. Even so, people in this country are healthier and live longer than their ancestors did. The person who accidentally had a few fingers or even an entire arm completely severed from the body has a good chance of having those very members reattached by a modern surgical team and even regaining their use. People with mental-emotional disorders are not

[6] Dennis Gabor. *Inventing the Future*. New York: Alfred A. Knopf, Inc., 1963; Boyd R. Keenan. "The Great Kahn." *The Saturday Evening Post*. Winter 1973. p. 50.

viewed with side glances today except by the uninformed. The terribly depressed are now known to have a chemical imbalance in the body which can be counteracted quickly with one of several tricyclics or with lithium. Some 8,000,000 persons in the United States suffer the agony of severe depression and nearly three times that number are affected to a lesser degree. There is a new ray of hope for victims of Parkinson's disease, and perhaps cancer, in the use of levodopa (L-Dopa) to increase their comfort and life span. Recent work with neurotransmitters in the brain, such as enkephalin which relates to pain or norepinephrine which affects constriction of blood vessels, also holds promise for persons prone to stroke and certain mental illnesses. According to the University of Texas Health Science Center, one of the side effects of the use of methadone in the treatment of heroin addicts was a 40 percent reduction in arrests of such persons for theft or burglary. On the other hand, a study for the Drug Abuse Council of Washington, D.C., conducted by Norman Zinberg, M.D., found that among 54 persons who had been controlled users of heroin (chippers) for a minimum of two years and as many as 23 years, *none* had become addicted (biologically dependent) and *none* had ever resorted to crime to support this behavior.[7]

Do you need a new valve for a worn-out one—in your heart? Or a pacemaker to jolt a tired ticker? There is good hope now that such repairs can be made successfully; and for the liver, the pancreas, the ovary. There is talk too in the medical world, more serious than not, about "medical-electronic repair stations" and about "artificial" parts of the body made *better* than the originals.[8] And that is only the tip of a scary iceberg! Radical thinking already widespread plays with development of knowledge of DNA and cloning to suggest that it seems quite possible to repeat the most desirable characteristics of certain individuals, to engage in deliberate genetic planning for the kind of individuals we want, and to duplicate them for as many as we want. Brave New World! But wait. Experiments with "recombinant DNA" and artificial genes can not only modify existing forms but can provide wholly new genetic forms whose function and control scientists do not yet fully understand. Most such experiments have been carried out by using the familiar bacterium, Escherichia coli—or E. coli, which is universally found in human intestines. One terrifying possibility that haunts many people, including scientists, is the accidental transplanting of cancer genes into bacteria and their subsequent escape from the laboratory to invade human bodies. What price progress! There is even talk of push-button control of pain and computer linkup with the brain: all we need is a miniaturized com-

[7] Ronald Kotulak, Science Editor. *Chicago Tribune*. January 18, 1976.

[8] Alvin Toffler. *Future Shock*. New York: Bantam Books, Inc., 1970. Chapter 9.

puter implanted in the brain. Thus might one person gain control of a staggering store of knowledge and be able to perform hardly imaginable mental feats. The gap between science and science fiction is fast closing! But who shall decide? Who shall control? Shall we have ten thousand Mozarts or Gandhis? Or single out the very top quality individuals in all walks of life we wish to continue, and replicate them to the optimum population that would sustain the happiest human condition imaginable? Transplants and implants, enzymes and mutations, test tube babies, automation and cybernation, humanoids and cyborgs: who will control the forms; who will push the buttons; who will pull the strings? The critical question is *who?*

One of the more interesting developments of science and technology has been the use of solar energy for heating and cooling. This involves using the sun's rays to heat storage units and managing the release of the heat to warm houses and other buildings. Both heating and air conditioning can be accomplished with this system.[9] This has been the response of science and technology to the end of the era of cheap energy in the more familiar forms of electricity, fuel oil, and natural gas. Solar devices used for heating household water have been in use in thousands of homes in the United States and elsewhere in the world. Special house construction and insulation required generate costs that are very high for the average consumer. In 1976, such costs were estimated to be approximately $8,000 for one home installation. It would take many years of effective usage for such cost to average out so that it compared favorably with the cost of fuels commonly used today. But what of tomorrow? If the supplies of wood, coal, gas, and oil are exhausted and the generators stop, the higher cost of utilizing solar energy may become entirely reasonable.

These are but a few of the conspicuous contributions of science and technology to the realities of our time. There are many more. Shall we grow energy-producing organisms? Shall we colonize space if our world population gets hopelessly out of hand? Shall we extract thermal energy from the ocean or build cities under the sea? Who owns the ocean floor or the water above it? Who has first claim on the moon or the Milky Way or outer space? What are the legal, the moral, the human issues at stake?

Leisure and Work. For many millions of our people, work is dreadful drudgery. But mass production, automation, the assembly line, all the products of creative intelligence, will soon provide more leisure time than we yet know how to manage. Modern mass production has dulled the very senses of workers with its monotony and boredom. The inhuman conditions in many lines of work have produced a malaise that is

[9] John L. Wilhelm. "Solar Energy, the Ultimate Powerhouse." *National Geographic* 149:381-97; March 1976.

devastating to morale. Add to this the threat of unemployment and the condition becomes explosive. Every supervisor has a personal responsibility for the success of each worker in his or her group. It is patently inhuman for any supervisor to watch the work behavior of an employee reach the point where termination may be suggested without doing something positive about it beforehand. Management owes it to the worker to provide feedback on performance, positive or negative. Where work is inadequate, the employee has a right to know specific reasons, and if the reasons are valid and correctable should be given appropriate time and assistance to make the required improvements. Where there is no prior effort on the part of supervisors to identify worker problems and to help plan solutions—where, in fact, the worker may be totally unaware that anything is amiss—when the termination occurs the effects can be ruinous. The loss of self-confidence, the diminished self-image, the feeling that one is not needed or wanted becomes a personal tragedy no one can bear gracefully. It is an inhuman condition.

Recent events in the world have required many kinds of adjustments on the part of employees. When a company has an unusually large work force, the individual is easily lost in the mass. Economic retrenchment may require reduction in the labor group. Over 60 percent of the labor force are in service occupations, and their proportion is slated to go over 70 percent by 1980. Changing technology and variations in public demand will create entirely new lines of work—and eliminate some old ones. But alert business and industrial leaders have known for a long time the importance of being sensitive to the human condition of workers: their life-styles, preference for certain schedules, early morning or late evening for example, family obligations that must be met, personal problems, and more. The position of personnel counselor in large corporations has been growing in popularity and significance. Many companies recognize today what Roethlisberger established in his research at the Hawthorne Plant of Western Electric in 1939, namely that when workers have opportunities for responsible participation in decisions affecting their work, morale and production go up together.[10] We know that work can be made easier, but more important, it can be made more enjoyable. And the length of the working day will surely shorten. The continued applications of science and technology will see to that. Though it seems something of a contradiction, if our insatiable desire for more and more material things should one day abate that too would reduce

[10] Fritz J. Roethlisberger. *Management and Morale.* Cambridge, Massachusetts: Harvard University Press, 1941; Fritz J. Roethlisberger and William J. Dickson. *Management and the Worker.* Cambridge, Massachusetts: Harvard University Press, 1939.

the number of hours of work needed from each person. So the work week that was shortened from 60 or more to 48 hours and then to 40 and in some instances to 32 hours, could quite possibly be reduced to 24 hours in the not too distant future. Nearly ten years ago, in 1969, a tire company in Atlanta moved to a 32 hour week and continued the same pay schedule that had been in force for 40 hours of work. According to Dennis Gabor,

> The present sum of working hours in the West, especially in the United States, is in no way in conformity with the level of our technology. It is kept up artificially, in the first place by enormous defense expenditures and in the second place by waste. This is only partly a waste of products; to a much larger extent it is a waste in unproductive man-hours.

In fact he views the "Age of Leisure" as one important part of the "Trilemma" facing the Western world today. The other parts are nuclear war and overpopulation.[11]

In part, our survival will depend on learning to *work* with each other in peace, justice, harmony. If people can manage that, it will be possible to arrange working teams and otherwise share the available labor. If we can manage that, we may not be *required* to work for so long a portion of our waking hours. There can be time for serious study and creative application to one's work, or even to reeducation for a second or third career as that becomes desirable. And almost certainly, we shall have more time for travel, for recreation, for amusement, for continued study of a purely private or avocational nature. It may not be necessary that *all* persons work for the *whole* of their lives; there could be such study of our personal selves and our human interrelationships, such flourishing of the arts, such widespread satisfying of all the major needs and interests of people everywhere, such release of creative talent in all facets of our lives as might bring on a new Golden Age to rival that of Greece in the age of Pericles. And it could include all people the world over. Is this totally in the realm of wild-eyed fiction or the lunatic fringe of the intellectual? Will the atomic bomb or the population bomb or the product-materialism bomb get us first? Is it reasonable, after all, to suppose that people *can* plan their future and make it happen? More and more individuals today are answering that last question with a resounding *Yes*.

Communication. Our communication systems are rooted in cultures and sub-cultures, in the whole network of our human qualities. In the area of communication, our rights are defined and protected by law and our facility is enhanced by technology. The effectiveness of our com-

11 Dennis Gabor, *op cit.,* Copyright © 1963 by Dennis Gabor. Reprinted by permission of Alfred A. Knopf, Inc.

munication depends very much on selection of appropriate modes, on rigorous standards of accuracy and validity, and on good taste. Satisfactory communication depends as much on the competence and attitude of the receiver as it does on the sender.

Difficulties in every sphere of life often have one base in communication. People don't say what they mean. People don't interpret accurately what they hear. People don't listen. Whether at the bridge table or in the halls of Congress, individuals who should be listening are often preoccupied with planning the next remark *they* intend to make; or worse, they simply pay no attention at all. Listening is only partly a skill that can be learned; it is largely a matter of human respect. So conversation problems develop between parents and children, between students and teachers, employees and supervisors, government officials and their constituents, husbands and wives. On every hand, failures in communication lead to or compound other problems.

We are only beginning to examine the more subtle facets of communication. Open hostility is easy to identify, so is genuine attention or acceptance. Body language or nonverbal communication can reinforce what is being said out loud *or* it can deny the verbal message completely. Some persons develop a level of sophistication that enables them to say the most appropriate things whatever the situation. This might merely illustrate falsehood or fraud, but it could also demonstrate tact or sensitivity or concern. It is important for us all to be able to tell which is which, and to make the effort to do so.

Of all the *mass media,* television certainly enjoys the widest audience. Approximately 96 percent of our homes nationally have at least one television set. It is estimated that by the time students are graduated from high school, they will have spent approximately 12,000 hours in classes and 15,000 hours viewing television. In the latter, people are offered objective reporting of the news, almost literal involvement in historical moments of our time and other times, flesh and blood portrayals of great masterpieces of literature, and living contact with famous and infamous individuals. Often we are offered mass trash. It is important to be able to tell which is which, and to opt for such programs as we can take pride in, for those that represent the better elements of style and taste and integrity.

The actual effect of mass media on behavior of consumers may continue to be an issue for years to come. It has been the growing subject of debate for the past several years. Some feel that, left unchecked, the media "could control the minds, actions, and destiny of our people."[12]

[12] Alan U. Schwartz. "Danger: Pendulum Swinging — Using the Courts to Muzzle the Press." *The Atlantic Monthly* 239:29-34; February 1977.

Others fear government intimidation or censorship of any kind, worst of all self-censorship. It seems clear that the negative effects of any product of the media, whether film or print, can be reduced drastically—hopefully to zero—by deliberate and careful discussion. Parents and children, students and teachers, groups of many kinds could observe carefully and critically in order to separate truth from fiction. They could check the objectivity of reporting and distinguish between violence designed to please sponsors and the realities of city streets. In our experience with the media there is no substitute for critical thinking, for knowing the language of the message, for analyzing assumptions, for identifying underlying values and the likely consequences of their acceptance.[13]

Communication is clearly one of the critical realities of our time. It fills one of the basic needs of every individual. It is the essential vehicle for association and cooperation among people. It is essential in every form of government, but most critically important to democracy. Yet it is fraught with danger. Free and open and honest communication enables us to examine human experience, so that we may distinguish what is right from what is wrong, what is informing from what is deceiving, what is degrading from what is ennobling. Thus we may shed what is unworthy and share what will enhance personal development and the social welfare.

The Human Population. The problem of numbers among the human species is one of the critical realities commonly recognized in most parts of the world. This, in spite of the *fact* of decreasing birthrates in many countries and in the face of family education efforts in some of the most highly populated nations. There are over four billion people on earth today. By the turn of this century, according to popular estimates, that number could reach nearly seven billion. Sickness unattended and starvation unabated are appalling wherever they occur. And they *do* occur in the United States. Here, however, they affect nowhere near the proportion of the total population that they do in less industrialized or so-called "underdeveloped" nations. In India alone, for example, well over one million human births occur every month, swelling further a nation that already numbers more than 600 million people. In the Indian economy which is mostly agrarian, providing the barest minimum of health, education, and human welfare services is a staggering problem.

The very old and the very young suffer most from food shortages, and hunger strikes first in the poorest countries. Malnutrition and ex-

[13] For an interesting report of how these matters were studied among teenagers at the St. Mary's Center for Learning on the near west side of Chicago, read *Me and My TV*, a research report on the role of popular television in developing verbal skills and bringing together adolescents and adults. This is a publication of the Journalism Education Association, 147 Tomahawk Trail, Shabbona, Illinois. 1976.

treme hunger over a prolonged period can result in brain damage from which children do not recover. With food reserves and energy sources now alarmingly low, the growing population of this earth faces enormous challenges.

Demographic studies have consistently catalogued problems associated with uncontrolled population growth. The quality of life suffers: all life, not just human life; though human suffering seems to touch us most deeply. Where space and particularly resources necessary to sustain life in the non-human animal kingdom are no longer available, tensions and conflicts develop—among previously friendly and cooperative members. It is the same in the human domain. Where numbers race on much out of control, it seems the most elemental logic that resources will also reach their limit, including those most essential for sustaining life, whatever the species. Conflicts have occurred over space, as between farmers and ranchers in our early West. Wars have been fought over resources, natural as well as human. The earliest modes of travel, crude, slow and uncomfortable though they were, yet enabled some people to see that their distant neighbors had a better quality of life. It is understandable that comparisons led to envy and tension, that resentment led to suspicion, that competition led to conflict. Whether the question is one of stark survival: Who shall get the food?—as it is in many lesser developed countries, or—Where shall we spend the tax dollars, for schools or for roads? as it is in more industrialized countries, the matter of numbers in the population is one of the critical realities upon which answers will hinge.

From where will answers come? How shall we provide for the growing numbers of people in the light of diminishing resources—made worse by capricious rampages of nature in extremes of heat and cold, floods and droughts, and even earthquakes? With advances in the sciences of food production, we may multiply our loaves and fishes sufficient to our needs. We may cultivate the ocean's floor. What we know of chemistry and nutrition may be applied to the production of little yellow pills, one of which could supply all the nutrients that the human animal requires for vigorous healthy living. Blue ones for the nonhuman animals and perhaps a food spray or food dust for plants more lush and beautiful than we have ever known. Perhaps, with Isaac Asimov, we shall colonize the heavens or build cities under the sea. Conventional wisdom recognizes the human tendency toward procreation, but there is some arrogance in the assumption that somehow, somewhere, someone—usually someone else—will take care of the offspring.

It is quite possible that, creative and inventive as we are, we will solve our population problems. Meanwhile we shall have to accommodate our lives to dwindling resources and reduced energy supplies. We shall have to reconsider our widespread tendency toward conspicuous consumption. Indeed we shall have to guard our freedom and our sanity. Sheer numbers can generate widespread feelings among people in the crowd that nobody really knows them as individuals, nobody is sensitive to their hopes and dreams. Such persons are easily convinced that the massive groups of which they are part are somehow running out of control, at least beyond any influence they could exert. This breeds such hopelessness and dissatisfaction with one's lot as to lead to complete apathy or purposelessness or impotence in the face of those who seek to exercise control over others' lives, whether for socially acceptable motives or not. "Too much organization transforms men and women into automata, suffocates the creative spirit, and abolishes the very possibility of freedom."[14]

The most successful "adjustment" to the problems that overpopulation brings may reveal the most severe mental illness. Huxley uses the work of Eric Fromm to show that the really hopeless victims of mental illness are to be found among those who appear to be the most normal. The more nearly adjusted people are to the abnormal, dehumanizing conditions in their society, the worse the state of their insanity. Where organization demands such conformity as to lead to uniformity in human behavior, freedom dies; the very biological nature of human beings, each unique from all others, is violated; the base for sound mental health is gone. Large numbers of mentally unhealthy people would constitute a gross negative factor in our environment: unhappy thought, a kind of people pollution.

Ecology and Pollution. As the family of humankind grows larger, institutions become more and more complex, greater demands are made upon available resources, and waste and destruction are often inflicted upon the environment in such increasing volume as to threaten the health if not the very life of all organisms. Pollution is one of the critical realities of our time. The population bomb of Paul Ehrlich is no more threatening to many observers than is Rachel Carson's silent spring. In our search for energy we pollute the air we breathe: a single power plant burning oil can belch out several tons of sulphur dioxide in a day. Add the oxides from great steel factories and others, add the pollutants from ocean liners, aircraft, trains, trucks, buses and automobiles. Although DDT proved to be an effective insecticide, at least before insect resistance to it developed, it also proved fatal to fish and birds. The spray-can culture we have been developing in recent decades has been a cause for

[14] Aldous Huxley. *Brave New World Revisited.* New York: Harper & Row, Publishers, 1958. p. 28.

alarm among those who fear the effects of releasing destructive gases into the upper atmosphere, inviting a breakdown in the ozone shield that protects the earth from excessive harmful radiation. Are nuclear power plants safe from fire, accidents, leaks? In 1976, the small town of Port Hope, Ontario, found that there were radiation effects lingering from a uranium processing plant that had been torn down 16 years before. Radiation levels in some homes now on the site were found to be 10 to 30 to 100 times higher than normal. The Atomic Energy Control Board has authorized a $67,000 study of costs required for cleanup and rehabilitation. And the total effects may not be apparent for another 20 years.

Jacques Cousteau warns us of the impending doom affecting the oceans of the world. It must boggle the popular mind to suggest that the largest garbage cans on earth might one day be filled! Something of this sort is happening: from innumerable plants and municipalities, industrial waste and sewage are discharged into streams that race to our lakes and oceans; from ocean liners and other sources come oil slicks and garbage and refuse of every kind, such as Thor Heyerdahl studied and reported he found in all parts of the ocean including the middle of it. We know who killed Lake Erie. Cousteau estimates that the vitality of the ocean is less than 60 percent of what it was only 40 years ago; fish catches have been reduced by 25 to 60 percent, depending on species.[15] When asked if he noticed any change in the condition of the oceans since 1970, Cousteau responded that the only change is that they are dying faster. There seems to be too much at stake economically for any nation to tackle the problem. That would involve massive battles with very large industries. We seem inclined to think pollution may somehow go away, or at least it won't affect us. Not here. Not yet. Cousteau reports that Italy felt that way in 1970. In 1972, hundreds of Italians were poisoned by contaminated mussels. By 1974, Italy had one of the strongest environmental protection programs in Europe.

There are more personal kinds of pollution to which many individuals contribute every day. Probably 75 percent of all cancer, very likely more than that, can be traced to environmental causes. Serious research reports inform us of the deadly relation between smoking and cancer. Daniel Horn, Director of the Clearing House for Smoking and Health of the Center for Disease Control in Atlanta, Georgia, summarized the results of long-term studies by stating that, in the United States, smoking tobacco is responsible for at least 20 percent of deaths caused by cancer and heart attack. Lung cancer could be reduced by 85 percent if cigarette

[15] From an interview with Jacques Cousteau by Casey Bukro, Environmental Editor. *Chicago Tribune.* January 4, 1976.

smokers would quit. Yet, in spite of official government warnings required on each package, the sale of tobacco soars on.

Every individual, every corporation, every nation needs to accept responsibility for controlling or eradicating pollution. Increased size or increased numbers make the problem more acute. Improvement of the human condition requires concern for the total environment. It is irresponsible behavior, in this context, to toss used facial tissue on the highway or empty beer cans on someone else's lawn. It is irresponsible to destroy the aesthetics of a whole region as some companies have done with strip mining. It is at the very least questionable social behavior to move major industries to other countries in order to escape from more comprehensive to more lax pollution controls, perhaps to tax the limits of ecosystems beyond their survival. The realities of pollution extend from one's personal private environment to the entire biosphere. Solutions will require a sense of cultural pluralism, transnational concern, world loyalty; indeed, loyalty to the universe.

Government and Politics. As the population of the nation increases, the size and complexity of government increase. With our advanced industrial system, the widespread uses of science and technology, the growth of urban centers and megalopoli, the spread of huge networks of transportation and communication systems, with hospitals and jails and schools: with the myriad facilities, services, arrangements, laws and regulations necessary to maintain satisfactory living in a modern society, the United States is required to mount government agencies equal to the task. There seem to be two major realities relating to government and politics in the United States, and they are in contradiction to each other. One is that our government *is* democratic. The other is that our government often does *not* seem concerned about the best interest of the people.

The government of the United States is democratic in the sense that *the people* do, in fact, rule. In other parts of the world, the losing contender for high office is often removed from the scene—by exile or by murder. Here the chief contender might be employed in high office. The people do have much to say, although the system isn't perfect, about nominations for high offices. They have even more to say about who shall be elected. Our Constitution and Bill of Rights provide conditions and guarantees that many other people can only dream about. We have them. In the judicial, legislative, and executive branches, our forebears established a system of checks and balances designed to ensure good government, responsive to the wishes of the people. In initiative, referendum, and recall we have the vehicles for keeping government in the hands of the people. In impeachment we have the means of removing the unworthy from our highest offices. Such measures serve notice that our public officials are accountable to the group who gave them authority. Laws may be made or repealed, officials may be elected or removed, according to the will of the people acting in the best interest of the nation at large. Probably we are more democratic in our government than in most other facets of our lives.

On the other hand, casual observation of the behavior of people in politics and government could well lead the average citizen to wonder whether his or her best interests were being served. Of course, we could act, but so often we do not act in the face of collusion and chicanery or fraud and exploitation, even in high places. Governors and legislators, judges and presidents have been no less guilty than ward heelers in our cities. Nefarious negotiations have been uncovered linking the military and private industry and government workers in our own country, and involving our multinational corporations with other governments. Graft and bribery and exploitation seem so much a part of everyday operations that many come to *expect* such behavior and actually display a tolerance for it among their government employees. Or again it may be the sheer size and remote power of the bureaucracy that causes the private citizen to feel somewhat impotent to affect government on specific issues. And one must wonder sometimes if the chief purpose of government officials is to serve the best interests of all the people—or to work tirelessly to preserve themselves in office. The whole world knows of Watergate and shoeboxes, and bankruptcy in great corporations bailed out by government. The whole world knows of "black bag" funds for legislators' jaunts and what Jerald terHorst called the greased-palm syndrome; or last year's action by Congress to increase their own salary by nearly 30 percent at a single stroke; or other abuses of public money through misuses, often fraudulent uses, of food stamps, unemployment insurance, and workers' compensation. The whole world knows of bombings and kidnappings and assassinations. The whole world knows too of internal conflict among different agencies of our government: the Executive and the Legislative, the CIA and the FBI, judges and the police. A judicial system that makes it possible for patently guilty criminals, even murderers, to be freed to continue their behavior; or one that permits a judge the option of sentencing a criminal either "15 years to life" or "free on probation" for a particular conviction; or one that seems obviously to protect the criminal over the victim of crime, surely tests beyond reason the belief of the people in the quality of justice in their government. The fact that our national image abroad may suffer is not nearly so serious as the deterioration of our faith in our own government here at home. If ever we reach the point where nobody gives a damn, we shall be doomed.

Conflict and War and Peace. The United States has been singularly fortunate that most of her major wars did not involve her own soil. That is not so likely to obtain hereafter. Nuclear capability is now in the hands of several nations; soon we shall have to say many nations.[16] To what point must resentment, fear, or anger build before some nation decides that the use of ultimate weapons may be worth the risk?

Antagonism and conflict we find on every hand. Often the private hopes and dreams of individuals are thwarted by the group. And groups oppose other groups with even greater ease and determination. The most obvious contestants within our boundaries at the moment seem to be labor against management and white against black: these conflicts both rest on long and ugly histories. Other conflicts have developed between political groups, religious groups, between the young and their elders, between criminal factions and the body politic, between those who are in control and those who somehow wish they were. This is not the place to delineate all the causes of war or all the reasons for conflict. But we have seen rather vividly that the need for oil generated dangerous international tensions. We know that the desire for power, the ambition to be better recognized, for higher status in the circle of nations, perhaps even the need for space as well as resources are some of the roots of conflict. Vietnam and Angola were recent proof that governments can be persuaded to do the wrong things for the wrong reasons.

There is a report that supposedly came from a study group of 15 eminent specialists in economics, sociology, anthropology, psychology, psychiatry, and literature, who met in a think tank somewhere, in the 1960's: it is known as the "Report from Iron Mountain on the Possibility and Desirability of Peace."[17] The report may be a complete hoax. The whole of it may have been fiction written with tongue in cheek. Yet reportedly there are those who believe that it was done only partly in jest. The major conclusion is that while lasting peace might be possible, it probably would not be desirable: that peace would be hell. Four supporting reasons are elaborated to show that war and preparation for war are essential to a stable society. First, military expenditures can be used to balance the economy because they do not relate to normal supply and demand conditions. Second, politically, war supports the continuation of national sovereignty; without war there would be less justification for nation states. Third, the draft and the army tend to remove overly aggressive antisocial persons from their communities: a sociological ad-

[16] *World Issues* (January 1977, pp. 24-25) reported that 19 nations had nuclear power reactors in operation, and 13 other countries had them under construction or on order.
[17] "Report from Iron Mountain." In: Donald N. Michaels, editor. *The Future Society*. Chicago: Trans-action Books, Aldine Publishing Company, 1970.

vantage. Fourth, ecologically, war can establish a better balance between the total population and the available supplies and resources to meet their needs. The Report recognizes the eugenic flaw in the last argument, since nuclear war would kill off the superior along with the inferior. Remember: a hoax, a fiction, tongue in cheek; but perhaps not entirely so.

The stark realities that must be faced include the fact of human differences, the uneven distribution of the world's goods, the determined reach for recognition, for fulfillment of personal ambitions, for status, for power, and the universal longing for a happy life in a just world. It does not necessarily follow that our own political system would be best for all other countries, or that our Christianity would save the world. Considering the enormous advantages the United States has been favored with among nations, we would be remiss not to strive for rational solutions to the critical problems in the world. We would be shamefully shortsighted not to join with other concerned countries in a multinational effort to reduce those problems. We could well provide leadership in the exploration of new creative ways to attack international issues: ways that rest not on force or violence but on genuine cooperation, goodwill, collective intelligence, perhaps on a body of world law that reflects deep concern for the human condition everywhere. All people everywhere on earth shall have to consider the alternatives to war, to annihilation. We could make capital of our differences, husband our resources and share them equitably, glory in our cultural pluralism, and create for the first time, *one* human community that embraced every person on earth.

Values and Life-Styles. The people of the United States are neither entirely clear nor completely together in the values they hold. For the past dozen years or so, we have been rearranging our priorities, shifting our moral and ethical beliefs, switching our loyalties and changing our life-styles. Not every one of us, but many groups and large numbers, and for many reasons. Our values permeate all of our behavior; they affect everything we do; they reflect our genuine preferences and govern every action. In this age of rapid change it is vitally important that we examine what is happening to the value systems we apparently are embracing and make judgments about their appropriateness. Everywhere in our lives today differing values, often opposing values, are contending for acceptance or dominance. Our determined choices will make all the difference in the nature of our human condition. *This* is the most pervasive and the most critical of the realities of our time.

Whether we are consciously aware of it or not, whether we do it thoughtfully or not, every one of us has been required to examine how we feel about such matters as: race, sex, work, leisure, technology, slums, schools, elders, media, crime, pollution, population, urbanization, transnationalism, space, nature, and humankind. It is expecting too much to assume that all our people might somehow come to agreement on the treatment of such matters. Every generation has certain rather more conspicuous value systems that govern their behaviors. And every succeeding generation tends to modify certain of the basic values of their ancestors. That is the nature of time, change, and hopefully, progress. As we examine the issues we face from day to day, we have to evaluate the alternatives, the human consequences of our actions, the value base of our decisions. It is particularly important that the young learn to do this, yet it is hardly less important for us all.

Where are we now and where are we going with marriage, family, and sexual behavior? Marriage agreements are entered more lightly these days, divorce is easier, less of a stigma than it used to be. Property settlements are fairer in some states. Younger couples often live together without benefit of marriage, share children and sometimes lovers in communal living. Older couples may live together but avoid marriage because that would reduce their separate social security receipts. Some married couples have been known to divorce in order to take advantage of individual income tax exemptions, and then remarry soon after filing. We have seen singles adopting children and same-sex couples officially married. Freedom in sexual behavior has greatly advanced in recent years, partly promoted by "the pill." It is only natural that we should have more factual information available today than ever before, including such research as that of Kinsey or Masters and Johnson; and that not only these kinds of research but information about all manner of sexual experimentation and behavior is widely disseminated by the mass media, particularly television. Things that were barely whispered in quiet corners only a few years ago now enjoy wide and quite public discussion: abortion, venereal disease, impotence, homosexuality, bisexuality, transsexuality, and more. The appearance in many schools today of sex education programs further illustrates a trend that was hardly recognizable a few decades back. What is right? What is tolerable? What is best?

The role of women in our culture has been changing radically. For many generations we have ignored the accomplishments, some highly conspicuous, of women who have worked in areas considered to be the special domain of men. Not so very long ago it was widely held that women's chief tasks were to keep house and rear children, that they were naturally limited in their activities by lesser physical strength and lesser mental powers. Women weren't expected to comprehend science or economics or politics or world affairs. Unfortunately, too many women seemed to accept this relegation to inferior status. Not so today. And the change has affected men in remarkable ways. Some are dismayed by this new female stance; some don't know quite how to deal with female executives or even female colleagues as they enter new areas of endeavour. Other men feel that the world should have opened to women long ago and are happy about the current situation. There are, after all, very few activities that cannot be engaged in as well by one sex as by the other. So men may welcome the possibility of housekeeping or caring intimately for children or perhaps shedding tears when deeply grieved.

How should we deal with delinquency and crime? The FBI Report of Crime for 1974 indicated that 1.6 million or one-third of those arrested were teenagers and that they accounted for 10 million crimes; that teenagers comprised 20 percent of those arrested for rape, 30 percent for assault and 65 percent for shoplifting. In one year, 1975, shoplifting alone caused a loss of about $5,000,000,000 nationally, which prompts a markup of 15 percent on "sensitive" items. Vandalism costs the Chicago School Board $1,000,000 per year just to replace broken windows in school buildings. Crime generally increased on an average of about 11 percent last year throughout the United States except for California; and the great majority of crimes are not reported. Merely by chance, the New York City police uncovered a bank teller's use of the computer to hide periodic thefts from the bank to support his gambling habit, which grew to $30,000 per week in losses; but only after three years and an embezzlement totaling $1.5 million. Crowded prisons have brought on the use of trailers (Arkansas) and tents (Florida) to house convicted criminals. *Each* cell in a new prison costs from $15,000 to $25,000 to build and $8,000 to $10,000 per year to maintain. What price we pay to "protect" the public! Add to this the fact that serious offenders are often back on the streets, through bail bond, in a matter of days, only to engage in further crime. Add to this what often turns out to be the sorry plight of the victim of crime. This person suffers personal indignity, perhaps serious bodily injury, loss of money or property, perhaps loss of work time and income. If somehow he or she resents all this and rebels in the process, the *victim* may well be arrested for infringing upon the rights of the attacker. Where such miscarriages of justice are visible and frequent, it is understandable that our youth might conclude that crime not only pays but that one has a good chance of getting away with it.

We know well enough the conditions that breed delinquency and criminal behavior. We understand their relations to government, business, unions, asocial organizations, unstable families, bad housing, easily available weapons, the more lurid aspects of the media, inadequate education, and to personal frustration, hopeless self-images and other personality disorders and perhaps health problems including chemical imbalance affecting the brain. We *know* this much already and more. Tackling these conditions would seem a fantastic undertaking, would cost an enormous price. Yet we shall pay a more fearful price for *not* tackling them. The question is very simple: How do we really wish to live? We shall never have a society without crime unless we prize such a community highly enough, consider it possible to attain, and *act* on that belief.

The young people of our nation have been in the forefront of activity in our changing values and life-styles, and that has been a mixed blessing. The demonstrations, protests, and rebellions of the 1960's made clear how strongly they felt about human life, personal freedom, the natural world, national integrity, and other values which many of us gave only lip service or denied altogether. We are better off now because they insisted that we pause and reflect and change. But many youths suffered. They were caught up in the habit of protest and found themselves protesting everything that was associated with "the establishment," all the old rules and regulations, all the old authorities or the old ways. Parental guidance was subject to disdain, teachers were ridiculed, police were pigs, anyone over 30 was hopelessly out of date.

After only a few years went by we began hearing about adolescents who felt "old" and youngsters who were "burned out" at age 30. Many of these people, exhausted by their frantic activities, became bored, depressed, hypochondriac. Many went from purposelessness to hopelessness to suicide. Yet their positive contributions are discernible. What does it take to get a society to look at its contradictions, its detrimental policies and customs and arrangements, its inhuman behavior? Its major beliefs and goals and values? People of all ages are asking such questions now.

Must certain groups continue to suffer systematic neglect: the American Indian, the Latino, the black, the poor white, women, and particularly elder citizens, perhaps even our children in school? Must we suffer impotence in the presence of gargantuan institutions? Shall we shed our conventional religious tenets and embrace astrology or witchcraft? To what extent *can* we hope to control our lives?

We shall have to learn to deal with what Toffler calls our super-industrial society. We shall have to learn to cope with more difficult problems, with a knowledge explosion of growing magnitude, with more influential mass media, with greater leisure and the more persistent pursuit of pleasure. Our compulsive attitude toward work will have to give way to increasing takeover by automation. Yet we must be wary that the control of human minds never falls to the computer.

And what of our elders? Not those over 30, but those over 60 or 70 or 80 years of age? There are 22 million persons past 65 in the United States today; they will likely comprise 25 percent of our population by the year 2000. All too frequently they are neglected or rejected by their children and by society. Their usually fixed incomes are decimated by inflation. They have awesome problems of housing, and sometimes the minimum essentials in food are beyond their means. Transportation and recreation that have price tags are virtually out of the question. Often they lose contact with old friends and companions, and live lives of quiet desperation. Some communities care. Many provide a meeting place where older people can gather socially on occasion; others provide meal service of a sort for persons who can't cook for themselves. An organization called Minneapolis Age and Opportunity provides help with all kinds of heavy work that elders no longer can do in their own homes. The city of Muscatine, Iowa, has made a concerted effort to provide inexpensive housing for older persons, and this in a city where housing has been exceedingly scarce. Still, millions of older citizens are frustrated, angry, sick, sad, and lonely. In some cultures, the elders are honored and revered, well cared for by the children. In some they can retire at 50 or 55 and live on with dignity. Sharon Curtin studied conditions of old age in the United States. Her report is a mixture of anger, outrage, praise and compassion for these people, and a challenge for us all.[18] Do people diminish in value year by year—after 30 or 50 or 70 years? When their formal years in the working world are completed, are they ready for the scrap heap? How do we *value* them?

Is it possible that we might one day change the depressed state of our older citizens, and the compulsive achievement-work ethic of the middle-aged, and the frantic deviant behavior of the very young, so that a happy community would result? Perhaps we may get help from the Walt Disney World. It was Disney's exciting dream to create an Experimental Prototype Community of Tomorrow—EPCOT.[19] The project is being undertaken by Walt Disney Productions and should be in full bloom in the 1980's. EPCOT will bring together artists, scientists, industrialists, and government officers in an integrated set of research centers for agriculture, communication, education, energy, health, oceanography, space, and the arts. The World Showcase will provide for the active participa-

18 Sharon R. Curtin. *Nobody Ever Died of Old Age.* Boston: Little, Brown and Company, 1972.

19 Horace Sutton. "Mickey's Global Mission." *Saturday Review* 3:53-55; February 7, 1976.

tion of people from about 35 other countries, through an International Village. The enterprise reflects the firm optimism that trusts the cooperative intelligence of people of goodwill to work together and solve the larger problems we face. In such an arena, with the help of specialists in a number of disciplines and natives of varying cultures, a shared analysis of personal-social values should surface those with richest promise for improving the human condition.

Valuing is a matter of setting criteria for decisions which order our lives. But how are values themselves to be determined? We are fortunate in this country to have a set of moral commitments to guide us. They developed from several sources and gained wide acceptance. These five major moral commitments were summarized by Counts in his Kappa Delta Pi Lecture over 30 years ago.[20]

First, the *Hebraic-Christian Ethic,* which proclaims the supreme worth and dignity of the individual human being, and the importance of the free development of each individual to the fullest potential. Hence, we accept the brotherhood and essential unity of all people, all races; none is superior or inferior and none is to be exploited. All are moral creatures living in a moral order.

Second, the *Humanistic Spirit* insists that the human is a rational being, has the power of choice, can sense the true and the good, and should be in control of his/her own destiny. Human progress is possible; the person is perfectible. Through effort and self-discipline, higher pinnacles can be reached.

Third, the *Scientific Method* provides the experimental processes to order inquiries into every sphere of interest. Thus more certain knowledge may be established, leading to better control and greater freedom in all areas of living.

Fourth, *Democracy* also prizes the worth and dignity of human beings, recognizes their intelligent judgment, insists that they can and should govern themselves; guarantees personal freedom and justice under law, equality of treatment and consideration and protection against arbitrary acts. Democracy promotes individual freedom *and* the general welfare. It assumes that common people will share the good things, and that everyone will willingly take on the political, economic, and social responsibilities and the obligations associated with this system.

Fifth, *World Peace* reflects our deeply rooted hatred for war. We feel that the military should be subject to civilian authority and that military-

[20] George S. Counts. *Education and the Promise of America.* New York: Macmillan Publishing Co., Inc., 1945.

industrial relations should be carefully monitored. We feel that war is hostile to democracy, to civilization itself; and peace *is* possible.

These commitments constitute an extremely critical reality for our time. Often it seems we have neglected or forgotten them. We should study them carefully, seek their deepest meanings, commit ourselves again to those we firmly accept and govern our personal and social behavior accordingly.

Respected observers of the critical realities in our life and culture have reached radically different conclusions. Heilbroner[21] expressed deep pessimism over the future because of the threats of overpopulation, nuclear war, industrial encroachment on ecosystems and resources, and detrimental effects of science and technology. Herman Kahn, as indicated earlier in this chapter, has been optimistic about the future, barring nuclear war. Not long ago, both Kahn and Eric Hoffer agreed that Western society was coming through a period of so many and varied changes that there has been little opportunity for recapitulations, absorption and consolidation of the innovations. Arnold Toynbee pointed out that while progress in technology ". . . has been immense, there has been no corresponding advance in human sociality."[22] He found people innately greedy, and the current system of sovereign states incapable of preserving peace or of solving problems of pollution and diminishing resources. On that score, the future looked gloomy. But he concluded with a spark of hope, indicating that we can make choices, can distinguish between good and evil, can opt for the better service of all human beings. We have *that* choice too. Professor F. M. Esfandiary, of the New School for Social Research in New York, predicts that the world will shift from scarcity to a new era of plenty in the next 20 years. Keith Davis, of Arizona State University, identifies the United States as the first nation to move within one century from an agrarian to an industrial to a service economy. More occupations are based on knowledge rather than manual skill, as we become more humanistic and socially concerned.[23] Speaking before ASCD assembled in Miami Beach in 1964, Harold Taylor observed that the characteristic posture of the world was *threat*. He identified three major national goals: (a) military-economic security, (b) the greatest possible technological progress, and (c) material well-being: first for ourselves, then for others. He insisted that these goals are

21 Robert L. Heilbroner. *An Inquiry into the Human Prospect.* New York: W. W. Norton & Company, Inc., 1974.

22 Arnold Toynbee. *Mankind and Mother Earth.* New York: Oxford University Press, Inc., 1976. Chapter 82.

23 See the *Arizona Republic* for December 26, 1976, pp. H-1 and H-4.

limiting and damaging to our national progress and he questioned our underlying value system.

It seemed useful, then, to bring together in a single chapter these critical realities of our day. Probably the matters included are familiar to observers of the social scene and the readers of this yearbook. And clearly, the list is not exhaustive. What of such matters as urban planning or transportation or medical services or tax reforms? It must strike even the casual observer that we are beset by many problems, that they are enormously complex, that they are intricately interrelated. It would seem an exercise in futility to try to identify *the* most crucial crisis that might generate our ultimate disintegration. We need to dissect our problems one by one, together with the related forces and factors that support each one of them. If we are feared in some quarters, it may be for valid reason; but we are admired too for the many good things accomplished over the past two hundred years: things that took courage, sacrifice, creativity, diligence, daring; things that represent the reservoir of resources and human qualities that made for moments of greatness. And we don't even know what the upper limits of our capabilities are! It has been predicted with much assurance that by the year 2000: a synthetic skinlike membrane will offer superior protection against the infection of burns; the Dvorak simplified keyboard will be far more widely used on typewriters; we may travel on flying trains, or go by subway from New York to Los Angeles in 21 minutes.[24] So many things are *possible*. But we do face issues and problems, mostly human problems. We need to marshal every resource at hand, particularly our most precious resource— the collective wisdom of our people—in a concerted effort to solve our most critical problems. Forces of disintegration are strong in our midst; but we can move toward greater integration, toward a vastly improved human condition. We can take just pride in the many good things we have done and build on that base. We can show more concern, build trust, foster integrity, share love. We *can* become what we want to be. But not without education, not without schools.

Selected Readings

Association for Supervision and Curriculum Development. Various yearbooks and booklets published over the past 20 years. Washington, D.C.: the Association, variously dated.

Theodore Brameld. *The Climactic Decades: Mandate to Education.* New York: Praeger Publishers, 1970.

Gurney Breckenfeld. "Coping with the Nation-State." (Special Feature: Multinationals at Bay) *Saturday Review* 3:12-22, January 24, 1976.

[24] Stephen Rosen. *Future Facts.* New York: Simon & Schuster, Inc., 1976.

Casey Bukro, Environmental Editor. Personal interview with Jacques Cousteau. Reported in *Chicago Tribune* January 4, 1976.

Arthur C. Clarke. *Profiles of the Future: The Limits of the Possible.* New York: Harper & Row, Publishers, 1973. (Revised.)

Sharon R. Curtin. *Nobody Ever Died of Old Age.* Boston: Little, Brown and Company, 1972.

Elliot W. Eisner and Elizabeth Vallance. *Conflicting Conceptions of Curriculum.* Berkeley: McCutchan Publishing Corporation, 1974. (NSSE Series.)

Allan A. Glatthorn. *Alternatives in Education: Schools and Programs.* New York: Dodd, Mead & Company, Inc., 1975.

Robert L. Heilbroner. *An Inquiry into the Human Prospect.* New York: W. W. Norton & Company, Inc., 1974.

Arthur Hoppe, editor. "Humanizing Secondary Education." *Thresholds in Secondary Education* 1 (3) ; Fall 1975. Entire issue.

James J. Jelinek. *Philosophy of Education: 1972-73.* Proceedings of the Twenty-First Annual Meeting of the Far Western Philosophy of Education Society. Tempe: Arizona State University, 1972.

James J. Jelinek. *Principles and Values in School and Society.* Tempe, Arizona: Far Western Philosophy of Education Society, 1976.

Herman Kahn and B. Bruce-Briggs. *Things to Come: Thinking About the Seventies and the Eighties.* New York: Macmillan Publishing Co., Inc., 1972.

Michael B. Katz. *Class, Bureaucracy, and Schools.* New York: Praeger Publishers, 1971, 1975.

Mark L. Knapp. *Nonverbal Communication in Human Interaction.* New York: Holt, Rinehart & Winston, Inc., 1972.

Mary Conway Kohler and Bruce Dollar. "An Antidote to Alienation." *The Center Magazine* 9:20-27; May/June 1976.

Ronald Kotulak, Science Editor. Regular Feature. *Chicago Tribune,* January 18, 1976.

Jess Lair. *I Ain't Much, Baby, but I'm All I've Got.* Greenwich, Connecticut: Crest Books, Fawcett Publications, Inc., 1969, 1972.

Michael Marien and Warren L. Ziegler. *The Potential of Educational Futures.* Worthington, Ohio: Charles A. Jones Publishing Co., 1972.

Donald N. Michael, editor. *The Future Society.* Chicago: Trans-action Books, Aldine Publishing Company, 1970. Includes "Report from Iron Mountain."

John P. Miller. *Humanizing the Classroom.* New York: Praeger Publishers, 1976.

Stephen Rosen. *Future Facts.* New York: Simon and Schuster, Inc., 1976.

Seymour B. Sarason. *The Culture of the School and the Problem of Change.* Boston: Allyn and Bacon, Inc., 1971.

Arnold J. Toynbee. *Mankind and Mother Earth.* New York: Oxford University Press, Inc., 1976.

2

Communications and Society

Gerald V. Flannery, Ralph E. Hillman,
Jerry C. McGee, William L. Rivers

MARSHALL McLUHAN, the modern guru of mass communications, once observed that there is really not much difference today between education and entertainment. McLuhan, author of many books and articles on mass media, along with many other writers, feels that which educates, entertains, and that which entertains, educates. Thomas Edison, Alexander Stoddard, and others early predicted that the motion picture and other communication innovations of the day would replace, or at least minimize, the need for teachers. Educational television generated similar predictions, raising the spectre of the master teacher, a dramatizer who would softshoe into the hearts and minds of students, all technique, no content. And so it goes, each new advance in communications threatens the old.

Communications is a relatively new academic and professional discipline. No one knows for sure quite what it is or what it will finally encompass. We once thought communication began with the cry of birth and ended with the sigh of death, but research in new fields like prenatal awareness, telepathy, cybernetics, and cryonics is expanding our limited knowledge. The parameters are forever changing. Contrast what you have learned from actual experience to what you have learned through communication; contrast your knowledge of society against your experience with it. Communication is interaction and we need only look to psychology and the stimulus-response research to realize that much is known but much is not understood. Communication is also reciprocal, thus it involves reversal of role; it is a function of the conscious and the subconscious. In short, communication involves individuals *and* society; therefore, it crosses all disciplines.

Will communications shape society and replace the traditional teacher? Will society and education mold and direct communications to extend and enrich the environment of both? What are the problems for teachers when one considers communications and society? This chapter attempts to review and project the implications of both as we move toward the end of this century. Communications may well be the key to both the problems and the solutions of the future.

Communications Overview

Communication for centuries was an interpersonal process, one involving individuals. It grew from prehistoric grunts and groans to signs and symbology, and finally to language and the sophistication of nuance, intonation, and meaning. Gradually the concept of group communication arose and consequently the study of the group and the individual process. Scientific research made us increasingly aware of the importance of the biological process, discovering in greater detail how the biological/physiological aspects of our being helped us function as living creatures; yet, even today, much remains to be done in the area of our communication processes, the very thing that helps us function as rational creatures. In earlier years, this function was neglected; after all, what's so special about speech? We've been talking since we were children. We looked elsewhere for importance.

The invention of the printing press in the middle of the fifteenth century forever changed the limited, transient, ephemeral quality of communication, catapulting it from primarily an oral process with societal traditions to one with both group, mass, and personal overtones. It borrowed from the group process in the way it was received, yet kept the personal in the way it was used. McLuhan views the development of the Gutenberg printing press as beginning of "linear" thought, the arrangement of communication and ideas in an orderly fashion, from point "A" to point "B," the subsequent breakdown of knowledge into steps and sequences. He sees the printing press as a turning point in the shift of societal communication from the aural culture to the visual; he even credits it with the introduction of privacy as a factor in general communication, creating the need for private spaces to read. Notwithstanding, it did alter the transient aspect of oral communication and introduced the residual aspect of the printed word. It also opened the door for the later development of public education for the masses in America.

Society, until this time, was a limited factor in the development of the individual; the community and the neighborhood (as such) were stronger determinants. Transportation and availability placed great limits on the experiential ability of the individual, and the communicator pretty much had full control over the message transmitted. The introduction of the written and printed word put a societal stranger in the midst of the community; it allowed reexamination of communicated material; it made independent examination of content possible and provided a continuing exactness in source material, not necessarily present in previous communication: the thought or message became frozen in time. It also sounded the death knell to the feedback aspect of communication, the opportunity for the recipient to respond to the communication and perhaps affect it at the source: here began the first trickle of what has become a tidal wave of "one way" communication.

Aristotle believed the true test of an idea was its acceptance in the marketplace. Print drastically altered things in that the originator of the idea no longer had to be in the marketplace; all manner of things could be discussed from the safe distance of print. The later interpolation of an editor in the process only acted to filter the communication, not provide a feedback element. The linear arrangement of data allowed information to be contrasted against information, removed the limits of time and space on its usage, and provided a step-by-step method that generated self-paced education: the key was reading, the tool, language. Print paved the way for the ages of reason and enlightenment that were to come. It must be remembered that when something emerges to affect humankind's social, economic, political, religious, and educational life, what is born, must, in turn, be affected by them, creating a related chain of affect-effect-affect.

The cumulative effect of the gradual development of the written and printed word, coupled with the interaction of group and interpersonal communication, gradually diminished the effect of the peer, the authority figure, the locale, shifting the emphasis to the communicator and the message. People reasoned and wrote, then reasoned and discussed from what was written, and wrote again, sure the effect of the process was meritorious, aware more of the message than the medium. Much attention was paid to what was said and who said it.

The nineteenth century brought the introduction of new carriers, the first being the telephone and the telegraph. The telephone was really a technological extension of the interpersonal process of communication. It allowed person to person communication, with feedback, but introduced distance and the loss of face to face proximity. The telephone was a giant technological step in personal communication and it generated a new spectrum of communication possibilities; it remained for television to be added to return the face to face aspect of interpersonal communication. The telegraph was sort of an electronic Gutenberg signalling the later birth of radio and television. The telephone and telegraph greatly facilitated the flow of information to and from the printed media and helped create the network of news transmission that made the wire services possible.

Other communication breakthroughs were introduced in the nineteenth century, one of them being photography. Newspaper publication was spreading across the land, photographs were being taken, circulation rose and papers prospered. The slow, time-consuming process of publication was gradually quickened as the nation moved toward the Industrial Revolution and the possibility of mass communication. The revolution first affected printed matter. It splintered the book into pieces called pamphlets, broadsides, newspapers, and magazines; it accelerated the painted picture in the photograph. More importantly, it shattered the pace that had made the book and the painting a slower, more considered piece of communication. The time between the creation and the communication was narrowed, the time between the event and the knowledge of it, reduced.

Mass communication forced attention from the past to the present, from history to current affairs. Radio came along later to extend the voice to unparalleled limits and to extend the ear in the same way. McLuhan believes any extension of one sense creates an imbalance in the others. Print reached an increasingly larger audience that received information in less time than ever before. This shift affected the classroom also in that the focus moved from the study of purely historical events to the consideration of current affairs: the newspaper entered the classroom. It took radio, however, to generate an instantaneous audience receiving the message simultaneously on a massive scale. Network radio came along and began to break down regionalism, opening the land. Transportation was no longer a problem for the message or the audience.

Newspapers challenged the book, photography challenged painting; both were forced in new directions and neither was the same as a result. Print communication broadened from information about the past, to the recent past, and finally to the present. Pictures went from the captured idea of art, to the captured instant of the photograph. The media began to compete in the areas of information, education, and entertainment; newness and accuracy were key elements.

The contrast of the printed word and the pictured event forced attention to the effect of the carrier on the content of the message. The controlled photographic "point of view" was also recognized as being present in the controlled printed view. The captured instant of photography was eventually expanded into film and motion pictures: the recreation of an event and the reexamination of an event became a repetitive possibility. It was possible to look at something over and over again, from several angles, to reexamine reality. Film also allowed the restructuring of material and the creation of new reality. The natural continuity could be altered and scenes juxtaposed for clarity or impact.

Communication, like society, is under examination today on all fronts. Computers contrast data against data using the systems of one discipline on another; information is brushed against information, creating new information. Technology fostered the spread of mass communication and society is continually showered with it. Society is in the midst of a communications explosion on one hand, and an information explosion on the other. Researchers still break down communication into two large areas—interpersonal and mass—but the study of it is now divided into (a) process and (b) effect: the general elements involving a communicator, message, channel, and audience. Most of the research centers on the process, very little on the effect. However, we now talk about communications in social, economic, political, and moral language, interspersing psychological, scientific, and technological terminology. The literature abounds with references to things like "channel noise, context, interface, dissonance, semantic noise, data flow, redundancy," and countless others.

There will undoubtedly be communication breakthroughs by the end of the century to the developments we know today. The field of mass communication will probably develop along predictable lines aided by technology now extant. The marriage of computers and communications will continue to beget the communication/information explosion but we will be inundated by its completeness and complexity. The major area for communication (s) breakthroughs, however, remains interpersonal and intrapersonal. The fledgling fields of ESP and brain wave research offer new communication nerveways; experiments in thought transfer will coincide with thought transport (special locomotion from a fixed position). Cryonics offers the potential of postdeath communication and hallucinogenic drugs are already opening minds to visionary experiences. Recent research with rats by Dr. Georges Ungar suggests it may someday be possible to feed people ideas and knowledge, learning and understanding, through some sort of synthetic formula. Ungar and his group performed a chemical analysis on more than 4,000 rats trained to avoid a dark chamber. They found a simple protein they called scotophobin that appeared only in the brains of the trained rats. They reproduced this substance using inorganic materials. When new rats were injected with the synthetic scotophobin, the results were intriguing: the new rats behaved as if they had been part of the trained rat group.[1] Who is to say

[1] James V. McConnell. *Understanding Human Behavior*. New York: Holt, Rinehart and Winston, Inc., 1977. pp. 379-81.

that regenerated or synthetic experience/communication is not possible?

The future shift in communications research, however, will undoubtedly be from process to effect; the societal aspect of communication will merit new emphasis. We will be concerned more with what the message does than with what it is, how it is packaged or delivered. We may investigate the effect of 11 years of a television western on a person, or study the effect of nightly war in the living room. Daily, more and more people share the same experiences through communication. Does the sharing of media experience lead people to a greater or lesser understanding of others? Do we ever really see the same thing or do we all withdraw something different from the same experience? The concern about sex and violence in the media has served to raise our national and individual thresholds in those areas. We have become both sexually and violently aware and have learned to distinguish the subtleties of each.

Parents, in one section of the country, are finding they don't like what is accepted in another section, particularly when it affects their children. Some parent groups are banding together to challenge the educational materials selected for their children. Citizen groups are joining forces to reject a group of books, widely used elsewhere, from being introduced in their local school system. They are demanding input on reading lists, homework assignments, and classroom materials. There is a conflict in the private vs. public aspect of education, particularly on the K-12 level. Do parents have a right to create their own school and use their own materials? If so, does this right then extend to the public schools? Are the civil rights of children infringed upon by discriminatory treatment of communication materials, by restriction of exposure and information?

Humankind's communication processes will be studied and charted in great detail over the coming decades, just as its biological processes are now. We have proven that the biological process is being seriously hampered by the uncontrolled influx of junk foods, that nutrition is seriously lacking in much of the food we eat, that well-intentioned additives are in fact harmful, particularly in combination with other additives; that large segments of our population are undernourished and overweight, dying from lack of exercise and a balanced intake. The psychological/societal well-being of the individual is being examined with the same indices we use to determine caloric and carbohydrate balance: biological balance is so closely related that the research is overlapping. Some say we are what we eat, others that we become what we eat; surely, the same thing is true for communication and learning.

What then is the result of the communication process? Is there some correlation? Life magazine once published a cover story on the hot dog, indicating that there was only about 13 percent protein/nutrition value in it, not enough to deal with the 87 percent junk in the rest of the dog. If we can produce a nation of overweight people, nutritionally deficient, emotionally tied to junk foods, in just a few decades, what is the result of decades of mass media, in uncontrolled doses? Where is the dietary balance to assure nutrition? Perhaps we need to develop caloric indices for communication (s) intake. The implications for the elementary and secondary teacher are clear. There will have to be programs developed to educate students in these areas; visual literacy programs expanded, media courses in elementary and secondary schools, exercises in criticism and understanding. What is the proper mix of mental intake to provide balanced growth? Perhaps the daily dose of society's ills we call news is really bad news in more ways than one; and the inane weekly television series is the hot dog we consume with relish? These are questions yet to be posed, much less answered; the force of communication (s) is such that it first demands consideration of other matters.

General Problem Areas

The problems facing society in communications are myriad; they tend to rise in direct geometrical proportion to the general problems of society and the specific problems of the individual. One specific problem is the trend toward more and more "one way" communication, more and more messages via the mass media with no real opportunity for interactive feedback; in fact, no opportunity for any type of feedback; even the individual seems more interested in telling us his or her opinion than in listening to ours. Circulation figures have replaced such commentary for the mass communicator and the massiveness of the media experience is replacing the effect of individual feedback in personal communication. If 30 million people got the message it is *per force* a better message than the one only ten million received; it is not important what you think, it is more important what I think. We select our ideas from an array of media messages and our peers from an array of media models, but we are finally left to deal with messages and people we did not select; we are driven in search of people who agree with us. As the mass of one way communication continues to escalate, we see an increase in group activity, in demonstrations, in massive feedback attempts, in staged media events designed to get a message across. We may expect a continuing rise in inner frustration and anger from one way communication, and we should expect it to manifest itself in those areas where face to face, one to one, situations still occur. Simply put, for educators, the frustrations engendered by this mass of communication will evidence themselves in explosions in the school setting since it offers the only real chance for students to feed back their feelings, ideas, and frustrations. The remoteness in school leadership and the largeness of educational systems only contribute to the problem.

Mass demonstrations, mob response, and violent attack are often viewed as the only societal means of feedback readily available to vent the stored disagreement. People will continue to use the media to feed back their opinions and feelings but it will be an "after the fact" response, not developmental interaction. Originally, personal, face to face communication allowed for personal, face to face response; the individual's ability to interact was ever present. Even with the rise of group communication the individual response survived, coupled, in some instances, with group and local response. Mass messages invite mass response: stored communication implies stored feedback. Kings often killed the messenger who brought bad news; a frustrated person often strikes out at the nearest link to that frustration, no matter how tenuous. Educators should consider ways to assure students, parents, and taxpayers access to media/communication both in and out of school.

The problem of privacy is another troubled area in communication (s). The explosion in communications technology, coupled with the information explosion, coupled with the accelerated computerization of both, makes everyone vulnerable to invasion of privacy. We all leave bits and pieces of us in a hundred locations in our lives, forms filled out here, data provided there, medical, dental, religious, social, economic. The interest of some in the activities of others will pose monumental legal and social problems in the area of privacy. The courts are having a difficult time in balancing the privacy rights of an individual with the public's right to know or the right of the press to report. We cooperate daily with organizations that seek to compile detailed accounts of activities, wants, backgrounds, and problems. We are all vulnerable to dossiers, profiles, and data banks; increasingly, what we do is computerized and the river of data finds its way into the mainstream where it mixes with countless other rivulets. Data are keyed to birth records, social security numbers, driver's licenses, charge cards, subscriptions, school and court records; cross breeding information banks operate continually and what they do may be legally defensible. The temptation to run checks on people will give way to psychological and sociological profiles drawn from legal, medical, and other types of records. Where will the right of privacy be drawn? How much information can a person be required to give, in what situations, in what context? If information is given willingly at point "A," is it then to be available at point "B"? For example, suppose I have a charge card and over a period of time purchase a hundred different items in numerous places; each action was a public one, yet each was private too. Does someone have the right to computerize those purchases and draw a profile of the person? To mate that data with other data? Will the legal principle that public figures have no privacy rights be extended to the public actions of a private individual? Will a student's activity in school be construed as public or private, and to whom? The Buckley Amendment is but one example of how the problem of privacy and open records may be dealt with.

The "sunshine law" controversy springing up across the country is extending into the school arena, into classrooms, faculty meetings, and disciplinary actions. The judicial principles now thought to apply to the governing of adults are gradually being extended to children; the result may very well be a "bill of rights" of students, educational "public defenders" for students, and "Miranda" readings by teachers. The private file of a student is a thing of the past; the student has increasing access to it and the student "public" feels it has a "right to know." School publications are demanding and getting First Amendment rights and freedoms, and they may soon demand and get Sixth and Fourteenth rights also.

The clash among the First, Sixth, and Fourteenth amendments is one that will erupt continually for the balance of this century: freedom of speech and press, the right to a speedy and fair trial, and the public's right to know; these will be tested on every front. The freedom to speak and to publish without "prior restraint" will be utilized on all levels of communication. Educators will find those rights being exercised in educational situations. For example, the school, as publisher of a student paper, may be able to exercise control over the budget and the distribution of the paper, but it will be powerless to censor or control what goes in the paper, prior to its publication. It may require that all articles be signed or that the editor assume responsibility for all unsigned pieces, but it will not be able to do anything about what is published until after it is published. It may suspend publication for a time but not without some judicial or quasi-legal action. The right of an individual to a speedy, fair, and public trial by a jury of peers will create difficult challenges to the process of jury (peer) selection and to the prospect of venue change. The Fifth Amendment rights of an individual may be extended to discussion, testing, or revelatory information of any kind. Will the trial rights of a defendant be more important than the information rights of a society? A principal can now search a student's locker or give police the right to do it if there is reason to believe some danger exists to other students or that some rule is being violated; however, the police must have a search warrant to do the same thing elsewhere in society. School "shake-downs" may be a thing of the past and evidence obtained through illegal search, unusable. Even so, will the young offender be judged by peers in a school committee, in a local court, in an administrative review board or by school officials? Is the trial public when it is held in a small area with limited access, or even in a courtroom built years earlier to hold 40 people? Can the defendant demand the proceedings be published, broadcast, or televised to a broader public? Who will decide such matters?

The celebrated trials of the past decades point out the conflict in vivid detail, yet leave the decisions clouded. The Warren Commission was created to satisfy the public's overwhelming "need to know" in the face of social danger; the rights of the individuals in the case were over-ridden: they eventually became academic by later events. The King assassination was viewed as an equally dangerous social situation but the public's "right to know" was superseded by the individual's rights: a guilty plea kept the defendant off the stand and the details out of public scrutiny. The My Lai massacre story would not have been told had not a reporter printed eyewitness accounts of the event by participants. What does a public confession in the newspaper do to an individual's Sixth Amendment rights? The Manson murder case went to trial despite one of its participants publishing a book detailing the event before the trial got underway. President Nixon was quoted as saying Manson was guilty and newspapers the next day headlined the story across the nation. Manson himself managed to sneak a newspaper into court and hold it up for the jury to see, but the judge ruled the jury was "unaffected" by that. There are countless other examples: the Pentagon Papers, Angela Davis, Watergate, the Chicago Seven, Berrigan Brothers, the CIA investigative report; all point out the conflict of these rights.

Another major problem is control and access. The print media for generations have had absolute control of who, what, when, where, why, and how in publication, opening their pages to whomever they wished, closing them likewise; it was considered a legal right. Then the electronic media emerged with guidelines developed by the Federal Communications Commission, the fair news doctrine, and the Federal Trade Commission. The FCC took the approach that the airwaves belonged to the people and that the limited number of frequencies available made it imperative that presentations be fair, balanced, and that access be open to differing views. In broadcasting, the right to reply is given equal legal standing with the right to speak (publish): counter advertising and editorial replies are but two examples of it. With this established, the next controversy arises in the area of access: who, what, when, where, why, and how? Internal media control is no longer viewed as fair, legal, or even desirable. There is growing external control being exerted by citizen groups from without and by professionals from within. The entire function and role of the mass media are under examination, their power challenged, their codes evaluated, not only as media of mass communications but as interpersonal ones as well. Fairness is considered a better goal than objectivity. Printed material is being examined using the legal and governmental criteria of the broadcaster.

The school board, county or district, will find it necessary to enter into the communications business on all levels, not just the limited few used today. It will publish its own newspapers, books, and magazines, set up its own broadcast and closed circuit facilities, develop and spread its own advertising, public service, and public relations messages. Much of this is being done now in some form at some level, but it is not coordinated; the business of education will require more skillful communication in all areas plus greater care in the selection of materials used in schools to ensure balance and fairness. Publication is being undertaken by more and more individuals, groups, and organizations, with special problems or special points of view, or special needs. Educators will be forced to establish conduits in all areas and open up existing ones to all constituents.

Copyright is yet another major problem area in communication and one with serious ramifications for educators. Copyright, as we knew it, is, for all practical purposes, dead. The original law was so antiquated that it could not effectively deal with the technological and libertarian advances in communication in this century. Attempts to revise the old law failed and new legislation stalled in Congress for years, bogged down by ignorance, selfishness, and indifference, on one hand, and by the challenge of continual change on the other. The onslaught of new technology made existing laws ineffective and unenforceable. The Xerox process and subsequent copying systems, coupled with film, computers, audio and video tape, and data transmission dealt a death blow to creative ownership. The decision by manufacturers and business people to put copying products in the hands of the consumer forever removed the possibility of effective copyright control of existing materials, or of new materials distributed in the old way. Materials to be copied were readily available and freely transmitted; copying tools were both physically and financially available.

A major southern university joint library system began copying the nightly network television news programs in the late sixties, viewing this as a needed service for scholars and the community. The rationale was sound in that there was no way to make readily available all the "published" television news material broadcast nightly in America.

If someone wished to "study or review" such material it was only available at the networks or by special arrangement and private screening through a local affiliate. There was no microfilm copy available at the local library, and there was no way to purchase a copy either. In a few instances it was possible to "rent" a copy of the program, months later, if it had been copied on film and made available through a rental agency.

It is interesting to conjecture why it took television to awaken libraries to the problem of access to such material; nothing had been done for decades about radio programs or films. The library system did not choose to videotape entertainment programs—had it done that the reaction might have been quicker and more decisive—just programs of news and public affairs offerings of a historical nature. Not much was done about the practice until people began using the service and the library system began making duplicate tapes for use by "people with a justifiable research interest." Film and television producers now realize they must make a copy of their offerings available and that the Library of Congress is one good place to start. The original case against the library in question was later quietly dropped; however, the matter will undoubtedly come up again while usage, access, and availability problems are fought. The library, rental, publishing, and broadcast systems can never control what has been already distributed. The only real and effective control may come in newly duplicated or distributed products—printed, filmed, taped, or broadcast materials—specially designed to thwart illegal copying, or priced at the point of purchase/distribution to cover the possibility of wholesale copying, or the resale of already copied materials.

The plight of the record and tape music companies best illustrates what the future holds for other media. "Pirating," the theft, copying, and wholesale distribution of material, will continue to spread. Pirating takes place today in every aspect of communication from mass to personal: we don't ask the distributor where the item came from; we don't ask the individual where the idea came from. Plagiarism is so rampant in educational and business institutions that it is ignored rather than dealt with. There may be some way to effectively control the individual's attempt to copy new material, perhaps by transmitting the material in a noncopiable form, or by making the copying process more expensive than one can afford; however, a video copier costs less than a thousand dollars, other types only a few hundred. The copying by individuals of material for their own use will continue—and will be unstoppable.

The concept of the used book store or eight-track tape swap store provides one model of how much of the material will be redistributed. Swap clubs, much like those that now exist for old comics, radio shows, magazines, and films, will spring up to facilitate the underground, individual transfer of material, while bootleg copies, from illegal sources, will continue to be mixed with the legitimate product and sold to unsuspecting consumers. Scholastic materials, such as tests, papers, and projects, will not be immune; "paper mills" are only the first such example. It is probable that the courts will view the process much the way they now treat the ownership of books and magazines, namely, that once purchased (or created), they become the private property of the purchaser and therefore are subject to barter.

Libraries and schools will undoubtedly be hardest hit by the new copyright laws since they provide an enforceable focal point, and their very existence is proof of their interest in controlled protection and distribution of materials. The business person will undoubtedly continue to pass on the enforcement problem to someone else. The sales potential for the copying process and materials is too great to be long fettered. The personal home copier is already a reality in every medium and the market potential is as high for them as was the television or stereo set. Any industry that can number its potential customers in the hundreds of millions cannot be stopped, even by a new copyright law.

The simplest way for educators to view the direction the copyright process will take is to examine what is now practiced and theorize from there. First, the newly created product, be it a book, play, film, article, song, or whatever, will be handled much the way a potential best seller is now; namely, the rights are divided and sold in different places for differing amounts: hardback one place, paperback another, film another, and so on. Most of the time these rights are negotiated before the point of publication/distribution and they are either done on an exact dollar basis or on a percentage. Educational materials will not be immune from similar pre-publication sale. Second, the price of copying materials already extant will be raised at the storage and distribution points in society, libraries, schools, and the like. The cost of copying material could be doubled quickly by changing the coin operated machines and upping the lease costs on others; the extra money would be earmarked for a special creative/copyright distribution fund.

The music industry and the newspaper business both have organizations handling such rights today. Looking at two of the most famous ones in music gives insight into how copying funds could be distributed. ASCAP and BMI charge subscribers a fee based on the completeness of the service/material available to them for reproduction and replay. That fee is based on what class the customers fall in and what rights they buy. Newspapers pay wire service organizations a fee to use stories, columns, and material, the fee based on the size and circulation of the paper. Television, theater, and film companies already have a royalty system in operation based on original contribution and final control of the product. Complex contractual agreements provide both access and control. The increasing computerization of material provides another enforceable method through coding, selection, distribution, price, and royalty. Educators should understand what is happening, what has happened, and what will happen in communications in order to deal with new developments.

Media in Particular

The newspaper in America is undergoing considerable change; circulation is on the increase but readership is on the decline. More people read newspapers today than ever before, but the average reader reads less of the paper. The one-paper family is the rule and the number of families receiving two papers is miniscule; however, more than one paper usually enters the house or is read by its members. The second paper is usually a specialty one, a suburban shopper, a trade or school paper, or a newsletter. The metropolitan or city paper covers less and less of the area it circulates in, preferring to extend further into the suburbs and surrounding counties. What emerges in metropolitan areas is a huge paper with multiple sections, some special inserts for the suburbs and counties, yet less specific coverage of the entire area. A paper distributed over a three hundred square mile area cannot cover that area; it does, however, provide a sophisticated package with an abundance of bad news from many places. The local paper does a better job on local news and gives a more balanced sense of community but it can't compete with the sheer bulk and variety of the city paper.

Newspaper advertising is varied and plentiful but news coverage tends to be narrower and narrower; specialty sections and special columns are taking over more and more of the space, leaving less of it for local news. Inserts appear daily in the bigger papers and the small, or weeklies, can't compete. The prospect is for increasing specialization and compartmentalization within the paper with more and more papers distributing the same sections. The Sunday edition of most papers is an example of where the daily paper will go. It's not inconceivable that we'll have the same national section of the paper distributed in several states, printed in several regions from a computerized control center or system tape. The regional section and the state section of the paper could follow suit, leaving only the local section to be locally gathered and printed; it may form the envelope for the other sections. This would preserve the logo (title page) of the *Daily Chronicle* while beefing up its inner sections to compete with larger papers and television coverage. The specialty sections may have utilization possibilities for the local school or school systems such as replacing the old "Weekly Reader" for elementary schools with something bought locally.

The newspaper may become a complex of sections arranged by special order for each customer; thus one could have the local paper delivered to the door with an international section, a regional and state section, with perhaps *The New York Times Book Review* magazine, the *Los Angeles Times* entertainment section, and the *Atlanta Constitution's* medical section. The paper will use its idle printing facilities to put out special local sections which could include school or college papers whose issues could then be distributed along with the regular paper. It may even provide a supplemental text adopted by local school systems.

Newspapers will increasingly be used as mass circulators of informational and educational material; some papers now offer correspondence courses with printed lecture materials, pictures, and assignments mixed right in with the normal news fare. Why not a series of multiple choice questions at the end of a news article? Or a suggested assignment, discussion activity? Newspapers will undoubtedly merge with magazines to offer their distribution services to all comers, first, because of their door-to-door delivery capability, and second, to combat the continual rise in postal rates. Newspapers will begin offering a whole range of community services, but now on special order. The bigger papers will contract with doctors, lawyers, educators, and professionals in all fields or will buy such services from national printing and distribution centers. For example, basic research results are available on poisons and antidotes; it could become a chapter in a larger work or be issued in paperback or a magazine style section, perhaps with holes punched for later insertion in a three-ring home medical binder (distributed as a circulation incentive), or it may be ordered on microfilm or microfiche and sold to subscribers as part of the paper's specialized computerized order service.

Newspaper distribution might eventually evolve into an electronic screen system hooked to cable television where we see the story projected on a television screen, are able to copy it with a home copier, order more data as a follow-up, perhaps in some other form, print, tape, or video cassette. Newspapers will continue to have a lock on news information and gathering, and that service will become one of their most valuable assets—provided it is indexed and available—the other being their current, demographic subscriber lists with daily access and delivery capability. The newspaper news, feature, and syndicate services will grow in specialization, combining and competing with library, school, and university systems to provide special order software that will be packaged, carried, and presented by specially bought hardware. Newspapers, magazines, libraries, and universities are the "information morgues" of society and their files represent unmined raw materials. *The New York Times* is already computerizing its present and past indexes and will be able to offer instant computerized research and information printout. What could evolve eventually is a system of information supermarkets, linked by computer, offering a variety of special products, packages, and able to provide a "special cut" to any customer willing to pay for it.

Magazines in America are becoming increasingly specialized, serving continually more homogeneous subscribers, reaching even further toward the select, special audience concept. The magazine is rapidly becoming one of the most personal of media choices. The general circulation magazine is largely a thing of the past since it cannot compete with television for the mass general audience; the two notable exceptions are service publications, *TV Guide,* and *Reader's Digest,* both offering condensed information and both connected to other media.

Advertisers want preferred stock when it comes to magazine subscription lists. The general magazine is increasingly a regional or local publication with the greatest rise coming in special institutional or trade magazines. Magazines are supposedly "intellectualized" over by readers more than newspapers, radio, television, or film, thus certain types of messages are best put there. Magazines will undergo a revolution in distribution in the coming decades to combat rising postal rates; home delivery in conjunction with newspapers is one possibility.

The national magazine will begin to treat content the same way it does ads, inserting different material for different sections of the country, and finally, like newspapers, providing a product computer packaged to individual taste. The specialty magazine and the special newspaper section will fight it out for acceptance by the same subscriber; it could result in the *Reader's Digest* concept of reprints being taken over by newspapers through special sections.

School boards and districts might well consider redefining their communication carrier decisions to allow distribution of materials in print form through both newspapers and magazines. Magazines will exercise great care about whom they "allow" to subscribe to their publications to control readership, and even newsstand sales will be curtailed except where location is related to demographic choice.

Magazines will be forced to create and use a service like AP and UPI to get material, and will sell their own material for use in competing publications out of their immediate circulation area or as reprints after initial publication. Magazines will be more concerned with reader response and will actively collect it; magazines today ignore a potent feedback opportunity through the postcard insert: most magazines contain postcard mail-back offers within their covers, often connected with sub-scription renewals or special product offers. Thus, the vehicle is already there to sample or test their own audience in numerous ways. Magazines will soon urge such response and finally pay for it through free gifts, reduced subscription prices, or more media of some type. This same technique could also be used by any print medium to extend the school year through the summer months for children K-12, or be used for children ages three through six as a preschool readiness activity. Maga-zines could combine with tape and record clubs to issue tapes of the audio portion of the message while the magazines provide the pictures or slides to go with the data, a sort of ongoing cassette/filmstrip program. In the coming decades, the magazine, the newspaper, and the paperback book will interchange content and directly compete.

The big story in books remains the rise of the paperback and the death of the hardback, the death of that type of permanence. The expense of printing and distribution will gradually force the hardback publica-tion off the market. Libraries and school systems will add a few unnatural years to its life but its size and expense will be counterproductive. Books will be standardized in size just as magazines and newspapers are. Pub-lishers, to combat the problem of disintegration, will develop special covers and treatment for school and library paperbacks; a plasticized cover is but one possibility. Schools and libraries will be forced to further categorize their holdings, marking some for permanent collections, others for transient use, in relation either to the life of the physical book or to the value of its contents over time. Libraries and schools will be able to microfilm/microfiche their holdings or purchase such material for use when the physical book is no longer usable or is taking up valuable space. Libraries and schools will be able to double and triple their holdings in view of the reduced size of the new books.

The book as fiction is still alive but is slowly being challenged by the book as nonfiction. New readers tend to pick nonfiction, and content is increasingly a spin-off of the reality of news and mass media presentations and decreasingly the work of creation that is developed for posterity. Pulp and fad material will move into newspapers and magazines to more readily become throwaway material; advertising sponsorship is also more accepted in those forms. The commercial break and the ad have already entered the book field through the full page ad inserted midway through the paperback; soon the content of the ad will be keyed to the type of book or reader involved, and that followed by ads of a special type placed strategically at heightened points of interest or breaks in the story.

Television and radio regularly clue their audiences to watch for special ads in newspapers or special issues of magazines and special sections of papers; many paperbacks are advertised in other media; soon, the same approach will be used to advertise content. The broadcaster might combine with the publisher/printer in promoting material or in providing data in depth. The viewer might see a story on television, be told the newspaper planned a follow-up series, be able to order a book related to the topic or request additional data by phone or cable television hookup. This will generate the return of fiction material and other paperback content in other forms, particularly the magazine format since it lends itself so readily to publishing an entire book or to serializing it, chapter by chapter. Sample segments, chapters, short stories, and excerpts will be sold to newspapers, magazines, and television stations at reduced rates to generate book orders and sales. Finally, look for the development of "best seller" of the month clubs only in paperback. The book is not dead, it will rise again in other forms, and this will have major implications for public schools.

Advertising and public relations were once different fields but they are becoming inseparable today and are often indistinguishable; the techniques of one become the tools of the other. Advertising seizes on whatever is current in society and trades on it as a communication tool. Businesses communicate with the public through advertising and public relations, thus they become filtering mechanisms for society, the web through which the societal nerve is tapped. Advertising is really the most persistent and pervasive of the communications media because it exists at the core of all of them: the message is the medium. The advertiser's function is minimal in the early stages of a medium's growth; the medium exists first as a carrier with a purpose and an audience; later, the inclusion of advertising helps underwrite the rising costs of production and distribution, until finally, the creation and distribution of the product is no longer possible without heavy advertiser support. Newspapers and magazines went from subscriber supported to advertiser supported: the large newspapers and magazines do not go out of business because they lack subscribers or circulation, they die from withdrawal of advertiser support. Books and films were always supported solely by audience purchase; radio and television, in America, are supported solely by advertisers. However, the picture is changing daily; advertiser support is now present in some form in every medium: the same is true for circulation revenue. One way for schools to cut costs in public school texts would be to allow advertising in the books but not without the perils described earlier.

Public relations is the soft sell of advertising and it permeates society today at all levels. Public relations has two prongs, the propagandistic, personal, informative approach, and the misdirected, after the fact approach, personified by the "cover-up" or "counter release." Advertising is the most effective line of communication with the public and that line is readily available and used for public relations messages. The public is becoming conscious that it can feed back along these same lines with startlingly effective results; witness the success of counter advertising suits in the case of cigarette ads or in corrective language requirements in other ads. It may be that misstatements in the public relations area will be scrutinized with the same results.

Counter advertising is effective as exemplified by the nonsmoking messages that were put on television, but it may be something that the schools will have to involve themselves in if it is to be done regularly and effectively. Consumer reporting is largely a farce in most of the media; only a few magazines devote themselves to it seriously: little or none of it exists in the media as a whole. No one is training the consumer to deal with the onslaught of ads and PR messages. There is a real need for courses in media understanding, message analysis, and consumer education, courses that make use of student involvement in the communication process. For example, research on shoplifting indicates that it goes up in direct proportion to the increase in advertising at peak buying seasons such as Christmas. There are dozens of organizations that can supply schools with information on how to monitor and analyze each medium; even the most cursory examination yields relevant educational material.

The film medium is one people still love and respect, particularly the young. The general distaste large segments of the population feel about other media is not true for film. True, content is coming under increasing criticism but not by the people who attend the most films. There is a selective aspect of film that protects it from any general "anti-media" feeling. People invest more of themselves in film selection than they do in other media selections. Radio and television are background sounds or random selections depending on time and place; people flip the dial in search of something to tune to. Newspapers and magazines get transient attention, depending on time and place. Film, however, is more like a book, or an evening at the theater, in that its audience selects it more carefully than the others, setting aside a large block of time and preparing for the experience through careful selection; this type of "individual investment" causes the person to be more pleased with the product. Public opinion surveys indicate that television is the "most trusted, most believed" medium, but film is the most loved.

Film technique, however, is being strongly altered by television presentations; the quick cutting, montage story line of the television commercial is one example; slow motion, extreme close-ups, and fast-paced openings are others. Film content is affected by news reports and the most successful film content (in box office terms) is something that was created for another medium, a book, play, or song. Film is one medium of mass communication that still is primarily supported by audience revenue (as the book was) , and thus it is often closer to the heartbeat of the public than other media. The public uses newspapers and magazines in different ways and the advertiser pays the greatest share of the cost of development and distribution; radio and television are totally dependent on the advertiser. Film, however, presently gets all its revenue "after the fact" of publication or release and thus is often a clearer index of audience likes and dislikes. The only difficulty is that a successful film is measured in terms of dollar response and the more mass the audience the more successful the film. The film producers now feel it is better to make fewer films for more profit rather than tie up production facilities for lower yield products. Fighting this is growing proof that film attendance is now a "young" activity; attendance drops off drastically with age, thus more films are made for young people, further ensuring the cycle. Newspaper, magazine, and book readership increase with age; radio listenership and record buying decrease with age; susceptibility to advertising and public relations messages decreases with age. The only way these trends are countered is through specialty productions, a return to the segmented-audience concept.

Film will undoubtedly move toward commercial sponsorship in the same way newspapers, magazines, radio, and television have done. Commercials appear regularly now in most movie theaters, but they are sandwiched between selections or at intermissions and audiences are not really aware that the "commercial break" concept of television has already hit them in the movie house.

Radio is one medium that is still alive and well and living in America. It's not as prosperous as it once was but there are three to four times as many radio sets in this country as there are television sets; that makes radio a medium with maximum saturation potential. Radio is used in newly developing nations as the most effective medium for reaching large masses cheaply, of reaching the illiterate, and for reaching out, through music, to cross and break ethnic barriers in multidialect areas. In this country, however, large segments of society turn off and tune out radio. The young view radio as an electronic jukebox and give it more of their time than any other age group. School children take the most advantage of radio's portability.

Educators mostly ignore radio as a viable communication medium, preferring to sink dollars heavily into television and books as carriers and information sources. Much of what is transmitted by school television is really visual radio; costs could be cut greatly by using radio when the message has no real visual dimension. School boards and libraries should invest in radio, just the way they have in print, programming for each age group with solid music interspersed with information and education capsules. Radio will become increasingly specialized much as magazines are today, serving smaller, more homogeneous audiences with material tailored for them. Sideband stations will allow the "request" concept now applied to music on the commercial station to be extended to data and information. The sideband station and the growing popularity of Citizen Band radio both offer real possibilities for educators. The CB craze is really just a societal attempt to balance the preponderance of one way communication and the lag in the maximum development of the telephone. CB equipment could be used in school management, security and patrol, safety and scholarship. It could open up direct communication between educators and community leaders, between students, their libraries and their institutions. The low cost of CB equipment will force the phone companies to make mobile units less expensive to own and operate and to financially foster more educational services.

Television, the newest medium in the arsenal of mass communication, remains the most persuasive and influential. Television has more effect on us than we realize. Television is a business, a technology, and a social force, and it affects people in all those areas. The commercial aspects of television are largely ignored by educators and this is a gross mistake. The statistics indicate that the average individual now watches 6½ to 7½ hours of television each day; that is one-third of the day, as much as people sleep, or work, or attend school. We understand how important the other two-thirds of the day are to an individual's growth and well-being, yet we neglect the obvious: more experiential activity and learning take place via television than via *any other life activity*. We worry about the school environment, the neighborhood, the home, hot lunches, yet neglect the most effective/affective one, the television environment.

If we were presented with a student who read for 7½ hours a day, we would see that as extremely relevant in educational terms. If we had a student who spent one-third of his or her academic years traveling from place to place, seeing plays, films, sports, and current events, we would know this was a vital element in the student's development and education. We would readily accept the fact that this wealth of experience should be shared with others and should be made use of in an educational context. A student who views 20,000 hours of television becomes a critic, experienced, sophisticated, knowledgeable, through saturation if nothing else. However, the most damning aspect of it all is that educators neglect the fact that commercial television is an experience shared in startlingly similar ways by the mass of their students. If a teacher found that over 80 percent of the class were, on their own, reading the same books, wouldn't educational utilization and response be mandated by that fact?

Television, even at its worst, teaches something, be it language, life styles, or socialization, and it does it in a way that overrides all other factors—if not by the force of its content then by the massiveness of its presence. Give any teacher 7½ hours of voluntary access to a student each day and that teacher will dominate that student's life, for good or ill. Who has the child for six years before school begins? The parent and the television set. Who has the child when school begins? The school, the television set, and the community. Which of these involvements is voluntary? Which is personally selected?

Television, with the exception of situation comedy, is moving to longer formats, both in dramatic and informational programs. The longer news and information programs demand more balanced in-depth coverage and presentation; the longer dramatic programs force greater character development, more subplots, and less emphasis on surface action: the changes, however, are gradual. The commercials are beautifully packaged, expertly filmed, and highly effective; they are a blend of information and persuasion in a capsule segment: they have impact and they work. The advertising module is designed to give an impression and to generate a response: it is painless and it works.

The dramatic content of much of television is, on the other hand, shallow and unreal. The 20,000 hour student of television is led to expect information in compact, entertaining bits, with choices clearly spelled out and results effectively associated with actions. The student has seen too many perky presentations; education is dull and drab by comparison. The dramatic involvements of the characters on television lead one to believe that there are simple, easy solutions to most problems, that institutions and officials are incompetent, and that solutions lie in direct personal action or avoidance. Problems are often presented in graphic detail and solutions in sugary vapor: more often than not the problem is killed or talked away.

The 20,000 hour student may realize that the educational program/ film and the entertainment program/film are different, but can one push aside the sophistication that 20,000 hours produce? Why not use that sophistication to lead students to a better understanding of what they are seeing, to making better selections from what is available? Numerous organizations send out free listings of upcoming television offerings, and television guides are available in all good-sized cities; educators could post and publish their own listings and distribute them both in and out of school, probably with advertiser support or as a special section in the weekly paper. One hour of assigned homework viewing a day could make a difference in a student's lifetime viewing habits.

The electronic potential of the televised signal far surpasses any other communication medium and allows the first true blend of technology, mass, and interpersonal communication. Television currently is divided into two types of signals, open circuit (VHF and UHF), and closed circuit (cable and megahertz transmission). Open circuit television is when the signal is sent into the air from a tower/transmitter and may be received anywhere within the range of the signal by anyone with a properly tuned receiver set: commercial and public television stations broadcast this way. Closed circuit television is the transmission of signals from point to point through cables, phone lines, or line of sight beams, and may only be picked up by someone who is connected directly in some way. This means that the open circuit program is sent out in search of viewers, while the closed circuit program is transmitted at the request of viewers. The closed circuit program or presentation is therefore like a phone call: limited, private, and, in most cases, not subject to the same standards, regulations, and considerations as the former. The course on sex education broadcast over a public television station could reach persons it was not intended for, while the closed circuit program would only go where requested. The closed circuit program does not come under the same FCC provisions as the open circuit one when used privately in business or education. Commercial cable television systems, however, do come under the FCC.

The normal television set today has 83 channels for reception, but the average viewer gets only three or four to choose from, usually the three networks and an independent. Cable television systems sprang up years ago to bring the signal to outlying areas. Cable operators then laid lines directly to the home set of each subscriber. The cable operator used a coaxial cable, one with multiple strands, capable of bringing many audio/video signals into the home. It was a quantum leap over the telephone company whose millions of wires had but one audio capability. The rest is history. Cable operators first sent their own pictures on one channel, usually a clock, temperature gauge, and the name of the cable company; eventually news reports, interviews, local announcements, films, sports events, and finally reruns of oldtime television programs were transmitted.

Today, the FCC requires all CATV operators to originate some programming, allows them to include commercials, and is gradually letting them compete with existing television stations. There is a requirement that two or three channels be set aside for local use; one usually for education, one for government, and one for the community. Most CATV systems provide hookups to educational institutions free and many also try to tie into school audio/video production centers, to learning resource centers, or to closed circuit centers. This means that students and school officials have access to the community and can send out their own information and public relations messages. Some CATV operators are even turning over their production facilities to students and educators to produce material during the off hours. This cable connection should be sought after by educators, not avoided.

The potential for in-service training using closed circuit television is well known by most educators. What is not realized is how useful the cable system could be in programs of adult education, continuing education, or general communication with parents and the community. The time to establish the connection with a cable system or to extend your own closed circuit system is now while those dozens of channels are empty and can be easily utilized. A CATV educational channel could make great inroads into student and community viewing habits by doing nothing more than taping valuable commercial or public television offerings and replaying them at more appropriate times or to select groups. New businesses are finding ways to utilize those vacant channels, hooking them up to burglar alarms, meter reading systems, to weather scanning or surveillance cameras; apartment complexes are setting up their own systems and tapping into the cable to provide their tenants with specialized services. Educators should be certain that they are aware of what is happening in cable television as it is or is planned in their communities. The time is now, the challenge is to involvement and excellence.

The Challenge to Education — A Viewpoint

In his incisive way, John Gardner, former Secretary of the Department of Health, Education, and Welfare, observed in 1971 that he was convinced that 20 years from now we would look back at our school system and ask ourselves how society could have tolerated anything as primitive as education today. "The pieces of an educational revolution are lying around unassembled."

There is no doubt that an educational revolution is all about us. And Gardner's metaphoric "pieces" and "unassembled" are especially appropriate, for the potential revolution has a major technological component. This revolution will engage the entire communications structure of society and will produce both great rewards and great changes in our society. Writing in *Computers, Communications, and the Public Interest*, James Coleman[2] warns of the danger of changes in communication struc-

2 James Coleman. *Computers, Communications and the Public Interest*. Martin Greenberger, editor. Baltimore: Johns Hopkins University Press, 1971. Copyright © 1971 Johns Hopkins University Press.

ture outside educational institutions, "powerful and persuasive changes that have unplanned and unanticipated effects on schools. These effects are often not recognized until after they have wrought their changes. . . . The indirect impact of changes in the communication structure of society has been and will be so great that the technological changes in the schools themselves must take place within the new frame that these developments create."

The new frame is being constructed by cable television and other new communication devices that are being linked to it. Its impact can be suggested simply: The broadcast television that has become so familiar to everyone during the past 25 years is like the passenger railroad, taking viewers to scheduled places at scheduled times. Cable television has the potential of becoming like a highway network, permitting viewers to use their television sets as they use their automobiles, selecting education, information, and entertainment at times and places of their own choosing. Cable, video cassettes, computer information systems, and communication satellites are now at a stage that permits us to create an "information utility" which can give instant access to society's information resources in every home and business. Educators can help direct the development of the new technologies, or they can become the passive and partial beneficiaries—perhaps the victims—of uncontrolled technological change.

Consider the way the communication structure is changing: Small cities like Gainesville, Florida (population: 64,000), that once depended upon television stations in Jacksonville can now have their own local stations to originate programming—not just relay stations that bring in programs from large cities, but stations that originate   programs. Even small towns like Brattleboro, Vermont (population: 12,000), are fully capable with cable of supporting local stations.

Because cable offers many more channels than does over-the-air television, those who argue that the commercial media stifle minority views can be given many more hours on television than they can possibly use. In fact, so many channels can be made available that public officials and others who complain that television devotes too little time and attention to their concerns will find cable a sturdy soapbox. Almost anyone who believes that television must promote "High Culture" will be able to read this epic poem or play the flute to as much of an audience as she or he can attract, and at little cost.

Cable can be designed to provide a two way avenue so that the receiver of information and entertainment can make choices to a degree that is not now possible and transmit those decisions upstream to the cable operator. Today, the sender—a television news producer or a newspaper editor—selects a few items from among the hundreds available and shapes the six o'clock news or the afternoon paper for everyone. The receiver can switch to another channel or buy another paper, but is still limited to the choices made by the senders. The new technology will make it possible for the receiver to order individually from those dozens of items. Some day it might work this way:

Sitting at the breakfast table or in the classroom, by touching a key, you cause the latest headlines to appear on a small display screen. These headlines might have been written five minutes before. You select one headline because you want its story displayed. If it is a continuing story, like a war or an election campaign, you might want to get either a report of the latest incident or background information or interpretation. For someone with a special interest, for example, particular legislation pending in Congress, it could be possible to retrieve the latest story whether or not it had received a headline, or even appeared in the latest edition of the newspaper.

With a slightly more expensive computer terminal, your news summary can be printed out for you while you are shaving or getting dressed. A wide variety of background information might be made available by an information utility, on demand by the receiver. Suppose you encounter a name of a person you would like to know more about: ask for a biographical sketch. Suppose you do not completely understand the economic reasoning behind an action by the International Monetary Fund; there might be a short tutorial program on some aspect of international economics, or you may just seek a brief explanation of some technical term. Suppose you do not see any sense in the actions of the local campus radicals and are genuinely curious about their motivation. You might request their own original statement. Suppose you want to have their actions interpreted in the framework of a viewpoint you already understand and appreciate: ask for the latest analysis by your favorite columnist. Suppose you want to see the supermarket ads. Instead of shuffling pages, you may just ask for a display of ads in a particular category. A child, home from school or at school, may wish to have the computer display what the *Children's Encyclopedia* says in answer to a question. Suppose a high school student wishes to search the equivalent of the local public library for information needed to write a term paper. He or she can quickly search the equivalent of the card catalog and soon be browsing in relevant material. A parent can select readiness activities. for a four year old child. Evaluation of the results can follow with suggestions of additional readiness activities. This two way capability is the most revolutionary as well as the most intriguing feature of the new technology. In its simplest form, home to cable station, it will enable us to shop, bank, take music lessons, and take a wide variety of courses, all without leaving home. As the system is made more sophisticated in a way that allows home-to-home, home-to-office, and home-to-school communication, we can consult physicians and educators, mail letters electronically—and privately—and it is even conceivable that we will be able to vote while sitting in the living room.

The Nonverbal Experience —
A Second View of Communications

Research in the area of nonverbal behavior emerged in the early 1930's; however, only during the past 20 years has it developed as a distinctive area of communication. Today, many universities across the United States offer training in nonverbal communication, and some high schools have included this area in their speech curriculum.

What are the nonverbal behaviors under the heading of *Nonverbal Communication*? Historically, nonverbal communication has come to mean communication without words, although this is not often a useful definition. Areas generally included under this broad definition include: facial gestures, body shape and appearance, personal space, territoriality, vocal qualities, and even aspects of the physical environment such as furniture placement and color.

More specifically, nonverbal behaviors are viewed as being part of the larger concept of communication where words are neither spoken nor written.[3] In effect, then, nonverbal behaviors are isolated only for the full understanding of the communication process.

Communication is frequently defined today in a transactional framework where meanings are assigned to experiences. Assigning meanings to experiences makes the analysis of communication far different than when dealing only with what the speaker intended; or viewing everything as a message with standard accepted meanings; or dealing with meanings selected by receivers. This current view of communication serves to clarify and expand our understanding of *Nonverbal Communication*. It is not the nonverbal experience that communicates, rather it is the meaning we assign to the nonverbal experience. This assigned meaning may be spoken or written about (made verbal), while the experience itself remains nonverbal. Nonverbal experiences do not communicate anything until we assign meanings to them.

In most cases, we have a fundamental commonsense understanding of the nonverbal elements in communication. However, we may not have

[3] Lawrence B. Rosenfeld and Jean M. Civikly. *With Words Unspoken: The Nonverbal Experience*. New York: Holt, Rinehart and Winston, Inc., 1976. p. 10.

taken the time to learn to manipulate these nonverbal elements to our communicative advantage. We may also not have allowed ourselves the opportunity of objectivity by finding out how others assign meanings to the way we use nonverbal expressions in our communication process. This is of particular importance in the teaching and learning process.

Functional Importance. The functional importance of nonverbal communication cannot be minimized. Leathers, in his book *Nonverbal Communication Systems,* lists six reasons for the functional significance of nonverbal communications.[4]

First, "Nonverbal, not verbal, elements are the major determinants of meaning in the interpersonal context." It is believed that nonverbal elements are responsible for well over half of the meaning assigned during interpersonal communication. How often do students identify the importance of an assignment not by what was said, but rather by the tone and intensity of how it was said. When the teacher says, "Yes, it is your turn to go to the water fountain," the child decides because of the smile pulled to one side, the tilt of the teacher's head, or the look in the teacher's eye that he is really not thirsty. Often when a person is given contradictory stimuli such as a verbal "yes" and a nonverbal "no" the nonverbal elements are the primary determinants of how the individual responds.

However, one phenomenon must be considered; when given contradictory cues, we place our reliance on the cues we consider harder to fake.[5] Only our personal experiences and preferences will determine whether we consider contradictory nonverbal cues harder to fake. These same preferences will function in determining which of the contradicting nonverbal cues we will consider harder to fake.

Second, "Feelings and emotions are more accurately exchanged by nonverbal than by verbal means." When asked how we feel we may respond with "great"; however, our gait, posture, and facial expressions reveal that we are, in fact, down in the dumps. When the phrase "I trust you" is verbalized it is believed if it is accompanied by nonverbal elements which reinforce that verbalization, otherwise the individual may suspect the statement to be untrue.

Third, "The nonverbal portion of communication conveys meanings and intentions that are relatively free of deception, distortion, and confusion." Most nonverbal responses come quickly and without intellectual preparation. It is believed that verbal communication can be used to

4 Dale G. Leathers. *Nonverbal Communication Systems.* Boston: Allyn and Bacon, Inc., 1976. pp. 3-8. Copyright © 1976 Allyn and Bacon. Reprinted with permission.

5 Rosenfeld, *op. cit.,* p. 12.

deceive, distort, and confuse because of our conscious control. It is often believed that nonverbal elements such as glances, posture, and movement are generally not consciously controlled and, therefore, harder to fake. While the face probably has the reputation of being the best deceiver around, we rely on the nonverbal cues as generally being free of deception because our personal experiences tend to reinforce that position.

Fourth, "Nonverbal cues serve a metacommunicative function that is indispensable in attaining high quality communication." Metacommunications are messages about communication. When someone says, "I'll give you $5.00 for that book," you may not believe this even though the person says, "I'm serious." However, when she presents the money, the nonverbal cue takes precedence and you are convinced the other person means business. Use of nonverbal elements in determining meaning often helps eliminate conflicting cues by focusing the listener on the intent of the speaker. This improves the quality of communication between individuals.

Fifth, "Nonverbal cues represent a much more efficient means of communication than verbal cues." Well-worn statements such as "a look says it all," and "a picture is worth a thousand words," add support to the efficiency of nonverbal elements. Nonverbal channels are very capable of efficient communication. A child that raises its hand signals instant meaning to a teacher. A teacher who closes the door may likewise signal meaning to a principal or visiting supervisor. The slides or film used on the national news may also signal nonverbal cues to the viewing audience.

Sixth, "Nonverbal cues represent the most suitable vehicle for suggestion." Nonverbal suggestion is the most efficient way to deal with our image of ourselves. We suggest that we feel okay by the smile we wear on our face. The teacher suggests that the child's verbal answer is correct in the way that he moves his head. The school's lunchroom garbage can suggest certain things about the lunch program and the socioeconomic class of the student body. We can suggest that we have a good-looking body by the clothes we wear and the makeup we apply to our face.

Nonverbal cues can suggest to the child that she is liked and respected by the teacher. They can also suggest that the teacher wishes the child would go away. Thus, nonverbal cues are efficient suggestions that deserve our attention.

Nonverbal Areas. Nonverbal communication can be more easily clarified if it is broken down into its presumed components. The following aspects of nonverbal behavior illustrate and briefly suggest the importance of this area of communication. Consider the impact on receivers when a trained person utilizes nonverbal behavior to the best communicative advantage. Consider also that these generalizations will differ with cultural groups.

Eye Contact. It is important to be sensitive to the type and duration of the eye contact used. In general, maintaining eye contact during interaction tends to increase an individual's capacity to communicate verbalized meaning and tends to provide the other person with current feedback on the communication process. However, prolonged eye contact (close to a stare) may signal negative meanings not necessarily related to the verbal message intended.

We tend to make less eye contact while we are speaking than while we are listening. We tend to make less eye contact when we are being shown negative feedback than when we are receiving positive reinforcement. We tend to make more eye contact when we want to include the other person in the conversation; when there is reason to expect approval; or when there is increased intimacy.

Facial Gestures. Increasing our concentration and sensitivity to facial gestures and expressions can greatly enhance our communication capacity. This provides excellent feedback from others on our ability to show meanings through nonverbal gestures. Most individuals need to check what they see in facial gestures with others in order to arrive at some common understanding of the assigned meaning.

Hand Gestures. The hands and their movement are obviously important to communication. In some instances hand gestures can substitute for vocal communication such as in nonverbally pointing out North; or the gestures can repeat what was said verbally as in saying the word "North" and then pointing. Hand gestures can also be contradictory as a teacher tells a parent to "come in, I have plenty of time," but is constantly pulling back a shirt cuff to check the time. But, regardless of possible contradictions, this is an important nonverbal area and we should seek to understand the meaning we convey to others through hand gestures we most frequently use on the job and in our daily life.

Body Appearance. Our body shape is closely related to our self-esteem. If we are excessively overweight many of our body movements and gestures are planned to avoid calling attention to that fact. A scar or birthmark can severely inhibit our communication efforts if we feel others have focused their attention on it. How others have typed our bodies (heavy, athletic, or thin) has a strong bearing on our communication behavior, and those who are viewed as physically attractive are more likely to be sought after for additional interaction.

Body types are associated rather consistently with specific personal characteristics. The first impressions of others are most apt to be influenced by these body characteristics regardless of the personal characteristics of the person in question.[6]

Often our image of our body is different from that perceived by others. We frequently involve ourselves in self-deception, and thus introduce contradiction in our interpersonal communication. We need to be aware of how others view our body so that we may compare our view with theirs.

Clothing. Clothes provide us with considerable information about the wearer. With your attire comes your identity. Uniforms tend to dictate conformity to the group and generate audience expectations about our behavior. Consider how you behaved the last time you saw a police officer.

Students who wear clothing unacceptable to their peers are often in conflict. This conflict is likely to affect their performance and generally causes unhappiness.

Cosmetics. Makeup can change the face so that the reflected image is closer to the desired image. This improves both the self-concept and the communication ability of the individual. When we are pleased with how our faces look, we are more apt to describe ourselves as self-confident.

Hair. Men with long hair are often perceived as less credible than men with shorter hair. This attitude is reflected most vividly during the initial job interviews. Mustaches and beards also elicit different nonverbal responses from different individuals. In general, if a man's hair is unclean, too long, or not neat, he is likely to be evaluated negatively.

Female hair color and length also follow some stereotypes depending on the age and circumstances of the individual. Need we mention the category into which we put the shapely lady whose hair is long and very blond?

Educators with unusual hairstyles may very well convey one image to the students and another image to the community. In the classroom the beard and/or mustache and/or long hair may be accepted by the students. However, in the community where short conservative hairstyles may be more prevalent, the teacher with extreme styles may be viewed with suspicion.

Voice. Vocal cues which accompany the words we utter have a great deal to do with determining the meaning our listeners ascribe to what we say.

1. Volume. The loudness or power of the voice conveys certain meanings. If the volume is such that people must strain to hear us, we

[6] Rosenfeld, *op. cit.,* p. 44.

may be perceived as being weak. On the other hand, the loud voice may be perceived as strong or even offensive.

2. Pitch. Most people rarely use the full range of tones and notes that can be produced by the voice. If too few tones are used by an individual, the person is often perceived as monotonous, boring, apathetic, or unemotional.

3. Rate. If the number of sounds per time unit are too many, speech becomes unintelligible. However, if the rate is too slow, audience interest is lost. The usual rate for spoken English is 150 to 180 words per minute.

4. Silence. The use of short pauses may so reduce the speech rate that the attention of the listener is lost. The use of longer pauses—silence —may be quite useful in indicating emotions and may have greater impact than the other paralinguistic variables for conveying meanings because of their infrequent use.

5. Voice Qualities. Voice qualities are probably the most important of the paralinguistic parameters. Your habitual voice quality can have a lot to do with how you are perceived. Paul Heinberg[7] indicated that if you expel excessive amounts of air while speaking your voice quality is breathy and you are perceived as mentally and physically weak. If you are tense and withhold air when speaking you are perceived as irritable or angry. If when you speak, you elongate vowel sounds like some ministers while preaching, an impression is created of an authority figure. This also conveys to the listener that care and thought are being given to the spoken word. However, if you mumble your words because you don't really move your mouth when you speak, you may be perceived as "cool" by teenagers, but sloppy or not caring by most everyone else. A too-low pitch results in a flat voice quality which is perceived as unemotional or unexcitable. A too-high pitch gives a thin voice quality often perceived as immature and insecure.

If when you speak you habitually open the lips wide and pull the tongue down and back slightly, you sound throaty and can be perceived as not being very bright. If on the other hand, you produce sounds at the front of the mouth very precisely you can be perceived as being overly precise. If when you speak you habitually resonate your sounds through the nasal cavity, you are nasal and can be perceived as irritable.

If you do not use the nasal cavity habitually when you speak, you are denasal and can be perceived as one who probably has a cold or sinus problems.

[7] Paul Heinberg. *Voice Training for Reading and Speaking.* New York: The Ronald Press Co., 1964. Chapter 5, pp. 152-80.

Knowing what voice qualities you produce may help you understand why people react to you in the way they do. Changing a voice quality is a relatively easy process which begins with awareness and is reinforced with practice. The quality of the voice plays a major role in the receptiveness of the listener.

Smell. Human beings both emit and perceive odors which elicit conscious and subconscious response. Body and/or room odor does make a difference in communication. In our American society most natural body odors are associated with negative values. Soap, mouth washes, deodorants, perfumes, and other products are used to help us conform to the nonverbal odor standards.

Touch. Each individual sends and receives messages through the skin. Some of the more obvious touching includes: handshaking, hand on the shoulder, and hand in or on hand. For most people, the concern regarding touch is when or when not to touch. In education, the teacher must identify times when a child needs and wants this kind of reinforcement.

It is important to recognize that there are some unwritten societal rules regarding the appropriateness of touch. A teacher may hold and guide the hand of an elementary child in forming his letters. However, it is quite possible that the same child would not allow the teacher to hold his hand under other circumstances.

Touch is an important nonverbal communication cue. Typically, individuals need to be more sensitive to reinforcement through a touch that expresses care and affection. Touching carries sexual connotations essential for the development of children.

Proxemics. How individuals use space communicates. The closer people are the more intimate are the interpersonal communication possibilities. As distance increases, communication possibilities decrease. In the classroom, students closer to the teacher frequently participate more than students in the side or rear of the classroom. When the talkative/active child is seated at a distance from the teacher, that child's attention-getting activities are frequently interpreted as misbehavior. The greater the number of students you have in a classroom, the more difficult it is to have student participation.

The organization of desks in a classroom may hinder or enhance the learning environment.[8] The location of the principal's furniture or teacher's desk also provides nonverbal cues about the individual. Neatness and order, clutter and mess, also provide informational cues.

[8] Mark L. Knapp. *Nonverbal Communication in Human Interaction.* New York: Holt, Rinehart and Winston, Inc., 1972. p. 25.

Probably the most important space we own is the space around us. While territoriality refers to objects and defined geographic areas, personal space is that area around each of us with us as the center. If someone we do not know gets too close physically to us (enters our personal space), we feel violated and respond by moving back, turning away, or changing the subject. If the space is too great between individuals, communication is equally difficult and frequently interrupted. As space increases, nonverbal cues become more difficult to read and understand. What constitutes personal space generally varies among the regions of this country. What is likely to be acceptable in the East, where we are likely to stand closer to talk, is likely to violate an individual's personal space in the South, where more distance for casual conversation is expected. When we enter a crowded elevator our personal space is violated and we generally compensate by not looking at anyone. When four people are all seated at a card table no one feels their personal space is violated. But remove the table and all four people will move back feeling the others are too close.

Territorial identification by students and individuals is the attempt to indicate ownership. When students enter a classroom for the first time, the initial choice they make regarding where to sit often becomes "their chair." They will return to it every class time unless reassigned to another chair.

Territorial behaviors also establish the pecking order within an organization. For example, the principal has his or her own office, the teachers may share several offices, while students may have a small desk in a room for 30 students. The further up you go toward the top of the order the more careful you must be about feelings of invasion. A student might open the teacher's office door and ask if a specific teacher is there, but the student would be expected to knock or perhaps even check with the secretary before approaching the office of the principal.

The Need for Greater Understanding. Currently we as a nation focus too much on the effect of the "overall feeling" regarding a person or an experience. We need to more clearly integrate what we know about how the effects work on us (how we assign meaning) and why we respond as we do to the meanings we assigned.

As a nation, we are generally unsophisticated and gullible about nonverbal behavior. If the television announcer looks and sounds good and uses the appropriate nonverbal behaviors (according to our evaluative assignment of meaning), we tend to accept or trust what is said. We tend to avoid asking important content questions because of the general impression of honesty we assign to the behavior of the announcer.

Most educators are not trained to recognize and deal with nonverbal behavior in students. The current training process is usually through one's actual experiences in the school. Long hair on a student a few years ago was a signal of nonverbal communication. It was an important nonverbal cue that we assigned meaning to and responded to as a result of the meanings we assigned. The meaning most often associated with long hair was negative in nature, and the response was most often punishment. A fruitful discussion might have been held if the communication intent behind the behavior (long hair) had been explored. Certainly, the punishment was to the ultimate disadvantage of both the educators and the students.

Often the term generation gap is used when two different frames of reference are applied when assigning meaning to nonverbal behavior. Whether the assigning is being done by the youth or the older generation the problem still is one of not comparing the meanings as assigned and discussing those meanings.

Often our expectations determine the meaning we assign to specific aspects of nonverbal behavior. Doesn't the student who looks slow (determined from nonverbal behavior) frequently do poorly on our tests? Sometimes, our expectations predispose the students to certain behavior.

It is important to know how others assign meaning to our attempts at communication. It is also important to understand that when contradicting communication signals (verbal and nonverbal) are given, we tend to rely heavily on the nonverbal signals. What are the critical realities and problems in nonverbal communication? The following is an attempt to identify critical problems of study that will expand our understanding of this area.

1. How can we assign meaning to all the available stimuli so that "good" decisions can be made?

2. How can we sort out all the stimuli available, so that those stimuli which are not important to consider in the decision may be disregarded?

3. How can teachers learn to incorporate, on the interpersonal level, nonverbal signals?

4. How can school programs train students to be discriminating nonverbal observers?

5. How can we know what meaning others assign to our nonverbal cues?

6. What personal resources are available for each of us to use in a nonverbal training program?

7. What implications does this area hold for the academic success and peer acceptance of students?

8. How do the mass media use nonverbal cues in their presentations?

9. Do we realize that nonverbal cues differ in meaning between cultural groups and geographical regions?

Trends. It is predictable with some certainty that interest in nonverbal communication will continue to grow in the future. It is also predictable that future research will expand our understanding and possibly clarify our assignment of meaning to nonverbal cues. If this can occur, it will be a major step to operationalize this dimension of communication. It is an area that can and will help us personalize communication in a mass communication environment. It is an area that needs to be researched if we are to maximize communication in a free society.

Role of Education

The strength of our Republic is dependent upon development of the potential of all citizens. Elementary and secondary schools have been charged by society with much of this responsibility.

To do this job, educators can harness the powerful forces of communications. This perhaps can be accomplished through the recognition of the following imperatives.

Educational Imperatives.

1. It is imperative that all educators understand and utilize the emerging technology and knowledge in communications available to us. This can make the most of the teacher's ability to teach and the child's ability to learn. It can enrich and expand the learning environment.

2. It is imperative that the schools and school leaders work with and through the mass media. This can enhance public understanding of the role and goals of elementary and secondary schools. It can also maximize the mass media's understanding of the schools and the school's understanding of the mass media.

3. It is imperative that school leaders understand the responsibilities and emerging patterns of influence by the mass media on society. This understanding can provide a basis for the maximum redirection of the mass media as a usable educational resource in the elementary and secondary schools. It can also minimize role and goal conflicts of both institutions as they seek to serve society.

4. It is imperative that we prepare students to be discriminating and

analytical viewers and listeners. This can place a major burden on each teacher to understand and share their understanding of mass communications and nonverbal communication with the students. This can also place additional responsibilities on system wide textbook selection committees, librarians, media specialists, and instructional leaders.

5. It is imperative that we continue to seek ways to personalize and humanize communications within the growing mass communications environment. This can allow us to maximize the advantages and minimize the disadvantages of mass communications. It can also help us overcome the remoteness which has frequently accompanied the growth of our institutions.

6. It is imperative that we be sensitive to the cost of communication technology. School leaders can work with developers to ensure that what is developed is within the buying power of the schools. This can ensure that all children in urban, suburban, and rural school districts have equal opportunities to experience and work in enriched environments. It can also ensure that local and regional goals in education can be maintained.

7. It is imperative that elementary and secondary teachers understand and utilize the expanding knowledge available in nonverbal interpersonal communications. This can reinforce and enhance the teaching and learning processes. It can aid in the personalization of the teaching process. It can aid in our understanding of teaching and learning styles. It can also aid in our understanding of cultural differences.

8. It is imperative that educators help clarify student (personal) rights and institutional responsibilities. This has implications for student records, school regulations, student publications, student safety, program funding differences, staff evaluation, and other school areas. Communications is probably the key to these and other very real problems.

Educational Involvement. What can educators do to work with and learn about the mass media? How can we understand and utilize new knowledge and technology in communications? The following are sample suggestions that can be considered.

1. Professional development programs for teachers should accept that both personal and mass communications understanding and skills are a continuing goal.

2. Communication developers and scholars should be actively involved in the planning and delivering of professional development programs for educators.

3. Mass media personnel should regularly be involved in school programs and classes for students. Appropriate school classes should consider including units on critical realities, responsibilities, and trends of mass communications in society.

4. The schools should work with the mass media to improve and expand student opportunities in radio, newspaper, and television. This can also serve to improve citizen understanding of school activities, goals, accomplishments, and failures.

5. School leaders should take advantage of existing and future technology and develop new opportunities through the mass media for interpersonal communication to and from parents, nonparents, and students. New opportunities can also be developed for governmental leaders and all school personnel.

6. Special publications or reports featuring programs, program decisions, or status reports should be disseminated throughout the community through the newspapers, radio, or television stations. This means the school system will need to budget funds for reporting just as funds are budgeted for evaluation, transportation, instruction, travel, and administration.

7. The colleges and universities need to rethink their teacher training programs to include a more fundamental understanding of interpersonal communication. This can complement classroom management, course content, skill development, and teaching methods.

8. The schools should focus more attention on verbal and nonverbal interpersonal communication skills (human relationships) for students and on nonverbal communication cues from students.

9. Communication techniques currently being used by school officials and teachers should be evaluated regularly for their efficiency and effectiveness.

Mass communications will continue to shape society in the future, that much is certain. The elementary and secondary schools will have to demonstrate their vitality to adjust, change, and adapt. Communications need not enslave our society in an Orwellian future. The Republic can survive, free and enlightened, and it undoubtedly will.

Selected Readings

Peggy Amidon. *Nonverbal Interaction Analysis: A Method of Systematic Observing and Recording Nonverbal Behavior*. Minneapolis: Association for Productive Teaching, 1971.

Les Brown. *Television, the Business Behind the Box.* Harcourt Brace Jovanovich, 1st Edition, 1971.

James Coleman. *Computers, Communications and the Public Interest.* Baltimore: John Hopkins Press, 1971.

Edwin Emergy, Phillip Ault and Warren Agee. *Introduction to Mass Communication.* New York: Harper & Row, Publishers, 5th Edition, 1976.

Charles M. Galloway. *Teaching Is Communicating: Nonverbal Language in the Classroom.* Washington, D.C.: Association of Teacher Educators, Bulletin Number 29, 1970.

R. P. Harrison. *Beyond Words.* Englewood Cliffs, New Jersey: Prentice-Hall, Inc., 1974.

Sidney Head. *Broadcasting in America.* Boston: Houghton Mifflin Company, 3rd Edition, 1976.

Paul Heinberg. *Voice Training for Reading and Speaking.* New York: The Ronald Press Company, 1964.

Mark L. Knapp. *Nonverbal Communication in Human Interaction.* New York: Holt, Rinehart and Winston, Inc., 1972.

Dale G. Leathers. *Nonverbal Communication Systems.* Boston: Allyn and Bacon, Inc., 1976.

James McConnell. *Understanding Human Behavior.* New York: Holt, Rinehart and Winston, Inc., 2nd Edition, 1977.

Marshall McLuhan and Quentin Fiore. *The Medium Is the Massage.* New York: Random House, Inc., 1967.

A. Mehrabian. *Nonverbal Communication.* Chicago: Aldine-Atherton, 1972.

A. Mehrabian. *Silent Messages.* Belmont, California: Wadsworth, 1972.

Ashley Montagu. *Touching: The Human Significance of the Skin.* New York: Columbia University Press, 1971.

Bernard Rosenberg and David Manning White. *Mass Culture Revisited.* New York: Van Nostrand Reinhold Company, 1971.

Lawrence Rosenfeld and Jean Civikly. *With Words Unspoken: The Nonverbal Experience.* New York: Holt, Rinehart and Winston, Inc., 1976.

Wilbur Schramm and Donald Roberts. *The Process and Effects of Mass Communication.* University of Illinois Press, Revised Edition, 1971.

Alvin Toffler. *Future Shock.* New York: Random House, Inc., 1970.

3 Environment and the Quality of Life

Pauline Gratz

THERE IS an optimal environment or a range of environmental conditions for every living organism. Such an environment constitutes a web of interrelationships among living things and their surroundings. Within limits, all living species can adjust to environmental change. With time some living things, through the process of evolution, become adapted to conditions their ancestors could not have tolerated. Despite this ability to adapt, an optimal environment is the first requirement for all organisms including the human organism.

The current environment poses a twofold threat to the well-being of the human organism. First, the current environment contains technologically made elements which are directly poisonous or otherwise harmful to us. Secondly, rapid, drastic, and in some cases irreversible changes underway threaten to overwhelm many of the natural systems upon which we are dependent for survival. Many environmentalists also feel that our capacity to adapt to the environmental changes is greatly diminished. These environmental changes threaten our natural habitat, the integrity of our support systems, and the quality of our life.

How did a critical environment problem occur?

If we talk about the environment, it is evident that the environment is everything but us. It is people, however, or ourselves, that are the leading cause of environmental change. We are responsible for much that we do not like: air and water pollution, deteriorated cities, poisons in food, endangered species of animals, and crowded park campgrounds. In order to correct such disagreeable, unhealthy, and unpleasant conditions we must understand the ecology of our environment.

Environmental abuse is not a recent development. The opening of the western part of the United States to farming, logging, and mining might be considered by some as an era of unparalleled disregard for the environment.[1] The slash and burn method of clearing land was used in the early extension of farming westward. Fortunately the soil was hardier than most kinds found throughout the world. However, an abundance of land combined with a limited population encouraged soil depletion. Depletion of resources by the early settlers was almost inevitable because of the profusion of wildlife and the apparent unlimited expanse of land. To the early settlers, land, timber, minerals, and wildlife were overabundant and a hindrance to living. The emergence of a "land ethic" had to wait to arise from those who did not struggle with dense forest or grasslands stretching to the horizon. The frontier people were not concerned about decimating the plains antelope, the buffalo, the heath hen, and the passenger pigeon. As a result these species were either totally exterminated or so reduced in numbers that there are now only protected remnants as survivors. The loss was brought about by thoughtlessness, callousness, and a lack of knowledge or a disbelief that the abundant numbers would ever run low. Today a list of endangered species continues to grow because of changing habitats, indiscriminate use of pesticides, callous methods of hunting, and economic greed.

The establishment of Yellowstone National Park in 1872 was the first sign of a break with the past. While it probably was not initially concerned with the preservation of nature, it was an approach that later spread to the preservation of other areas of the United States. Although President Theodore Roosevelt and Gifford Pinchot, his Chief Forester, had a narrow conception of conservation by today's standards, they did succeed, in the early 1900's, in the adoption of better forest management and recognition of the danger of depletion of the natural resources.

It was not until the early 1930's, however, that the nation was jolted into looking into its depleting resources as a result of drought, dust storms, and a collapsed economy. The Soil Conservation Service, the Civilian Conservation Corps, and other federal agencies were established to cope with the damage to resources, but the examination of the issues was confined to depletion and scarcity. As a result of 150 years of soil abuse in the Midwest, the productivity of more than 280 million acres of farmland was impaired and the topsoil of another 775 million acres had been eroded by the time the government examined the problem in the early 1930's.[2] There was some improvement as the drought lifted; the shifting soil was brought under control and the economy improved.

[1] L. G. Hines. *Environmental Issues*. New York: W. W. Norton & Co., Inc., 1973. p. 2.
[2] Hines, *ibid.*, pp. 5-6.

World War II brought with it, however, concern for national survival which meant maximal industrial and agricultural output and shoved aside considerations of environmental abuse.

After World War II there was still little concern with environmental policy, perhaps because of a fear of returning to the mass unemployment of the 1930's. The war had over-utilized the national resources; however, in 1952 the Materials Policy Commission under President Truman found the domestic resources reasonably well off. It was during this time that long-lived pesticides, high-nitrogen fertilizers, and disposable containers were viewed as huge improvements in our life. The harmful side effects of these improvements would only begin to occur with increased use over an extended time.

The side effects of industrial improvements and overall environmental abuse went largely unnoticed, with the exception of a few unheard and unheeded voices in the 1950's. However, environmental changes were at work. In the post–World War II period the population growth spiraled sharply upward increasing the congestion of already densely populated cities. Technology produced a wealth of new products and processes. Industry increased its output. We enjoyed increased affluence and leisure. Rachel Carson, one of the earliest environmentalists, was maligned by many scientists for her warnings about the results of their technological achievements. By the late 1960's, what had been random cases of environmental damage became a matter of serious concern.

Almost overnight the rivers had become fouled, the air polluted, and the bird and animal species endangered. Of course, the environment had not changed so rapidly. It was an insidious and long process. But once the ability of the rivers and streams to recuperate had been exceeded, the change in water quality from acceptable to intolerable was rapid. Once the air above our cities became overburdened, air pollution could produce near-lethal conditions overnight. As Rachel Carson tried to warn us,[3] the threshold point at which pollution of air and water endangers humans is not the same for plants, birds, fish, and other animal species. Some species are less resistant to environmental abuse than others. Human beings are not satisfactory indicators of environmental stress.

The environmental deterioration that seemed to arise so suddenly in the later 1960's and early 1970's was not due to the specific causes as in earlier times, such as overgrazing of livestock, poor timber practices, inappropriate farming procedures, or erosion of land by wind and water. These causes played a role, but the major factors were the results of advances in technology, growth in population, and increased industrial

[3] R. Carson. *Silent Spring*. New York: Houghton Mifflin Company, 1962.

and agricultural output. The question asked could no longer be a narrow conservative one of how to minimize natural resource depletion but rather a broader question had to be explored: whether our planet as a habitat for all living creatures, including ourselves, could be effectively protected against some of the destructiveness of a rapidly expanding industrial system and a growing population.

While there was almost universal agreement on the need for environmental protection in the early 1970's, there was little general accord on the basic causes of the environmental deterioration. Some claimed that the environmental abuse was caused by rapid population growth and advocated the need to bring the birth rate under control. Others indicated that economic expansion and high living standards were the basic reasons for environmental deterioration. They urged a no-growth policy. Still others believed that the technological advances in products and production techniques during the late 1960's were the basic causes and recommended that technology be somehow channeled toward less harmful effects.

Environmental deterioration can no doubt be traced to any number of causes. It is for this reason that sharp disagreement has developed among individuals and groups concerned with the problem. Barry Commoner and Paul Ehrlich, two leaders in the movement toward environmental improvement, emphasize different viewpoints in explaining environmental deterioration. Barry Commoner believes technology to be the contributing cause, while population growth is emphasized by Paul Ehrlich.[4] The difference of opinion between these nationally and internationally famous biologists is important because it illustrates the complex and multicausal nature of the environmental problems.

The above controversy is not the only dispute over the identification of causes of environmental deterioration. The largest dispute involves the issue of economic growth and its contribution to the decline of environmental quality. The release of a computer simulation study by MIT[5] discusses the role of economic growth as an environmental influence. The growth controversy has brought significant attention to the economic nature of the environmental problem. It cannot be denied that the abuse to the environment is primarily physical and biological. Its persistence, however, is due to those who produce abuses, including ourselves, and who do not wish to bear abatement costs or change their life-style. Protecting the environment involves using resources for abatement rather

[4] See the review of Barry Commoner's *The Closing Circle* (New York: Alfred A. Knopf, Inc., 1971) by Paul R. Ehrlich and John P. Holdren in *Environment* 14; April 1972, p. 24; and the rejoinder by Barry Commoner, *ibid.*, p. 25.

[5] D. H. Meadows *et al. The Limits to Growth*. New York: Universe Books, 1972.

than for profit. Hines states[6] that if unlimited resources were available, we could have both products and abatement with no need to make a choice. Reality tells us, however, that almost all resources are scarce to some degree since they are available only at a price. The availability or scarcity of different resources is indicated by the range of prices established in the economy. In addition, environmental abuse has been accompanied by a change in the pattern of abundance and scarcity. The atmosphere and ocean, previously thought beyond the power of people to reduce or permanently change, have been degraded by the pressures of population growth and waste disposal. At the same time the supply of material products has vastly increased.

Environmentalists and others who have raised the growth issue see the changes and the environmental deterioration as the consequences of industrial output, and postulate a future in which we will be overwhelmed by wastes or exterminated by the depletion of resources unless output is checked. Economists do not foresee the same future. They believe there is a mechanism in the economy for corrective adjustments. Unfortunately, these corrective adjustments fall short in the case of environmental abuse. This is most likely due to the system's goal of private gain from resource use. It would appear that through different kinds of tax incentives and legal enforcement of industrial behavior, the economy can be made to function so that the choices of producers and consumers can protect the environment rather than damaging it. The problem is not confined to the private sector of getting and spending. It is also found in governmental decisions concerning highway development, defense budget for the military, and pollution abatement. The decisions made by governments affect what is done in the private sector from the local to the national level. Controlling pollution and protecting the environment must be viewed as components of a broad and interacting system as we reach the 1980's.

What are the critical environmental problem areas?

The central problem, of which many specific environmental difficulties are but symptoms, is that we are systematically diminishing the capacity of the natural environment to perform its waste disposal, nutrient cycling, and other vital roles at the same time that the growing human population and rising affluence are creating larger demands for these natural resources. Cornfields are replacing forests. Huge single cultures of new high-yielding crops replace the broad assortment of traditional crop varieties. These vast effects of agriculture are reinforced by

[6] Hines, *op. cit.*, p. 9.

additional assaults on nature's complexity in the form of urban sprawl, highway systems, and the release of toxic industrial chemicals. Whole species of plants and animals are being decimated or exterminated by intentional or inadvertent poisoning, by too intensive harvesting, and especially by the destruction of their environmental habitats.

These losses represent dangerous and irreversible manipulation of the ecological systems upon which the planet's carrying capacity for the human species is dependent. They are not trivial losses to be mourned by bird watchers and naturalists. Ecology or the study of the environmental habitat is not a fad. It is a scientific discipline whose scientists attempt to decipher the complex relationships among organisms, including the human organism, and their physical and biological environment. Slowly, painstakingly, but steadily, ecologists are providing scientific substance to ideas once held by conservationists on aesthetic grounds primarily. The basic tenet of environmentalists is that we do not exterminate any population or species lightly; that our future is inextricably tied to nature; that all of us, including those billions who may never set foot in the wilderness, have a stake in unexplored land. The elements which threaten our environment are collectively called pollution.

Pollutants are classified according to their physical and chemical natures. They include such unwanted side effects and products as heat, noise, radioactive elements, dust and other particles, hydrocarbons, carbon dioxide, pesticides, and toxic metals and chemicals. Pollution is also considered in terms of what is polluted, air, water, soil or food. For preventing pollution or controlling it at its origin, the polluter must be identified. Agriculture, industry, mining, power plants, transportation, domestic and municipal wastes, the production and refining of petroleum and people are all major sources of pollutants and pollution.[7]

What are the environmental effects of pollution?

People may be affected by pollution either directly or indirectly, through changes in the environment. Many living species have had a long time in which to adapt or become compatible with external change. The evolution, however, is fragile and consequently any drastic change is more likely to be harmful than beneficial. Many pollutants are being introduced into the environment with which we have had no evolutionary experience and against which we have no defense.

Waste Heat. Waste heat production is inevitable. As long as large numbers of people continue to use huge amounts of energy, we will have

[7] N. D. Levine *et al. Human Ecology.* Massachusetts: Duxbury Press, 1975. pp. 394-95.

to learn to deal with it. Until now, the amount of heat released at a particular site was small when compared to the total energy flow in that site. In addition, the total amount of energy used by the population was negligible compared to global energy flow. Both situations have changed rapidly.

Waste heat, no matter how it is disposed of eventually ends up in the atmosphere. During its loss from the earth, the heat, since it is a form of energy, brings about many changes which are detrimental to the environment.

The most notorious producers of waste heat are electric power plants. Large amounts of waste heat are also released in urban areas as a result of transportation, space heating, and by industrial processes requiring heat. At the present time most environmentalists do not see a diminished use or increased efficiency of energy. Consequently, the best that can be done is to find uses for waste heat wherever possible and ultimately to discharge it in a manner in which it can do the least harm.

Waste heat discharged into the atmosphere may cause local climate modification. Of immediate concern, however, is the problem of thermal pollution of water. In the generation of electricity and in industrial processes, waste heat is conventionally transferred to cooling water which, after passing through the system once, is discharged much warmer than when it began. This warm water causes major changes in the physical and biological environment.

Every organism has a characteristic temperature range in which it can survive. Within this range is a much smaller temperature range that favors optimal growth. The temperature range determines the direct effect upon the organism and the effects of the plant and animal communities that thrive in that range. The presence or absence of food, parasites, pathogens, competitors, or predators may determine the ability of an organism to survive at a particular temperature. Game fish vanish from warm water not because they cannot live there any longer, but because the organisms which they eat cannot.

The optimum temperature for an organism is usually toward the upper end of the temperature range in which it can survive. This upper end of the natural temperature range in a body of water may be so close to the lethal temperature that additional waste heat becomes the critical cause of death. The effects of waste heat vary with the season of the year: it is most likely to be beneficial in cold climates and harmful in hot ones.

Temperature influences the behavior of tiny plankton as well as great game fish. The disposal of waste heat on this behavior is unknown. For example, the migration of some fish is triggered by temperature. If fish are caused to migrate by exposure to a discharge of warmed water, potential difficulties arise at their destination. Conditions unfavorable for spawning, development of eggs, survival and/or growth of the young, and appropriate food may occur.

Most plant and animal species of value to people thrive at lower temperatures than those less valuable. An example of this is the blue-green algae problem. Diatoms, basic elements of many food chains, flourish at low temperatures. Green algae, also important in food chains, thrive in warmer water. Blue-green algae can grow at a vast range of temperature, but tend to grow best in very warm waters. Consequently, as the water temperature increases, so do the blue-green algae. Since blue-green algae are not part of the food chain of most organisms, they flourish in the absence of predators, at the expense of green algae and diatoms, driving away fish that feed on green algae and diatoms. When the blue-greens die, their decomposition by microorganisms further depletes the oxygen supply already low due to the increased temperature.

Once the blue-greens have become established in a region of warm water, they have the opportunity to colonize water relatively unaffected by waste heat. What begins as a small problem begins to have far reaching effects resulting in deterioration of a water habitat called eutrophication. The rate of change is further enhanced by addition of nitrates, phosphates, and organic carbon from agricultural runoff and sewage.

Not all effects of waste heat are unfavorable. An increase in temperature can result in more rapid development of eggs and faster growth of all fish of all ages. There are schemes to use waste heat in nurseries for fish and shellfish. However, there is much to be learned about the effects of heat on aquatic life before predictions can be made as to the effects of thermal pollution. Current concern centers around the continued growth in use of energy which will ultimately result in our inability to assimilate waste heat.

Radioactivity. The development and testing of nuclear weapons and the threat of nuclear war resulted in knowledge of the potential hazards of radioactivity. Today, we live with the realization that "peaceful uses of nuclear energy" may not be peaceful after all. This realization accompanies the rapid development of nuclear energy among industrialized nations. The nuclear power plant is not the only source of radioactive pollutants. Problems also arise from mining, transport, processing, and disposal of nuclear fuels and radioactive wastes.

Some radiation to which we are exposed is natural, arising from cosmic rays, solar radiation, and radioactive elements in the earth. It varies with the latitude and the altitude at which we live, with the composition of the rocks beneath us and the buildings around us. The fact that people have always lived in this level of radiation does not mean that it is without effect. Many scientists believe, even though they cannot quantify it, that some fraction of the cancers, genetic defects, and diseases of aging from which people have always suffered is caused by the natural radiation around and in them, and that any increase in exposure will bring about a corresponding increase in radiation-induced disabilities.

At present, the United States standards for maximum exposure to manufactured radiation are set at an average of 0.17 rem per person per year for the general population, with a maximum of 0.5 rem per year for an individual. Medical exposure is not included in these limits. There is widespread concern that the standards are not strict enough even though the permissible dose of manufactured radiation approximates that from natural sources. Since we seem to be planning to rely upon nuclear energy for our increased energy needs, there is also the question as to whether we will be able to meet these standards at all.

The half-lives of radioisotopes and the rate at which they are released are only two factors related to their presence in the environment. For radioactive wastes that are gaseous in nature, wind and rain patterns must be considered. For those in liquid effluents, bodies of water receiving them are significant. Radioactivity from one power plant using the cooling capacity of a river might have no effect on the environment. But what would a twofold or tenfold increase do? Lakes are especially complex, each lake having a characteristic time required for a complete renewal of its water. For Lake Erie the time is about three years. On the other hand, Lake Michigan may require as much as a century and Lake Superior, it has been estimated, 1000 years. Obviously radioactive material discharged into Lake Erie is not as potentially dangerous as it is in Lake Michigan or Lake Superior.

Air Pollution. Air pollution is the result of a high concentration of material and heat by-products which have become airborne. The by-products are inevitable. Our options involve trying to use less energy— the most sensible option, decreasing the proportions of the various substances produced—and altering the ways in which we deal with by-products. The last option, if carelessly undertaken as a "solution," leads to further water pollution and solid waste pollution.

The atmosphere has tremendous capacity for diluting, dispersing, and eventually destroying a large variety of substances that we discharge into it. As air pollution in most of the world's cities indicates, this capacity is not infinite. Furthermore, although the largest concentrations of pollutants remain near their source, deterioration of air quality can be found long distances away. Particulate matter and carbon dioxide have increased everywhere, with carbon monoxide levels very high in the

Northern Hemisphere as opposed to the Southern Hemisphere. Weather satellites have detected bands of polluted air circling the globe around the latitudes of the United States, Europe, and Japan. Currently these occur occasionally and are broken up by the mixing of air over the oceans. Nevertheless, these zones of intercontinental air pollution must be carefully considered as a threat of what may happen without some abatement.

As in the case of radioactivity, the setting of standards for air quality is surrounded by controversy. Scientists cannot agree as to whether thresholds exist in the relationship between concentration of pollutant and effect. Nor can they agree on the level at which cost for reducing the risk becomes excessive. The situation is further complicated because some poisons, particularly lead and mercury, are cumulative and may also be concentrated in the food chain. Most air pollutants eventually end up in the soil, water, or food supply, in some form. In Europe, Japan, and the United States the effects of air pollution on health are real and well documented, and are conservatively estimated to cost between two and four billion dollars in health care annually.

For many health problems today there is no single cause. Involved are a wide range of genetic, environmental, nutritional, and other cultural factors. The synergistic interaction of pollutants results in a combined effect of several substances resulting in a greater effect than one individual effect. For example, chronic irritation of the respiratory tract may enhance cancer-producing effects. There is some evidence that pollution enhances the susceptibility to infectious disease or disease commonly associated with stress. It is difficult to specify the cause among the various factors involved. Disease is primarily multicausal, but pollution, particularly air pollution, plays a major role.

The adverse effects of air pollution are found in zoos, outside cities, citrus groves, truck garden crops, and other agricultural areas. Evergreen and deciduous forests have also fallen victim to air pollution. Acid rains have caused extensive damage to agricultural fields and property. They result from the solution of the oxides of nitrogen and sulfur in atmospheric water, and their subsequent precipitation. Nitrates washed out of the air by precipitation may be a significant source of excess nitrates in water. Thus air pollution becomes a source of water pollution.

Water Pollution. Water has universally been considered the solvent for all kinds of waste disposal. At one time we could confidently assume that running water purified itself and that the ocean was so vast it could assimilate all the wastes we dumped into it. Today we can amply document the fact that we have overtaxed the ability of water to purify itself and have fouled the oceans. Water pollution is a relative term in that water polluted for drinking may not be polluted for agricultural use. Paradoxically, water fit for drinking may be polluted for industrial use. However, difficulties in defining water pollution do not make the phenomenon disappear. The most common definition is that water pollution is an unfavorable alteration of all bodies of water through changes in physical and/or biological constitution. The difficulty arises in deciding what is "unfavorable."

Many of the natural cycles on which we depend are mediated by organisms in aquatic ecosystems, and we hope to increase our harvest of food from aquaculture. However, in the United States our water usage is over 400 billion gallons per day. About half of this is used by industry, 40 percent by agriculture, and less than 10 percent for domestic use. We know that after such use the water is returned to the environment; but it has been altered, as evidence of massive fish kills, rivers that become inflammable, and so on show. There can be no argument that these conditions are "unfavorable." How unfavorable, however, is cause for considerable debate. Some scientists claim that since there have been no devastating epidemics of water-borne diseases there is no danger even though the bacterial count in many municipal water sources is higher than public health standards allow. Other scientists warn that there is more danger in the unknown than in the known.

Sources of water pollution span the range of human activities. Mining leads to acid mine drainage. Minerals that are insoluble in nearly neutral water dissolve in acid water from the mines, thus becoming toxic to life in the waters. Mining also produces pollution by sediments and radioactive materials. Thermal pollution has already been discussed as a by-product of electric power. Agriculture pollutes water with herbicides and pesticides. Municipal sewage contains excess organic and inorganic nutrients and infectious agents. Even when sewage is treated, nitrates and phosphates remain. Industry produces a complexity of organic and inorganic wastes which are highly toxic to living organisms.

Ecologists are extremely concerned about threatened aquatic ecosystems. Some have given up hope for the Great Lakes, one of the largest reservoirs of fresh fish in the world. Catches of shellfish have been drastically reduced in all coastal regions of the United States. There is an overall decrease in the number of species of plants and animals found off the coast of most countries, accompanied by an increase in species of plants and animals associated with polluted water. Most ominous of all are the reports that ocean waters thousands of miles from land are coated with oil and floating debris. Jacques Cousteau has reported in a variety of ways a sharp decline in marine life, with the extinction of numerous species in the past 50 years. The problem of water pollution is only one example of callousness, thoughtlessness, and ignorance of our fragile habitat.

Solid Waste Pollution. Our life-style depends on a massive conversion of resources to waste, several billion tons each year. We dump our waste on the land where it is unsightly and can lead to pollution of air, water, and soil. We burn waste, creating air pollution, while leaving a residue which still must be disposed of as solid waste. Some wastes are dumped at sea and have become a tragic source of water pollution. Other wastes are used to fill in wetlands, destroying callously a beautiful and fragile ecosystem. No one as yet has come up with any imaginative or economical way in which to dispose of solid waste. Recycling, which makes the most ecological sense, is currently uneconomical to many because of a shortsightedness and unwillingness to understand that *not* using solid waste is an even more uneconomical choice.

Efforts at reclaiming land that has been mined have been incomplete and unsatisfactory. Currently the Supreme Court of the United States opened more land to strip mining without adequate provision for environmental control. Thus, with inept legislative control, three billion tons of waste rock and mill tailings are still dumped near mine sites each year which is a cruel waste of the material being mined; and heaps of rock and mill tailings are available for erosion by wind and water, leading to air and water pollution. The land loses its productivity and becomes ugly.

It has been estimated that there are more than two billion tons of agricultural wastes each year. One-quarter of this is of plant origin, the remainder chiefly manure and dead animals. This is due to agricultural methods that have interrupted nutrient cycles and destroyed the interrelationships that keep ecosystems in balance. Animal droppings are no longer used as fertilizer for fields providing animals with food. Instead animals are crowded together in feedlots. For example, in Kansas, 5.5 million cattle and 1.5 million hogs cover about 200 feedlots producing waste equivalent to that from 70 million people. Another example involves chickens. A single chicken farm may contain 200,000 birds which produce as much solid waste as a city of 20,000 people.

About three-fourths of a billion tons of solid wastes each year come from residential, commercial, institutional, and industrial sources. This includes the litter that is carelessly left wherever people are. Levine *et al.* indicates that the amount of litter strewn by people in one year would cover a superhighway from New York to San Francisco to a depth of one foot.[8] Included are also seven million automobiles that are junked each

---

[8] N. D. Levine *et al.*, *op. cit.*, p. 417.

year, as well as growing amounts of virtually permanent radioactive wastes and the familiar trash and garbage of everyday life. Most of the production in our industrialized society appears quickly as solid waste. Most of the garbage dumps are ugly and unhealthy.

Pollutants in Food. Our source of food is from a food chain which progresses from primary producers such as aquatic microorganisms and plants to herbivores, plant eaters, to carnivores and higher order carnivores, the meat eaters. The concentration of harmful materials in food chains is of extreme importance. Plants to some extent concentrate pollutants from the water they draw into their roots and which, upon evaporation from the leaves, leaves behind many harmful substances. In a similar manner, aquatic organisms accumulate high levels of pollutants because of the large amounts of water they filter. At higher levels of the food chain, about 90 percent of organic matter is converted to energy. However, many pollutants cannot be converted to energy and consequently they become concentrated in the food chain. The top carnivores in the food chain are relatively few in number and slow to reproduce. They cannot afford the consequences of the poisons that they eat. This is a partial explanation of why game fish may be dangerously contaminated with a variety of poisons, from heavy metals to DDT to radioisotopes.

Many other substances have been introduced into the foods we eat. These substances, which may be considered pollutants in that they have been added to the natural food, include almost innumerable food additives as well as antibiotics and hormones used to increase the yield and growth rate of poultry and livestock. Whether they are actual or potential health hazards for the general population is not known.

In 1924, more than 150 persons died and 1,500 in the Greater New York area suffered from acute diarrhea and other forms of gastroenteritis. This was the great "oyster scare" which caused the federal government to become more interested in food pollution.

But 54 years later this federal interest has not yet been translated into prevention. People are still suffering and dying from polluted seafood. Too often, federal protection has seemed to be more readily available to the polluters than to the public. However, the gradual disappearance of seafood from our coastal waters has in some ways protected people from a significant health hazard.

Pesticides and Heavy Metals. Since the publication of Rachel Carson's *Silent Spring* in 1962, public awareness of the dangers of pesticides has sharpened to a point where the benefits of these chemicals are often overlooked. Countless lives have been saved by pesticide control of malaria, encephalitis, cholera, Rocky Mountain spotted fever, and typhus, to name a few.

But in controlling the insects, rodents, and predators, pesticides frequently kill off desirable life forms, or more subtly, they attack the reproductive powers of fish, birds, and animals. To date, there has been no conclusive evidence that pesticides harm humans directly, but as in the case of cigarettes and disease, the suggestion of such danger is so strong that it cannot be ignored. The pesticides belong to a group of chemicals called chlorinated hydrocarbons. The best known of these are DDT, endrin, aldrin, dieldrin, parathion, malathion, chlordane, and lindane.

One of the problems with pesticide use is that a little bit can do a lot of damage. DDT, for example, seems to last almost indefinitely. The same batch that kills bugs on a North Carolina farm can go on to pass through the fatty tissues of many successive fish, birds, animals, and humans. It may drain through the river system toward the sea, or circulate halfway around the world in normal atmospheric currents. For example, a small concentration of DDT can inhibit growth and photosynthesis in marine plankton. It has been noted that a shrimp population can be destroyed in two days by as little as 0.00006 parts per million DDT in sea water. Shell formation in oysters is impeded by equally tiny concentrations of DDT. Endrin had been responsible for several massive fish kills in the Mississippi River during the early 1960's and a closely related substance, endosulfan, caused an excessive slaughter of fish in the Rhine in 1970. However, the evidence of DDT and other pesticides' harm to humans is skimpy. What is known for certain is that humans, like birds, accumulate and store DDT in body fat.

Heavy metals usually reach a water source by leaching from mineral bearing rock and soil, but increasingly in recent years they are in water from industrial emission. There has been much research designed to determine the toxic effects of these metals on aquatic organisms. This toxicity can be modified by a variety of factors; the water's hardness or temperature, the presence of other chemicals, or a combination of one or more of these. As an example of heavy metal toxicity, mercury has become an increasing concern because biological as well as chemical interactions in the environment can be responsible for increasing its toxicity.

Mercury is found in a variety of forms; elemental liquid mercury (quicksilver), elemental mercury vapor, mercuric salts, and organic mercury. Not all of these forms of mercury are equally toxic to people. Methyl mercury, an organic form, is the most toxic. Inorganic mercury can be transformed into methyl mercury in the environment.

The Minimata disaster in Japan brought widespread attention to mercury's potential as an environmental polluter. Here 110 people became the victims of mercury poisoning between 1953 and 1960 as a result of eating fish taken from Minimata Bay where a vinyl chloride plant released methyl mercury as one of its waste products.[9] Brain damage is the result of methyl mercury poisoning.

It is now recognized that inorganic mercury can be transformed in nature into methyl mercury which can then be accumulated by fish and passed on to humans in this highly toxic form. Mercury can be methylated by bacteria and molds found in lake or river sediments. This reaction can be carried out by any microorganism that can synthesize vitamin B-12, that has a large supply of organic substances as a source of food, and that has a supply of inorganic mercury. Methyl mercury is not bound by the organic material in sediment, but is easily released into the water where it is soluble and available for consumption.[10] While many industrial firms have halted or reduced mercury discharges, the great accumulation of inorganic mercury in the sediments of the aquatic environment provides a continuing source of methyl mercury and ensures continuing contamination of the food chain.

Noise Pollution. Physicians and acoustical engineers are increasingly alarmed at the continuous exposure of humans to levels of everyday noise which not only destroy the cilia of the inner ear, resulting in neurosensory hearing loss, but also cause measurable physiological harm as well as suspected psychological and emotional damage.

Sound is measured in decibels, which represent the smallest difference of loudness that the human ear can ordinarily detect between the loudness of two sounds. Noise specialists rate decibels according to the A scale, which is weighted against low-frequency sounds to reflect the fact that high-frequency sounds are more unpleasant, and apparently more harmful, than low-frequency sounds of the same loudness.

Conversation in a relatively quiet setting ranges around 60 decibels, and the roar of traffic or sounds of factory machinery are typically at about 80 decibels. Anything above 80 is likely to be uncomfortable. At 90 or above, the experts start worrying about effects on health.

One common household appliance, the food blender, emits 93 decibels, and a subway train screeching around a curved track goes up to 95. The motorcyclist revving up his bike generates 110 decibels, and a jet plane taking off will assault unprotected ears with 150 decibels.

Like air and water pollution, noise has crept up insidiously and is only now gaining appropriate recognition. We are currently floundering

[9] L. Goran with M. E. Duffy. "Birds Give Warning." *Environment* 11: (2) ; May 1969.

[10] J. M. Wood. "A Progress Report on Mercury." *Environment* 14; January-February 1972.

in our inability to control noise; however, there is increasing recognition that noise pollution is as much a threat to certain people as air pollution is to those who have asthma or emphysema. Studies have shown that prolonged exposure to noise or sudden, sharp noise produces involuntary responses by the vascular, digestive, and nervous system. The danger to hearing is obvious, but the more subtle physiologic and emotional responses to noise are more difficult to measure.

Legislation to control noise has not gotten very far in many local governments or in Congress because there just is not enough public pressure for strong antinoise laws. Indeed some people seem to like noise. In some cases, a quiet piece of equipment will not sell. For example, a nearly silent vacuum cleaner, which is technically feasible, is not likely to sell very well. Unless it sounds powerful, many women will not believe it is really cleaning.

The references listed at the end of this chapter contain information on the amounts, sources, and effects of various pollutants. Many discuss the technology and institutional arrangements for the control of pollution. In addition, Levine has a useful list of some common pollutants, where they came from and what they do.[11]

Is environmental deterioration altering the climate?

There is a constant exchange of matter and energy among air, land, and water. This exchange is carried to all parts of the earth by the atmosphere and the oceans. For instance, water polluted by spilled oil evaporates a fraction of the oil and pollutes the air. Other fractions wash ashore to deface beaches. Hydrocarbons in the polluted air are washed out by rain and pollute the sea once more. Much of the residue on the land may also find its way back to the sea. Almost everything that pollutes the air and land eventually reaches the sea. The processes that spread pollution around the earth are the same processes that determine weather and climate, and they may be modified by pollution.

The atmosphere can be likened to a great heat engine that runs on solar energy, moving the surplus of energy that falls in the equatorial zone to the poles, where there is a deficit. The oceans are another such heat engine, running on the same principle and interacting with the atmosphere.

Warm air rises at the equator and moves toward the poles, where it is cooled, sinks, and moves back toward the equator again. The rotation of the globe produces bands of prevailing winds which add to the complexity. In addition, modifications in the atmospheric circulation

---

[11] N. D. Levine *et al.*, *op. cit.*, pp. 409-18.

occur because of the irregular distribution of continents and oceans and of the location and topographic features of land masses.

Ocean currents occur by means of differences in temperature and density of water. They are modified by the prevailing winds. Some 20 to 25 percent of the energy carried from equatorial regions to the poles is carried by ocean currents. In addition to the heat directly redistributed by the oceans, almost 20 percent of the energy carried toward the poles is in the form of latent heat in water vapor, most of which evaporates over the oceans. This heat is released in the atmosphere when rain or snow falls.

Thus climates of the earth are determined not only by amounts of energy received from the sun and radiated back from earth, but by the way in which energy is distributed over the earth. When the distribution is uniform, the climate is mild. When circulation is restricted between the equator and the poles, an ice age results. World and local climates have undergone many fluctuations since the last glacier receded 11,000 or 12,000 years ago.

Climatic change has been a major force in evolution and in the rise and fall of human cultures. There is no reason to believe that our present climate is infinite. The questions that concern us are what is the "natural" trend and how are we influencing it. We are on very shaky theoretical and observational ground when we try to answer the questions because of the number of variables involved and the complexity of their interactions. Consequently, it is extremely difficult to determine the relative contributions of human beings and of forces beyond human control.

Cities modify local climate and the climatic effects of cities are well documented. However, when we try to determine the effects of pollution on global climate, the sequence of cause and effect is seldom obvious. The problem is compounded by our uncertainty about the magnitude and direction of the natural trend in world climate. Many hypotheses have been formulated about climatic change and many computer models have been developed. Different models, however, lead to conflicting results and paradoxes. It has been suggested, for example, that an ice age could be started by an increase in solar radiation, which would lead to increased evaporation of water, increased cloudiness, increased rain and snow, and decreased temperatures. Most scientists, however, do not believe that a hotter sun would cause a colder earth.

When we think of modifying the climate, we often think of another ice age or melting the polar ice and flooding all our coastal cities. Many other changes would come before we froze or drowned. A slight but persistent change in temperature or humidity can tip the balance in favor of organisms pathogenic to plants, animals, or humans, or insects that spread those organisms. The result could be severe epidemics of diseases and pests that formerly were held in check by climatic conditions. Major epidemics affecting crops and forest trees have often been associated with just such changes.

The effects of pollution upon the climate is another area that is unknown. Research is needed to make the unknown known. We can only hope that after the unknown becomes known, it may not be too late to do something about it.

What can we do to improve the quality of the human environment?

A discussion of how the environment deteriorated and what some of the critical realities are in the realm of environmental quality is incomplete without some consideration of population limitations. The consequences of "people pollution" is in many ways more acute in the United States than in less prosperous lands. If it weren't for people and the constantly expanding technology that it engenders in our industrialized society, air pollution, noise pollution, food and water pollution, and radiation pollution would be far less of a problem.

Pictures taken of the earth from the moon show us graphically how finite is the nature of our planet. Do we know what is the capacity of the earth to support people? Although theoretical limits can be calculated there is no simple answer to this question. It has been pointed out that we are on the logarithmic phase of a typical growth curve after a long lag period. In nature no animal, plant, or bacterial population has ever maintained a logarithmic phase of growth for very long. The major factors that slow this rate of growth are exhaustion of food supply, accumulation of toxic products, decimation through disease, or the effects of some outside lethal agent which kills a high proportion of the population. Can these factors be applied to the human population? It is difficult to predict. However, it is evident that our survival is related to the growth of world population and a decreasing food supply.

The current birthrate in the United States does show a marked drop since 1971. However, in dealing with population problems the focus must be on the earth as a whole because it has become a single, closed-loop feedback system as far as human activities are concerned. Pollution is a global problem and an excessive population in one area of the world creates problems for all other areas.

Biological evolution is conservative in its chaotic striving to enable organisms to continue to adapt and evolve, to be a little better. Much of our social and cultural evolution has been similar. To many people today, cultural and social change means change that will permit the "American" way of life to continue. Our national policy is to develop technology for producing gasoline from coal, so that we may continue our transportation system based on the private automobile, and in many other ways to maintain the status quo. Without realizing that we, not "they," are the polluters, we look for pollution control not through a change in life-style but through a technological fix, so that our life-style will not have to change.[12] Cultural and social adaptation, however, does lead to many cultural adjustments which accumulate until a life-style does change. With neglect or positive approaches, in dealing with pollution, it will no doubt change our life-style further. Solutions to the improvement of the quality of life through environmental improvement can be regarded from three vantage points: the technological fix, social and cultural change, and a realistic curriculum.

People tend to think in a linear fashion, in what is referred to as cause and effect thinking. It is this type of thinking which gives rise to the search for technological solutions to problems. Pollution is merely a symptom that something is wrong with our relationship to our environment. Pollution is not the basic problem and alleviating pollution lulls us into a false belief that the problem will disappear. No intelligent individual could argue that concerted efforts at pollution control are not desirable. The technological fix is needed to buy time for reexamining global, national, and individual goals and for adjusting them so that they are compatible with the limits imposed by nature.

If we continue our present course, our use of energy in the year 2000 will be three times the level of 1970.[13] This is a forecast based upon estimates of the gross national product and population, which falls in the middle range of future projections. Most of this energy will be used to maintain the status quo, with a small growing part of it used in pollution control.

The Environmental Protection Agency indicates that the cost of pollution control based on its recommended emission standards for 1975, assuming these standards will be met, for the year 2000 will be about two percent of the gross national product.[14] These estimates involve control of particulates, hydrocarbons, oxides of nitrogen, biochemical oxygen demand, suspended solids, and dissolved solids. Such pollutants as radioactive materials, heavy metals, and persistent biocides, however, are conspicuously missing, and the future for their control is not promising.

[12] N. D. Levine *et al., op. cit.,* p. 432.
[13] Environmental Protection Agency, Office of Research and Development. *Alternative Futures and Environmental Quality.* Washington, D.C.: Government Printing Office, 1973. p. 95.
[14] *Ibid.,* p. 73.

Some pollution problems may be fairly easy to solve, while others may remain intractable. An example of a difficult problem is the emissions from the internal combustion engine. Control of hydrocarbons and carbon monoxide cannot control the emission of nitrogen oxide because the solution to the former problem leads to increased emission of the other. In agriculture, the nutrient cycles we have interrupted could be reestablished to balance agricultural ecosystems by returning agricultural wastes to the soil. We could alleviate two problems: the disposal of agricultural waste and the pollution from runoff in inorganic fertilizers. This solution, however, will further increase the price of meat and milk. Yet, if we do not do it, pollution will make them more expensive anyway.

The United States generates 200 million tons of garbage yearly. Solid waste, as it is now called, is fast becoming the quicksand of modern society. Garbage is one of the few things in today's world that is free. All it needs is some pioneer to exploit it. Garbage needs to be reevaluated and regarded as a resource that is not currently being used effectively. In the past, waste disposal has been based on spreading out the garbage and depending upon natural systems either to destroy or dilute it. By spreading waste around we have not made it go away, but by coupling larger numbers of ecosystems we are causing a general instead of localized pollution. One solution envisioned is a closed agricultural system in which all nutrients and water are recycled. We can still count on natural systems to handle some pollutants if we do not overtax them. But the process of producing further pollution of the atmosphere and the ocean must be stopped.

There are many ways for turning waste into resources. Japan and Europe have already put many into practice. There is some indication that they are on the horizon for the United States. Some of these include the pollution-free burning of municipal waste for the generation of electricity; the production of natural gas from sewage or agricultural wastes; the use of waste heat for space heating, for fish and shellfish nurseries, for defogging airports, or for increasing the rate of decomposition of sewage; the incorporation of fly ash into construction materials, and the use of wastes from agriculture and the food processing industry for animal feeds.

The technological fix has its limitations; technology can only solve technological problems. A more serious problem with pollution control is related to growth. If for any source of pollution we decrease its production by a factor of two and then double the number of pollutants we have not gained very much. Growth can rapidly cancel out any improvements that technology can bring in the control of pollution. In any case pollution control which relies on a technological fix can never be total. No technology is perfect because there is a fundamental economic and physical limit. Pollution is only one manifestation of problems that require social solutions.

New knowledge has shaken our perceptions of reality, increased our conflicts with our traditions, and is gradually changing our cultural patterns. Sociologists believe that our traditional linear thinking (simple cause and effect) needs to be replaced by pattern thinking (multiple causations and interrelationships). We can no longer be oblivious to the rest of the universe and the ever changing interrelationships within our environment. An extension of the past and present is not an appropriate approach to the future. What is needed is a systematic plan that will bring about cultural change in such a manner as to really improve our environmental quality. The Environmental Protection Agency has devised a hierarchy of human needs that is appropriate to our culture.[15] The hierarchy as shown in the following figure is obviously based on Maslow's hierarchy of needs, possessing a variety of curricular options for the teacher. It must be understood that such a hierarchy of human needs cannot apply to any culture but that found in the United States. The suggestion is included here to emphasize the point that the goals and priorities of a culture change in relationship to where that culture is in terms of satisfying the needs of its people. It is also included to indicate the relationship between learning and cultural change.

There is a growing conviction that we are already entering a post-industrial state of cultural evolution. The Environmental Protection Agency identifies what it sees as some basic changes:

1. From primary and secondary industries (agriculture-manufacturing) to tertiary and quaternary industries (service, knowledge activities) ;

2. From goods to services;

3. From goods and services produced by muscle power to those produced by machines and cybernetics;

4. From the material to the sensate;

5. From "things" to experiences;

6. From physiological to psychological needs;

7. From scarcity to abundance and eventually to superabundance;

8. From a few stark choices to a bewildering array of choices;

9. From durability to disposables and planned obsolescence and back to recyclables, reclaimables;

10. From self-interest motivation to a broader social and humanitarian outlook;

15 Environmental Protection Agency, *op. cit.*, p. 107.

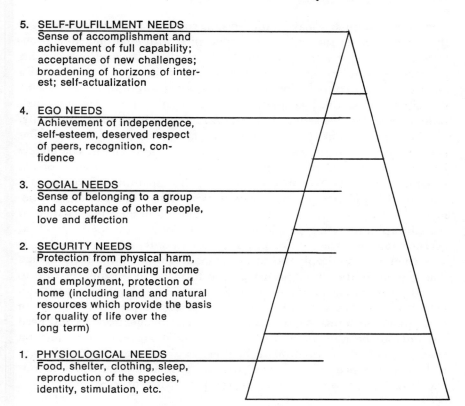

5. SELF-FULLFILLMENT NEEDS
   Sense of accomplishment and
   achievement of full capability;
   acceptance of new challenges;
   broadening of horizons of interest; self-actualization

4. EGO NEEDS
   Achievement of independence,
   self-esteem, deserved respect
   of peers, recognition, confidence

3. SOCIAL NEEDS
   Sense of belonging to a group
   and acceptance of other people,
   love and affection

2. SECURITY NEEDS
   Protection from physical harm,
   assurance of continuing income
   and employment, protection of
   home (including land and natural
   resources which provide the basis
   for quality of life over the
   long term)

1. PHYSIOLOGICAL NEEDS
   Food, shelter, clothing, sleep,
   reproduction of the species,
   identity, stimulation, etc.

Figure 1. Hierarchy of Human Needs

11. From independence and self-sufficiency to interdependence;
12. From individual freedom to voluntary restraints to mandatory restraints;
13. From Puritan hard-work ethic to leisure as a matter of right;
14. From Darwinian self-survival to humanistic security;
15. From atomistic to large-scale, pluralistic institutions;
16. From national to multinational and "one-world" scale operations;
17. From decentralization to centralization and eventually globalization;
18. From irrational chaos to creative, long-range planning.[16]

These changes are in various stages of being and becoming. Environmental deterioration has been evolving for generations and new knowledge and new ways of thinking are also evolving slowly. It is possible that no final solution to environmental problems exists. Or, a change in

[16] Environmental Protection Agency, *op. cit.*

environmental quality may require social, economic, and political changes that we cannot yet imagine. People concerned with environmental problems object to the term environmental crisis not because our current problems are not critical, but because the use of the word "crisis" implies an impotent citizenry waiting for an omnipotent solution. We are not in that situation; we can take and have taken, in many instances, sustained, rational, and creative action. In other instances we have failed abysmally.

Perhaps the most basic reason for our environmental deterioration is ignorance. For over two generations we have been almost completely ignorant of the concepts and principles of ecology. The paradox of the situation lies in the fact that we do have the capability of rooting out some of the underlying causes of pollution. There are human, technological and financial resources at hand. What is needed is a change in the education of young people who are our future voters and practical decision makers. The task of restoring the stability of the ecosystem is vast, complex, and deeply rooted in economic, social, and political issues. The responsibility for preparing people to make judgments relating to the vast restorative program lies with curriculum developers and ultimately with teachers capable of teaching young people relevant facts in understandable terms. As the custodians of knowledge, teachers will need not only to be able to inform students about current environmental crises but also about what might be done to avert crises, if possible, and to help young people to discover why we have not done better in our efforts to manage our ecosystem in the past two centuries.

What should be the underlying philosophy of a curriculum to educate people, especially the young, concerning environmental quality?

Information is not enough. The student's way of thinking must be developed to make it readily apparent that an extremely serious threat is involved that calls for action and sacrifice of an individual and collective nature. The basic approach to ecology is not difficult to teach. What is difficult to teach is how to analyze controversy. The population-environmental problem is controversial from a social, political, and economic view. In every one of the environmental areas, legislation has its proponents as well as opponents. Students need to learn how to weigh information that is controversial if education for restoring environmental quality is to be accomplished. The stress in learning must be on the interrelationships that exist between the various components in the environment. Students need to discover and comprehend that millions of years of a slow gradual process were needed for fragile ecosystems and their interrelationships to be established. It will be almost as slow reversing some of the havoc that has disturbed these relationships. Any curricular response to our environmental problem must be so constituted as to impress students with the fact that people are not divorced from the environment but are an integral part of it.

It is apparent that there needs to be some curricular change that will prepare people to understand and make decisions relating to environmental quality. Unfortunately, most human problems do not fall into neat academic categories such as sociology, history, economics, psychology, or biology. Human problems and their solutions require a multidisciplinary curriculum. Many universities are quite determined to perpetuate disciplinary myopia; nevertheless the loosening of rigid departmental organization is evident at some colleges and universities, such as Stanford University. Stanford, with the help of the Ford Foundation, has developed an interdisciplinary undergraduate program in human biology preparing students to attack current human problems.

The majority of and most exciting progressive changes in curriculum during the 1960's had their roots in student activism. It is hoped that these same people may produce equally good changes in society as a whole. Perhaps they have become the teachers of elementary and junior high school students who have demonstrated their concern for environmental deterioration through various activities. Many teachers have encouraged interest in population and environment. Since Earth Day, 1970, in particular, there has been a widespread effort to introduce environmental concern into schools at all levels. A program to encourage environmental education is available through the U.S. Department of Health, Education, and Welfare. Education dealing with the knowledge and issues of the environment draws together multiple strands of knowledge and goals for a common focus. It would appear that teachers can be encouraged to focus upon environmental problems by drawing upon interests and concerns at the neighborhood, community, city, state, regional, national, and international levels. The understandings and skills for analysis and action can be developmental through all levels of learning, but they must be interdisciplinary to be effective.

Effective teaching of environmental issues demands students be encouraged to look at cultural, social, economic, and political issues surrounding an environmental problem. For example, let us consider the issue of why environmental control is the challenge of the late 70's and early 80's. We have learned that Earth Day demonstrations are not enough to improve our environmental quality. Firm decisions are required in the political arena and the economic market. The life-style of people may require more emphasis upon self-restraint and self-discipline to achieve environmental quality. This implies a combination of voluntary personal action and organized political action needed to achieve a less polluted environment. For students to understand how complex solutions to environmental problems are, they could role play a Senate investigation committee with several students playing the roles of consumers, consumer advocates, business tycoons, and the vast variety of political and legal roles involved. Some of the following questions may help them explore the difficulties and the alternative courses of action:

1. Should there be a national ecological authority with power over all technological industries to prevent environmental hazards?

2. Should the quality of the environment have priority over the rights of private property or private enterprise?

3. Should tax incentives or punitive measures or some combination of both be used to achieve environmental standards?

4. Should a pursuit for a higher and higher standard of living in the United States be changed?

5. Can the Ninth Amendment be used to make the quality of the environment an inalienable right?

The details of such a teaching strategy are complicated, no doubt, but the benefits would far outweigh the difficulties. There is no other way to change a growing rigidity of roles in our society. Virtually everyone must be brought into the decision-making processes that affect all our lives.

An understanding of the relationship between ourselves and our environment, natural, technological, social, economic, and political, can help us to consider the consequences of our actions. If we comprehend our relationship to the environment we will be somewhat equipped to do something about the environmental problems that beset our world. Achieving a prosperous, humane, and environmentally sustainable life cannot be realized without some fundamental changes in our social, political, economic, and other institutions which influence all aspects of our human behavior.

Selected Readings

Melvin A. Benarde. *Our Precarious Habitat.* New York: W. W. Norton & Company, Inc., 1973.

Lester R. Brown. *Seeds of Change: The Green Revolution and Development in the 1970's.* New York: Praeger Publishers, 1970.

Neil W. Chamberlain. *Beyond Malthus: Population and Power.* New York: Basic Books Inc., Publishers, 1970.

David W. Ehrenfeld. *Biological Conservation*. New York: Holt, Rinehart and Winston, Inc., 1970.

Paul R. Ehrlich, Anne H. Ehrlich, and John P. Holdren. *Human Ecology*. San Francisco: W. H. Freeman and Company, 1973.

Environmental Protection Agency. *Alternative Futures and Environmental Quality*. Washington, D.C.: Government Printing Office, 1973.

John Kenneth Galbraith. *The New Industrial State*. Boston: Houghton Mifflin Company, 1971.

Edward Goldsmith, editor. *Blueprint for Survival*. Boston: Houghton Mifflin Company, 1972.

Frank Graham, Jr. *Man's Domain: The Story of Conservation in America*. New York: M. Evans and Company, Inc., 1971.

Laurence G. Hines. *Environmental Issues: Population and Economics*. New York: W. W. Norton & Company, Inc., 1973.

Donella H. Meadows *et al. The Limits to Growth*. New York: Universe Books, 1972.

Gunnar Myrdal. *The Challenge of World Poverty*. New York: Pantheon Books, 1970.

National Academy of Sciences. *Rapid Population Growth: Consequences and Policy Implications*. Baltimore: Johns Hopkins Press, 1971.

Gustav Ranis, editor. *The United States and the Developing Economics*. New York: W. W. Norton & Company, Inc., 1973.

U.S. Department of Commerce. *Automobile Fuels and Air Pollution: Report of the Panel on Automotive Fuels and Air Pollution*. Washington, D.C.: Government Printing Office, 1971.

U.S. Department of the Interior. *United States Energy: A Summary Review*. Washington, D.C.: Government Printing Office, 1972.

Barbara Ward and René J. Dubos. *Only One Earth*. New York: W. W. Norton & Company, Inc., 1972.

4 Science and Technology: Humane Purpose and Human Prospect

Paul F-Brandwein

OURS IS a self-examining society. So it is in a constant state of renewal, of despair and hope; constantly we destroy and repair. Now a continuing crisis faces our society and, as it must be, there are conflicting views on the anatomy of the crisis.

Science and Technics: Human Purpose for a Self-examining Society

Somewhere in the depths of the Antigone we come to know that nothing enters the life of humankind without a curse. Then—as now—what was vast was man's overwhelming greed—the need not only to be free, but to be free on his own terms; he called this *justice*.[1] The curse was then—as it is now—the permanent one of social being, how to be one within the many, to permit diversity within the obliged unity. The permanent question of the human agenda then, as now, remains: How to reconcile the claims of the individual with the claims of society. Then, as now, we thought we knew. We thought we could divine humane purpose and, therefore, human prospect.

But then those of us who have survived and can contemplate man have survived, as well, the varieties of doom—the doom of physical "extinction" implied in the fall of species and the doom of social extinction implied in the rise and fall of civilizations. Nevertheless, modern man undergoes almost a cadenced progression of crises, each one surely the last, each one with its own rituals of doom and gloom—plague—famine—nuclear warfare. And now our society stands—as the first society to do

[1] In this book the word *man* is used in the generic sense; in no way is the term exclusionary.

94

so—on the threshold of the post-industrial era. We are at a true turning point.

Nevertheless, the merchandise of a teacher is hope. In his book, *So Human An Animal,* René Dubos speaks of the "new pessimism":[2]

As the year 2000 approaches, an epidemic of sinister prediction is spreading all over the world, as happened among Christians during the period preceding the year 1000.

He speaks of the "new optimism," stating

The new optimism finds its sustenance in the belief that science, technology, and social organization can be made to serve the needs and urges of mankind, instead of being allowed to distort human life.

This chapter is in the service of the "new optimism," an optimism based partly on the notion that what scientists and technicists can do they can undo, ameliorate, or improve; further it is based on a technology known as curriculum. Curriculum reform is based not only on the art-sciences of education, psychology, and sociology, but on the technics of teaching *per se*. Curriculum reform makes ethicists of us all.

Now we also "know" that our knowledge of doom is more than phrenology, more than the pattern of entrails or Tarot cards. The lesson of evolution seems to be that species died of that which made them great—at the particular time of adaptation to the environment. In simplistic terms—we like simple resolutions—we recall that the Ostracoderms died of their armor, the dinosaurs of their size. It is too early to extrapolate; surely we are about to die of that which has made us great—our technology. Surely this time we are doomed; there is no hope for future generations; there is no escape. Surely this time it is real; surely this time our woes are not merely the idealist's pique. But I anticipate.

Ours is an unkempt world in a century unkempt until now—at least. Historiography has not yet put sufficient cadence into the events of the past 75 years so that we see analysis and synthesis both. So, as we have always done, we grope for definitions. As scholars, we seek dispassionately for hidden likenesses in events in a search for meaning. As individuals committed to an open society, to an electoral democracy, we seek to set aside determinism and to supplant it with a society in which balance is sought in opposing opinion without coercion. We say, in effect, we are responsible for what happens to us; we are the architects of a future harmony. Indeed, to prepare our young to be architects of a future harmony is one of the major objectives of schooling and education. We

2 René Dubos. *So Human An Animal.* New York: Charles Scribner's Sons, 1968.

would say that man will survive if in effect he would apply this axiom to life and living: *Between impulse and action, to interpose evidence; failing this, reason and judgment; failing this, compassion.*[3]

We declare that man can assert his humanity, can make use of invention subject to the human use of human beings, can build an environment sanative for all life and those who will live, can indeed, in the words of Hammarskjold, become truer, kinder, simpler, quieter, firmer, and therefore wiser and stronger. Perhaps our crisis is not technological but moral.

Science and Technics: Humane Purpose

We seem always to edit out complexity, to conspire for simplicity; so it is easy to separate science and technics. So Da Vinci would express it this way: "Science is the captain, practice the soldiers." Or to make the distinction this way: America was discovered, the United States was invented. We may pursue this distinction in order to clarify thought, but in anticipation and in effect, in our time, science and technics are the two arms of the same organism, society.

For purposes of schooling and education, it is perhaps useful to attempt a distinction between the scientist and technicist, between science and technology. One such distinction has been offered here: The scientist is concerned with *discovering concepts which help him EXPLAIN HOW the world works, the technicist is concerned with discovering applications of these concepts to help him DO the world's work.* The scientist seeks to understand in order to explain; the technicist seeks to understand in order to do. Scientists are interested in light, technicists in light bulbs. Scientist and technicist both use the methods of intelligence, of inquiry through observation, investigation, and experiment; both insist on empirical evidence to test their hypotheses; both use theory not only as an explanation of facts, but as a guide to imagination and speculation. In both, imagination is the bridge from the seen world of unordered objects and events to the marvelous world—orderly, beautiful. Hans Zinsser goes on to say that the "marvelous orderliness" uncovered by the scientist is a "final refutation of purposelessness and chance." He posits a faith of the scientist: The regularity of the universe. The technicist is no less obedient to it. If scientists have uncovered the regularities of magnetism and electricity, valence and quantum theory, genetics and evolution, the unity of cells and homeostasis, then technicists have

[3] Here I think I am, without intention, modifying one of John Dewey's statements. I cannot find the source—it may have occurred in one of his lectures. I used it in *A Discipline of Responsible Consent.* (See the list of Selected Readings.)

brought to use aspirin and penicillin, lasers and cyclotrons, automobiles and airplanes, and surgery, the Kantrowitz heart and transplanted heart, Kanred wheat and tree cropping, Herefords and Holsteins, 1R-8 rice and the Iowa and Maine potato, hybrid corn and Poland hog, nuclear bomb and nuclear reactor, radio and television, computers and printing machines. Not to say, gasoline and pesticides, calculators, digital watches, and vinyl coverings; not to say the creation of the machines that make our machines which in turn make buttons, computers, poison gas, carpets, or nuclear bombs.

Scientists and technicists both search out the "hidden likenesses" (Bronowski's term) in objects and events, both create new and original works, both use the past. In written and oral traditions, both are valued by an open society.

It follows that the schools are the resource of our scientists and technicists—and also, of utmost importance, of our ethicists. If we weigh carefully the impact of science and technology on society, then we must weigh the impact of the values we hold on the scientist and technicist of the future; the children, the boys and girls in our schools. For all the scientists and technicists—and I repeat, ethicists—are in our schools. Their education and schooling—in terms of curriculum and instruction —has now become critical: Their survival and ours is now based on the choices we and they will make.

Nonetheless, here we are in the twentieth century faced with this dilemma: Which is to dominate, man or megamachine? Humanity or technology? Which is master, which servant?

Human Works and Values: Crisis as Continuing Reality

As always, science and technics create; as always, technology is voracious. This would be true even if global population were stabilized, for in the end the earth's resources are limited. The best evidence forces us to the bleak conclusion that a limited earth cannot nourish an unlimited population. We are required to face this as continuing crisis. But one we must and can make subordinate to human need and human values.

Ehrlich and Ehrlich state it this way:[4]

No geological event in a billion years—not the emergence of mighty mountain ranges, nor the submergence of entire subcontinents, nor the occurrence of

4 Paul R. Ehrlich and Anne H. Ehrlich. *Population, Resources, Environment: Issues in Human Ecology.* 2nd Edition. San Francisco: W. H. Freeman and Company, 1972. p. 1. Copyright © 1972. Altogether an essential and indispensable book in the development of philosophy and practice of a curriculum for environmental science and/or ekistics, the science of human habitation.

periodic glacial ages—has posed a threat to terrestrial life comparable to that of human overpopulation.

If curriculum responds to the realities, and the realities of shortage are monumental, then what is to be our response? The assumption that the issue will be decided against us is not tenable if we hold life-affirming and life-preserving values: The essential one being that the future belongs to the humane and human prospect. *Idealistic?* Or without other recourse, *realistic.* Perhaps the remedies belong within the area subtended by the basic assumption that no people, no nation, no country wishes to die, that is, life is better than death, although death is part of life.

We propose, then, to discuss these matters under a series of curricular thrusts which could, in our view, be developed into specific curricular and instructional materials.

The sketches of "continuing crises" which follow will, of course, present a variety of questions, therefore choices, to the curriculum specialist who, by the very nature of his work, catalyzes social change. For example:

Are the areas embraced by the "reality" within the responsibility of the school? If so, in what segment of the school curriculum is major emphasis to be given: primary, intermediate, junior, or senior levels? If the area is not within the responsibility of the school, should recommendations be made to other agencies: family, church, communications media, local and state government, federal government? Other questions and other means will occur to the reader.

The Continuing Crisis. Planet Earth is the present site of human habitation; we may assume that a space module will be inhabited on a continuing basis before the end of this century. Similarly, human needs are served by earth's resources and these are limited not only by the nature of geological constraints but by the constraints of our knowledge. It is customary to discuss the limits of the earth under renewable (for example, food, water), nonrenewable (for example, fossil fuels, minerals), and perhaps inexhaustible resources (for example, solar radiation). This is a convenient and suitable catalogue from the customary viewpoint. But it is not suitable from the viewpoint of humane purpose and human prospect. Rather, it is more useful to display the continuing crises under heads which fit an art-science of human habitation, namely ekistics (*oekos*—home). Ekistics, as art-science, and as curriculum, is not limited by science and technology per se but subtends the social sciences and humanities as well as science. The art-science of ekistics[5] is then

    [5] Constantine Doxiadis (Athens) has indeed developed a School of Ekistics concerned with the art-science of human habitation.

more than ecology, for it includes ecology among other aspects of human concern. If you will, as a physician heals bodies, an ekistician heals environments. It is therefore, for our purposes, more appropriate to discuss the problems which face us under two heads: The Continuing Crisis: *Shortage for Life and Living;* The Continuing Crisis: *Quality of Life and Living.*

The Continuing Crisis: Shortage for Life and Living. We should, it would seem as a matter of priority, discuss the grim prospect of *annihilation by nuclear warfare* as a "crisis" prior to *shortage.* We are of the view that prospects of shortage catalyze national and international crises which may, if we are stupid, serve the final solution: nuclear warfare. We acknowledge that national pride, or that combination of assertion of need, deprivation, and pride we call national policy aggravate the possibility of reasonable and compassionate solution. It seems clear to most that shortage and its recognizable danger of national deprivation, and possible national failure, will stimulate dark thought of warfare.

We shall discuss *shortage* under these conceptual orderings: population, human nutrition (food and regulating substances), energy (fuel for industry), industrial nutrition (minerals).

PROSPECT: POPULATION. At this writing, some four billion (4,000,-000,000) people inhabit Planet Earth and some 220,000 join us each day. In 1850 there were some one billion people on earth; 80 years later (1930) it was about two billion; 30 years later (1960) it was about three billion; 15 years later or so—now—it is four billion. If this trend continues there will be five billion by 1985 or so, and by the end of this century some six billion or more.[6]

The rate of increase of the global population is thus roughly 2.0 percent, ca. 20 people per 1,000 of population. This means a doubling of world population every 35 years. This would mean 12 billion or so in 2035. Carried to its absurd conclusion, at the rate of increase of 2.0 percent per year, in 3,500 years the mass of the population of the Earth would equal the mass of the Earth.

At this writing, in the United States the annual increase (births over deaths) is roughly 0.9 percent. One reason adduced for this reduction is: In an industrial nation children are generally seen as consumers, not producers. In agrarian societies, children are also seen as producers.

As a result of application of the newer medical technologies (for example, preventive medicine, spraying to control malaria, immunization to control smallpox, and the like), the world increase in population accelerated from 0.9 percent in the decade 1940-1950 (a doubling time

6 Personal communication from Population Reference Bureau, Washington, D.C.

of 77 years) to a population increase rate of 1.8 percent in the decade 1950-1960 (a doubling time of 39 years).

Projections for population in the year 2000 for selected countries are as follows:

Year 2000, in billions

China	1.5
India	1.1
USSR	0.4
U.S.A.	0.35

We should now assess the portent of the foregoing on the demands of a modern society on at least several critical prospects. It is clear that not all prospects (synonym: problems) can be discussed within the limits of this paper, but we have selected those which may be considered as *limiting factors* upon further advances of society. The theory of limiting factors proposes that any "advance" in a given system is conditioned by the factor in short supply. Thus, a green plant may have light, nutrients, temperature, all appropriate conditions but a limited supply of water. Water is then the factor limiting the growth of the plant.

Similarly, population, energy, nutrition, mineral substances for industry are the major limiting factors for growth of a society. When we say underdeveloped country (UDC), or less developed country (LDC), we say in effect that these countries are limited in their social and technological development by the absence of one or more of these factors.

PROSPECT: NUTRITION. The question: Will our food resources put a limit on population growth?

Generally speaking, food production has been outstripped by population growth. It is difficult to realize that before 1940 a number of countries in Asia, Africa, and Latin America were grain exporters. By 1965 the exporters had turned to importers. In 1969 there was no net increase in *world* food production over 1968. Indeed, there was a per capita decline because of population growth of 2 percent in 1969. This situation continues; Africa, Asia, and South America continue to be grain importers; indeed, the Soviet Union has become one—although it has the technology to be a grain exporter. At this writing, there is probably no more than one year's grain supply to feed importing countries. At present, North America (that is, the United States and Canada) remains the reliable exporter, barring adverse climatic conditions.

The connection between population growth and food supply will probably continue to be an inverse relationship: In the immediate future, say 30 years, the greater the population growth the lower the food supply, even given improved technology. Many food scientists would maintain that food supply will never outstrip a population growth of 1.5 to 2.0 percent.

It is estimated (United Nations Food and Agricultural Organization) that in 1965, some 2,420 calories (to convert to Joules multiply by four) per capita per day were available; that is, enough food to feed the then-existing population. But food is not distributed equally; furthermore, to say 2,420 calories are sufficient is not to say there are sufficient amounts of proteins, vitamins, and minerals as well. Further, losses due to spoilage, and insect and rodent pests, range on an average of 10 to 20 percent—a low estimate according to some. Nevertheless, to feed the population of 1985 world food production should be increased by some 45 to 50 percent over 1965, assuming that population growth will have been reduced by some 30 percent. Further, distribution will need to be improved. It is predicted that the UDC's requirement for food will greatly increase; the requirements for such countries as India, Bangladesh, Brazil, may double unless there is a decline in population growth. Protein demands may increase more than 150 percent. An adequate diet to prevent kwashiorkor (a protein deficiency) requires some 50 grams of protein per day (pregnant women and children requiring more than mature men). Under present conditions, many UDC's cannot maintain this standard.

Deficiency diseases such as marasmus and kwashiorkor are common in UDC's. Marasmus is the result of general malnutrition: low calorie as well as protein diet, low in vitamin and mineral components; it is related to early weaning and subsequent continued failures in diet. Kwashiorkor is due to protein insufficiency.

Add to these a host of other diseases categorized as malnutrition (lack of proper food substances) rather than undernutrition (insufficient calories per se). Widespread in UDC's are beri-beri, a deficiency of thiamine; anemia, a lack of iron or vitamin B-12 (folic acid); rickets, a lack of vitamin D; scurvy, a lack of vitamin C; and pellagra, a deficiency of niacin. Cases of scurvy and pellagra are less numerous than other vitamin and mineral deficiency diseases.

In any event, the best estimate—if we can increase worldwide food production some 45 to 50 percent by 1985, and if we can reduce population growth by 30 percent—we may estimate a population of five billion, of which some 10 or 20 percent may be undernourished, and 30 to 40 percent malnourished. A grim and unpleasant prospect.

Of course one may argue that cause of death due to nutritional deficiency and cause of death due to viral, bacterial, and protozoan and other invertebrate organisms (flatworms and roundworms) are different in category. Nevertheless, it is well established that weakening of resistance caused by poor nutrition is often antecedent to death caused by infectious organisms. Furthermore, studies of undernourished and malnourished children in a variety of UDC's indicates that both physical and mental activity was impaired. Undernutrition and malnutrition, coupled with parasitism, generally produce listlessness and low productivity.

What of the United States? In 1968 a report to the Senate Select Committee on Nutrition and Human Needs revealed that between 10 to 15 million Americans were undernourished. Another 10 to 15 million Americans did not have adequate diets because of low incomes. Kwashiorkor and marasmus do exist in the United States although the cases are few. That they exist at all is hard to understand, considering these diseases are easily preventable in a country which produces as much food as the United States. This applies as well to the findings of deficiency diseases where vitamin A and vitamin D are concerned.

However, with the institution of free lunch programs and the expanded food stamp program of 1970-1972, malnutrition and undernutrition, altogether embarrassing and unnecessary presences in the United States, are being controlled. But seven million are still to be reached if the estimate of some 24 million poor is correct. However, it is sobering to know that even in an affluent country such as the United States ignorance and poverty still affect the well-being of about ten percent of our population. Certainly the schools have a great function in this area if only because all the children can now be *seen* by teachers and any deficiencies can be ameliorated.

PROSPECT: ENERGY. The question: Will our resources in energy put a limit on population growth?

We must understand, first, some natural laws which bind us. Mainly these are the Laws of Thermodynamics. Stated without the benefit of mathematics, we recognize that energy cannot be created or destroyed (the First Law of Thermodynamics). That is, oil or coal when used are converted into other forms of energy, such as heat energy, energy of motion, and the like. The total sum of energy thus remains constant, but it may not be energy precisely useful to us, for example, heat put into the atmosphere or the environment generally may, for all practical purposes, be forever lost to us.

The conversion of available energies such as coal, oil, hydroelectric power, solar energy, and the like into useful energy for technological use is subject to the principles subtended under the Second Law. Simply put—high energy sources such as oil, coal, and the like are degraded into low energy sources as heat is dispersed into the environment.

Thus the First Law tells us that the total amount of energy in the universe is constant (is conserved). The Second Law tells us that such energy moves in a constant direction—the amount of energy useful to us is being diminished because it is constantly being degraded. There is in short, as many ecologists have put it, "no free lunch." Or, "you don't get something for nothing."

Having said this we are confronted by these probabilities: Our high-grade fossil fuels, oil, coal, and natural gas will last some 300 to 400 years assuming the rate of present consumption. Coal will probably be the fuel last consumed, with world oil and natural gas reserves estimated at a life of some 100 years. Implied in this understanding are increased energy costs in the future for Americans, not to say for people in UDC's and LDC's.

There are other sources of energy which are in use, however. First is hydroelectric power, and devices (wheels and turbines) which use wind and tides and geothermal sources. Of course, the utilization of water, wind, and tidal power depends on the availability of sites. Roughly estimated, these sources of power (reserves if you will) are large; potentially they could supply about one-half the power now available from fossil fuels. Since most of the potential hydroelectric power is in UDC's and LDC's, we must consider it unavailable until these countries become industrialized. Another serious question which must be considered is the advisability of controlling rivers by dams; the environmental impact of such devices must be considered.

Energy from the utilization of wind and tides is an unpredictable source. The former we know is intermittent. The latter is localized, supporting specific regions (for example, the St. Lawrence Waterway region). Although they are utilizable they cannot be considered, at this writing, of basic importance in answering the question posed at the beginning of this section.

Geothermal sources—related to tapping the heat of earth's interior —seem more hopeful but there are no reliable estimates of the scale of the underground reservoirs. Iceland has tapped these sources and they are utilizable. Experts vary considerably in their estimates and again we must consider geothermal energy as exploitable but not a preeminent source of future energy. In other words, wind, tidal, and geothermal energy are auxiliary, not fundamental, sources. Certainly, where feasible and desirable, these sources need to be exploited, especially since their environmental impact may be low.

Two useful sources of energy, solar energy and nuclear energy, need to be harnessed on a larger scale, but the technological problems standing in the way of feasibility and durability have not yet been solved. The sun is a so-called inexhaustible source of energy, assuming that we understand that present theory acknowledges that our sun—a small star by standards of the universe—will become a nova in some eight to ten billion years. Then it will envelope its planetary system and incinerate it—Planet Earth included. (Since we are dealing with the limits of Planet Earth, this postulated limitation on existence might as well be included.)

Nonetheless, it is estimated that the efficiency of solar energy—with present technology—is three to seven percent, depending on site. Some experts calculate that a solar-energy plant could be 25 percent effective but this has not yet been accomplished. In any event, present solar devices are utilizable year-round where solar energy is sustained year-round (southern regions) and in regions where the land is not primarily useful for agricultural purposes—desert, mountain areas, and the like. Thus, with present technology a solar-collecting area covering some 15 to 20 square miles, with a conversion factor of solar energy to electric energy of ten percent on the average, would supply enough power to furnish electricity for a city of some 75,000 people—say 1,000 megawatts. However, this source of energy should be vigorously exploited, especially in view of its favorable effects on the environment if further research demonstrates its feasibility and desirability.

At first glance, nuclear power seems to be a major source of energy for the future and it should be, if science and technics combine to solve present problems. At the beginning, and for the present, it should be realized that nuclear power plants produce only electrical energy. The importance of this fact is highlighted when we consider that about 25 percent of the total energy utilized in the United States is electrical energy. Therefore, one should not assume that the utilization of nuclear energy can indefinitely postpone exhaustion of our fossil fuels. It is probable that in the year 2000 about one-half of U.S. energy utilization will be electrical, *but* it is estimated that at least 50 to 60 percent of it will be generated by nuclear power of the "burner" and "breeder" types—possibly, but certainly, by "fusion" types of reactors. For the UDC's the utilization of nuclear reactors remains a problem if only because the source of energy necessary to UDC's must be local, that is, where industrial sites or cities or connurbations using large amounts of electricity are located. Similarly it would not be feasible—at present—for a region (two or three countries) to utilize the same source of power. In short, one or two nuclear plants could not be utilized for an entire country because of the high cost of transmission of the electrical energy.

What of the United States? It is estimated that by 1980, ten percent of our electrical energy will be produced by nuclear reactors; by the year 2000, some 40 to 50 percent will be so produced. At this writing, there are 58 units of licensed nuclear reactors in the United States. In addition, 69 more construction permits have been granted, and 25 of these are presently under operating license review. The number of nuclear reactors in the United States projected for 1980 is 93; projected for 2000—725 nuclear reactors.[7] Perhaps, in view of the current doubts with regard to the safety of nuclear reactors, this goal will not be realized. To all intents and purposes, by exploitation of its energy sources, power produced from fossil fuels (including mining of shale, and wide use of coastal waters), hydroelectric generators, nuclear reactors (including fusion reactors), solar energy, geothermal sources, and the like, the U.S. might be self-sustaining in energy by the year 2000. At a great expense, naturally. For example, one should include the high cost of construction of safe nuclear reactors in estimating the cost of electrical power. At present, coal-fired plants (of modern construction) produce electricity for about four to five mills per kilowatt-hour. So do modern nuclear reactors.

PROSPECT: INDUSTRIAL NUTRITION (MINERALS). A bird's-eye view, or perhaps a worldwide view of utilization of mineral resources would read somewhat as follows: At present to the year 2000, assuming present rates of consumption, the DC's (developed countries) will probably be able to maintain their present utilizations of mineral resources, if only because the LDC's and UDC's will not proceed with too-rapid industrialization. If the present trends of use continue, all populations will be required to exercise restraint in view of the limitations of readily available extractive industrial sites. It is estimated that the costs of energy needed to utilize less favorable sites—that is, oil from shale, minerals from granite rocks, etc.—may well be prohibitive. What are the underlying reasons, given our current knowledge?

Standards of living of the DC's depend in large part on the availability of certain staple substances—oil, coal, rubber, iron, aluminum, copper, zinc, cobalt, tin, lead, phosphate, other essential substances—in tiny amounts necessary for industrial utilization of many of these staples, such as molybdenum, tungsten, vanadium, thallium, tantalum, and the like; these last are sometimes called "mineral vitamins" in the industrial diet in an analogy to the function of vitamins in our diet.

Consider, however, that the DC's account for about 30 percent of the world's population yet consume about 90 percent of the steel produced on Planet Earth. Ehrlich and Ehrlich estimate that "to raise all of the

[7] Personal communication from Nuclear Regulatory Commission, and Energy Research and Development Administration, Washington, D.C.

3.8 billion people of the world of 1972 to the American standard of living would require the extraction of almost 27.3 billion metric tons (30 billion tons) of iron, more than 454 million metric tons (500 million tons) of copper and lead, more than 273 million metric tons (300 million tons) of zinc, about 45.5 million metric tons (50 million tons) of tin, as well as enormous quantities of other minerals. That means the extraction of some 250 times as much tin, 200 times as much lead, 100 times as much copper, 75 times as much zinc, and 75 times as much iron. . . . To raise the standard of living of the projected world population of the year 2000 to today's American standard would require nearly double of all the above figures."[8]

By the year 2000, we shall probably be near the end of our known easily "mined" world reserves of uranium, tungsten, copper, lead, tin, zinc, gold, silver, platinum; the United States will still have sufficient reserves of coal, iron, molybdenum. Although at present we produce about 25 percent of the world's oil we do consume about 3019 litres (800 gallons) per capita per year; in the ensuing years up to 2000 our consumption will be approximately double our proven reserve.

Another view of U.S. demand would be expressed somewhat as follows: Except for coal, the United States is dependent on resources outside its boundaries for most of the basic mineral resources which feed its industry. We are, in fact, a have-not nation because of the industrial maw which is ever unsatisfied if it is to meet our incredible demands.

WATER: In all this we have not considered water—as a substance needed in huge quantities to produce food (and to use food within the body). At present, each year we use approximately 6226 litres (1650 gallons) per capita for all purposes. By the year 2000, almost 7547 litres (2000 gallons) per capita per year. To produce a kilogram (2.2 pounds) of cereal grain (dry) utilizes ca. 415 to 498 litres (110 to 132 gallons) of water; a kilogram of rice, 1660 to 2075 litres (440 to 550 gallons); a kilogram of meat 26,400 to 49,811 litres (6600 to 13,200 gallons); one automobile ca. 377,358 litres (100,000 gallons).

Consider the requirements of the LDC's and the UDC's in water-hungry areas. Of course, 97 percent of the world's supply of water is contaminated by salts, namely sea water. Of the three percent fresh water remaining about 96 percent is tied up in the ice caps of Arctica (and Greenland) and Antarctica. The latter cannot be used with our present technology since freeing it would raise our sea level some 36.6 to 47.5 metres (40 to 50 yards) and this would flood our cities and our crop lands. Consider too the depletion of our water supplies in the

[8] Ehrlich and Ehrlich, *op. cit.*, p. 19.

forms of evaporation or transpiration, severe pollution, and discharge into oceans.

Be that as it may, the average supply—that is, runoff (from water-shed areas and the like) is approximately 4.52 x 10^9 litres (1200 billion gallons) per day. Considering that much of this runoff occurs during wet seasons, present runoff will not meet our needs in the year 2000, particularly in the western half of the country (excluding Oregon and Washington). Our technics will require considerable innovative devices to secure a useful water supply—but this below.

The Continuing Crisis: Quality of Life and Living. Stewart Udall, Secretary of the Interior, writing in 1968 but titling his book *1976: Agenda for Tomorrow,* tells us,

A tranquility index or a cleanliness index might have told us something about the condition of man, but a fast-growing country preoccupied with making and acquiring material things has had no time for the amenities that are the very heart and substance of daily life.[9]

In the foregoing "The Continuing Crisis: Shortage for Life and Living" we chose certain critical aspects of modern life for discussion: population, energy, nutrition, among others. We might, for instance, have added space, forests, pure air, and the like. But recall our purpose: to assist in the development of curricular and instructional modes fit for a curriculum which responds to modern realities. To forward schooling and education requires more than the cataloguing of information which, after all, not only cannot be complete within the limits of this paper, but which must be left as a matter of professional choice through a suitable bibliography to those who will develop a total curriculum. Our task is clearly to document direction and provide a framework. A useful category, given this view and our position, is to turn now to other elements of the problem under the enormous import of "Quality of Life and Living." We shall not concern ourselves directly with pollution, which is generously treated by Dr. Gratz in her chapter, but we cannot discharge our task without reference to certain aspects of it under a variety of concerns directed mainly to developing a kind of Tranquility Index.

The thrust of our discussion will come under these heads: prolongation of life, annihilation, purity of the environment, privacy, psychological safety, purposelessness, and the principle of minimum suffering. Again we shall find that principles of curricular organization require unity and confluence and these topics do indeed merge, overlap, and coerce each other into easy structure.

9 Stewart Udall. *1976: Agenda for Tomorrow.* New York: Harcourt Brace Jovanovich, 1968.

PROSPECT: PROLONGATION OF LIFE. Whether one considers immunity against viral and bacterial disease: influenza, measles, polio, diphtheria, typhoid, and the like; amelioration of nutritional deficiency disease: pellagra, scurvy, rickets, anemia, and the like; reduction of functional deficiency: heart malfunction by means of electronic pacers, the Kantrowitz plastic heart, the DeBakey valve, or heart transplant; kidney malfunctions by means of kidney transplant, and the like; elimination of malaria and plague by spraying of pesticides; the net effect is prolongation of life. By a variety of means, then, life in the United States and Western countries is now extended to an average 75 years—as compared with an average of 40 years in 1840.

In essence, 27 years have been added to the average life span in the past 27 years through a variety of biomedical procedures. Medical history tells us that this is not really an addition to longevity but largely an elimination of childhood diseases, which results in a lengthening of the average life span when statistically computed. It is also conceivable, by the same token, by means of "life-sustaining" machines to extend an individual's life span without his or her express consent.

One might say that all this is a beneficent accomplishment of science-technics, that is, the scientific theoretical accomplishments of Pasteur, Koch, Salk, Noguchi, Ehrlich, Lister, Goldsteiner, among a host of others have been extended by a host of technicists into vaccines, vitamins, drugs, and machines—all extending the life span. The other side of the coin is the moral dilemma imposed on the immediate family and the interested public when machines maintain life without consent.

In addition, one should consider the effects of technology in what students of population control have called "exported death control." (Why not call it "extending potential for life"?) For example, in 1945, the death rate in Ceylon (Sri Lanka) was ca. 22 per 1000. In 1971, after sprayings with DDT, the death rate mainly from insect-borne disease (mosquitoes mainly) dropped to 8 per 1000. Remarkable reductions in death rate (with resulting prolongation of the average life span) have resulted as deaths from malaria, smallpox, cholera, yellow fever were reduced.

But recall that these remarkable and, if you will, felicitous effects were a result of environment change: the removal of infectious agents. It was not necessarily accomplished in the UDC's by a similar change in institutions as in most of the DC's. That is, there is a growth in population without a necessary adjunct growth in production of food, energy, housing, and personal-social medical care. But disease as contravening longevity may not be the major problem which confronts civilization. Given sufficient time and funds and encouragement of ingenuity (synonym: creativity), most of the major diseases that affect humans can be brought under control. This estimate includes heart disease and cancer. These are, of course, partly caused by pollutants in the environment (internal environment, smoking, and the ingestion of additives and pesticides) as well as external aspects, stress, crowding, and the like. Such diseases as emphysema, lung cancer (due to inhalation of asbestos and other pollutants), can be controlled if our air and water are not used as sewers for a host of pollutants. But only, or mainly, political solutions may protect us against global annihilation.

ANNIHILATION. The atom of Democritus was not quite the atom of Dalton, nor was it the atom of Marie Sklodowska Curie, Albert Einstein, Lisa Meitner, Niels Bohr, Enrico Fermi, or Robert Oppenheimer. The atom of the 1940's—and the present—is awesome in potentiality for great good or great evil. This, of course, is the double face of almost all invention in science—or technics. The bow and arrow can be used to still hunger or to kill, penicillin can eliminate early syphilis but by its easy intervention lull the young into a false sense of security; too much aspirin can kill; so can too much food.

There is, then, the possibility of a source of energy which could energize national economies with the development of nuclear fusion or the destruction of entire populations by uses of overkill by nuclear bombs.

Clearly if potentials for developing the nuclear bomb proliferate— as they are indeed doing—are we not faced with destruction through intent or accident? Surely if China, Russia, have the bomb, as do the United States, England, France—as will numerous other nations—will the bomb be used, to repeat, by accident or intent? Either intent or accident will do the job of annihilation. Agreed. Then we shall take the view that, having the weapons of destruction, we will destroy ourselves. So say those who, without hope, define the reality of man's past inhumanity to man as a continuing inhumanity.

There is little doubt that we have the capacity to destroy "civilization" as it exists today. It is a kind of ultimate madness to contemplate using nuclear weapons which could, if used in total warfare, destroy humankind. The dead in World War II numbered 35 million; the *first* nuclear attack (without retaliation) would—it is estimated—result in deaths of 60 to 80 million. Put another way, one estimate assesses the megatonnage of the nuclear stockpiles of the United States and the Soviet Union combined could yield the equivalent of 13.64 metric tons (15 tons) of dynamite for each individual now on earth. Put still another way, the United States and Soviet Russia alone have enough atomic bombs to destroy the major populations of Planet Earth leaving—if any

life would be left after radioactive fallout has done its work—only isolated bits of humanity. Consider too that plant life would also be affected; genetic monsters in both flora and fauna would result. There is
no need to cite numbers. The blunt statement is enough: warfare on the
levels of World War II, but using strategic and tactical nuclear weapons,
would mean total devastation; no one alive now can say what would
remain.

But suppose they are wrong. Suppose—against odds—we gain time
by negotiation, by whatever honorable means, by SALT, by detente, by
all diplomatic means available. Suppose we press forward with attempts
to help the United Nations (or whatever alliance) to strengthen peace-
keeping activities. Suppose the United Nations is given power by its
signatories of enforced arbitration of all national disputes on the road
to war. Suppose the international community outlaws nuclear warfare
with complete inspection enforced. Why not? What are the alternatives?

Suppose leading nations with peaceful intent—the United States first,
certainly—join in assisting the less developed countries (LDC's) to
achieve sufficient technological progress to maintain their populations
(assuming that policies for population control are generally accepted).
Suppose at the same time we advance nuclear technology for peaceful
purposes—namely, nuclear fusion for the necessary energy to ensure at
least temporary development of all populations with sufficient fore-
thought and control to secure a beneficent life. To save our nation and
the world, for our nation could not exist in a world destroying itself, to
save technics itself, we need to control our technology, to place limits
on its expansion.

It is not a new thought but it is an essential one: *All things may be
possible but it is also admissible that all possible things are not necessary
or desirable.*

Suppose, then, we concern ourselves as much with moral development as with technical development; suppose we uphold the legacies of
Moses, Jesus and Mohammed, Buddha and Confucius, and we use them
to direct our technics for humane purposes and truly human prospects.
Impossible? Why?

Suppose we face these problems in our schools, colleges, and universities—worldwide—and begin the dialogue, opposing ignorance by knowledge of the elements of nuclear energy and nuclear warfare.

C. P. Snow reminds us that the scientist, by virtue of his special
knowledge, has a direct and moral imperative. He has a moral imperative
to say what he knows. And citizens in an open society have a right to
knowledge. It is possible, some medical scientists postulate, to extend our
life span past 100 years. But if this is so, into what kind of a world?

A fundamental question remains: What kind of a world do we want for our children?

PURITY. The past three, perhaps four, decades are witness to a phenomenon unique in the history of humankind: the chemical and physical poisoning of the environment, its airs, waters, lands. Not that the environment hasn't been "poisoned" before as a result of human activity. In the United States, for example, from the 1870's to the 1920's, poor sewage disposal, poor sanitation generally, and inadequate preventive medicine resulted in a high incidence of bacterial infection—smallpox, cholera, typhoid, puerperal fever ("childbed fever"), and the like. Largely, medical science and technology have eliminated these and other diseases (see the previous section on "Prospect: Prolongation of Life").

Now "technologically induced disease," if we may use the term, is on the increase. That is, the simple and life-giving activities of eating, drinking, and other modes of exposure (touching, etc.) may expose highly industrialized peoples to a host of malfunctions—among them an increase in chemically induced cancer, heart and lung disease. There are self-inflicted diseases such as cancer from the carcinogenic tars found in cigarettes, high ingestion of alcohol, polychlorinated biphenyls (PCB's), polyvinyl chlorides (PVC's), DDT, asbestos fibers, nitrites (as food preservatives) which turn into dangerous nitrosoamines, and the like. The assault on the human body becomes even more outrageous when we add to this incomplete list the colossal dangers from self-prescribed drugs—barbituates, amphetamines, heroin and other opium derivatives, nicotine (from cigarettes), and the like.

Add to this additional hazards not only from the mild effect of radiation from overexposure to the sun but the greater effect of radiation from excessive X-rays and nuclear fallout.

Add to this the effects of the nitrogen oxide and carbon monoxide from the exhausts of cars, sulfur dioxide and other impurities from industrial smokestacks. Add to this the industrial effluent into streams and oceans which includes not only alkali and acid wastes, but toxic amounts of mercury, copper, and the like. (We have not yet had outbreaks of the serious Minimata disease caused by effluents of mercury in Japanese waters, which destroys parts of the nervous system.)

Add to this discharge of oil waste into the ocean due to oil spills; the runoff of fertilizer into streams and lakes; the deposit of nuclear waste into the ocean. The effects of intensive nuclear radiation have been documented; survivors of the Hiroshima and Nagasaki nuclear attack have evidenced a significantly higher incidence of cancer of the brain, colon, and breast, and of leukemia. Consider, too, possible dangers to the ozone layer, which protects us from excessive radiation from the sun, due to the spraying of aerosol products in cans of deodorants, hairspray, and the like. The list grows . . . of some 1,400 substances (drugs, pollutants), 20 or so are held to be carcinogenic. But we cannot know of other possible dangers to the body mechanism, i.e., emphysema, hereditary malfunctions, nervous disorders, and the like. The list grows.

Nor can we be assured that drugs administered by physicians are always safe. Witness the incidence of malformations caused by administration of thalidomide during pregnancy. Witness the incidence of vaginal cancer in the daughters of women who in early pregnancy were prescribed the synthetic hormone diethyl stilbesterol (DES). Iatrogenic diseases may be on the increase.

Aside from this, we poison carcasses of sheep to kill hyenas and in so doing kill other animals—such as the bald eagle. We spray pesticides on lakes, or dump chemicals, and through the effects of biological magnification, the pollutant is concentrated in successive food niches, that is, small amounts in the plankton, larger amounts in plankton-feeding organisms, even larger amounts in organisms (say fish) that feed on them and finally the fish or fowl lands on our table with the concentrate of the pollutant to be focused in our tissue. Mother's milk can concentrate high amounts of DDT in this manner. So can the tissues of eagles and so can their egg-producing mechanisms so that the young do not hatch.

Our excellent yields of cereals—corn, wheat, oats—due to large applications of fertilizer may also be a hazard. The soil nutrients may be washed into lakes or streams, or oceans where the algae material and other surface plants may undergo vast growth. The bottom layers of the mat of growth may not be exposed to the sun's energy and fail to photosynthesize sufficient oxygen, and die. As the detritus increases, the oxygen supply may be diminished to such a dangerous level that the flora and fauna of the lake or pond may be destroyed. This is the process of eutrophication, or overnourishment, if you will, of the plant life. This aside from the effect of biological magnification.

No doubt, this litany is not new to the reader. In an "experiment" conducted by the writer, a good number of high school students were given a list of some 25 endangered mammals, that is, mammals in danger of extinction. They were asked to add others. More than 80 percent added "human beings."

For the large part, all this need not be. True, judicious use of pesticides—carefully controlled—is at this point in our technology required to control invasions of insect pests: for example, cotton boll weevil, gypsy moth, potato beetle, and the like. Fungicides are necessary as well. But uses of biological controls are growing; witness the use of sterile Mediterranean fruit flies to control an outbreak of the insect in southern fruit groves—the normal insects mate with the sterile ones and cannot reproduce. This is not to say that biological controls are capable of the constant vigilance required to maintain our food, wood, and fiber. But the application of insecticides can be controlled.

Recently the National Institute for Occupational Safety and Health, the U.S. Food and Drug Administration, the Occupational Safety and Health Administration, the U.S. Department of Agriculture, the U.S. Department of the Interior and their subsumed agencies have begun the massive confrontation necessary to bring these abusive practices which are an assault on the purity of the air, water, food we require for health and life under sensible controls. An Environmental Protection Agency has also come into action.

Within the next decade or so we can, *as informed citizens,* bring our magnificent technology to bear in the problem of securing a sanative, that is, a healing, environment into existence. This is not to say that selective use of our technology to prevent deprivation of food supply and assure delivery of appropriate medical services is not paramount. To repeat, a sensible, sensitive, responsive, and responsible balance between use and abuse can be struck.

The Western countries, the UDC's, have become the spearpoint of this effort because their demands on technology have, in effect, produced the abuses. The same abuses are now noted in LDC's which do not balance appropriate use and abuse.

For we did ban DDT for general and indiscriminate use once the case had been made; dieldrin is no longer responsible for fish-kills, "clean-air" standards are being slowly, ever so slowly, but surely, enforced; the automobile industry is responding ever so slowly, but it *is* responding. Environmental impact studies are now required, before a massive change in an environment is implemented, where a responsible community is on the alert. We are beginning, but only beginning, to turn the corner. There is considerable hope. But our schools have not yet taken up the curricular cudgel.

To the end of securing a sanative environment, the schools have a significant function to which we shall attend once the case has been made for the overriding responsibility of the individual who is not only competent in his or her vocation but a passionate and compassionate advocate of a sanative environment. That is, an ethicist and ekistician, both.

PRIVACY. The sad spectacle of the phenomenon we now call Watergate alerted the American public to the possible assaults on privacy by electronic devices. Again we have an abuse of magnificent adjuncts to life and living by those who would mismanage them. We find a President, and a group of plastic men, "bugging" themselves, their friends, their real and supposed enemies. We find government agencies using electronic devices illegally or, at the least, unethically. We find private agencies like telephone companies recording conversations, if only to determine whether their services are being delivered in an efficient way. We find computerized listings multiplying. We find government agencies compiling dossiers because computerized information and computers capable of controlling hordes of pieces of information are now available.

Our technology, in short, makes it possible for an industrial and postindustrial society to invade the privacy of its citizens; that is, unless the invasion of privacy is under the surveillance of those whose privacy is at stake. Watergate has had its blessing. "Freedom of information" laws enable us to call up our own dossiers—if such dossiers exist in government files. (This is not yet as easy as it should be.) Wiretapping regulations are being scrutinized; laws to control indiscriminate use of "electronic snoopery" are being considered, and the like.

Much more can be said about the dangers of invasions of privacy. Totalitarian states could not exist without manifest invasion of privacy; democracy cannot exist with it. The possibility of condoned secret invasion without "due process" must be a crime excepting those cases where the life of the individual, community, or nation is endangered in a clearly demonstrable way. The legal, ethical, moral constraints on an open, life-affirming, self-examining society require no less.

Here too curricular cures are possible, if desirable.

PSYCHOLOGICAL SAFETY AND PSYCHOLOGICAL FREEDOM. The right to privacy is akin to the requirement of psychological safety and psychological freedom (Rogerian terms) but are for the purposes of this discussion somewhat different in the areas subsumed. Psychological safety refers essentially to those areas related to the *protection* against intrusion of an individual's life and integrity. Thus, the right to determine whether or not one will be subject to medical-surgical treatment or biomedical interference is within each individual's terrain of choice and decision. We have but to recall Nazi subjugation of individuals in this regard and the unbridled uses of "truth serums" by self-serving totalitarian governments and their agencies. Similarly, psychological freedom is at the initiative of the individual to determine what kind of biomedical instrumentation he or she will seek or submit to.

We are at a point where biomedical engineering may become a major aspect of our technology. Of course, our immunological and chemical techniques (ameliorating disease on an international scale) may well be considered a biomedical technology. To mention but a few items: With regard to amphibians we are now able to produce laboratory organisms from the egg only; thus the organism has only the genetic traits of the female. We are able to imitate embryonic development of certain mammals *in vitro*—to put it obligingly, in test tubes. We are able to clone individuals in certain invertebrates and vertebrates, that is, produce twins at will. We are able to preserve sperm not only of livestock but of humans for later use in artificial insemination. We are at the beginning of cryogenic research which enables us to freeze (at minimal body function) organisms and organs to be revived later. We are able to substitute machines for organs (for limited times), or substitute transplanted or a variety of artificial hearts or kidneys to prolong life. Bionic limbs are being constantly improved and bionic surgery is being refined.

Genetic transformation is not new for certain organisms. Muller's production in the laboratory of Drosophila (fruit fly) mutants has long been known. But with the increased knowledge of the heredity code, DNA (deoxyribonucleic acid) and its chemistry pioneered by Woodward and others we have come to a new frontier. Geneticists have been able to exchange portions of the DNA complex, (that is, introduce new pieces not originally within the hereditary complex of the organism) in varieties of the bacterium Escherichia coli—a colon bacterium which also frequents sewage-laden waters. The result—to deliberately produce mutant forms. It is to the credit of the high integrity of the scientists involved that they personally agreed—in convention—to halt their investigation until appropriate safeguards had been established. Reason: While we can control the pathogenicity of established forms, a mutagen may run rampant and decimate populations. The science and technology, once established with Escherichia could, of course, be applied to a host of bacteria. And, if so, why not eventually to higher organisms?

Already in humans the technique of amniocentesis has been developed. Cells in the fluid from the amnion surrounding the human fetus can be withdrawn and their chromosomes (complexes of DNA) can be examined. Early in the life of the fetus, certain hereditary diseases (for example, Kleptonuria, nervous disorders resulting in death prior to 30 years of age) can be diagnosed; in such cases, the fetus can be aborted. Individuals with an XXY chromosome picture (there is *incomplete evidence* that such individuals tend to asocial, even criminal behavior) can be detected through amniocentesis. The list grows; recall that science and technology, in combination, put enormous potential within our grasp.

And, of course, it would not surprise us that biomedical, biological, and chemical technology can be put to other uses. Countries, including the United States, do either have arsenals or the potential to produce the equipment and material for purposes of biological warfare with possible results exceeding present calculation. Herbicides can defoliate forests and vegetation. Insects, new to an environment, can wreak havoc on agriculture. A variety of gases and biological poisons can destroy life immediately or act on the nervous system. Viral and bacterial agents can be introduced into food and water supplies to spread disease. It has been aptly remarked that we do not need nuclear weapons to destroy the life of this planet; to put it grimly, we can do it quietly with a "whimper," not a "bang."

PURPOSELESSNESS. Technology in its widest sense implements our ways of doing things, of extending life-asserting functions. Aspirins, alcohol, tobacco, heroin are as much part of our technology as TV, airplanes, computers, oil refineries, space laboratories—and buttons and Saarinen chairs. So it is nothing strange to find our technology serves purposelessness—even mindlessness.

Do we want to escape problems imploring use of knowledge and common sense? Then, the techniques implicit in "escape," alcohol and drugs, are useful. To become "spaced out" has become an accolade. Do we disagree with our institutions? Then we can make plastic bombs and other terrorist tools which enable those so inclined to hold innocents hostage, to kill indiscriminantly. Do we despair of life-affirming activity? Then we can become mesmerized by certain incredible programs on TV which "space" us out in their own way. We use our technology too often to escape a "discipline of responsible consent."

Our whims and fads in schooling are no less free from being victimized by technology. Find a new device and it may sweep the "school mind" into ecstasy. Recall how radio was once an answer to a host of problems? And TV? And programmed instruction? And computers? Long ago, Rousseau, then the Montessori School, now Summerhill, now "open schools." Progressive education? Recall how we embrace movements only to go to the newer ones without testing, testing, testing our preconceptions? Too often we proceed from word to word rather than from work to work. So "inquiry" displaces "discovery" and "discovery" displaces "learning by doing." And with the change in words comes new applications of print technology and machines. The list is endless.

If we are indeed *in loco parentis* must we not present a more critical view of all new devices (meant and honorably devised, to be sure, by their inventors) intended to change the behavior of the children and youth entrusted to our care? The central problem of education remains: How social stimulation is to be utilized honorably so that the young can acquire capacities and attitudes (aptitudes and permanent dispositions) which result in life-affirming changes in overt and covert behavior. Knowledge of the means of appropriate social stimulation (by teachers) is not acquired easily. The effects of prosaic instruction can be measured. *But teaching remains a personal invention. It is a performing art.*

PRINCIPLE OF MINIMUM SUFFERING. All that has been said prior to this has been meant to lead to the suggestion of a *principle of minimum suffering*[10] which a society in transition from a preindustrial to a post-industrial state should consider. A postindustrial society, as we shall see, possesses the theoretical knowledge to advance its science and technology at a rapid rate to this extent: Some 10 percent of individuals can produce the products required for life and living for the other 90 percent engaged in service, to wit, research, education, medicine, engineering, publishing, communications, transportation, and the like.

To develop a principle of minimum suffering one must ask questions grounded in values: Should any individual suffer death for causes which can be remedied? Should any individual—child, woman, man, go hungry? When we know the elements of beauty, should we suffer ugliness? When we know the nature of a sanative environment, should we suffer its pollution and desolation? When we know how to live and die with dignity, need we impose suffering? What suffering, knowing the remedy, are we willing consciously to permit without, at least, a dissenting statement?

A highly educative experience of the writer's is to the point. In 1952, at a conference devised for the purpose of developing national, then international, modes of worldwide discussions of the depredation of the environment, the fate of such conferences befell this one: Agreement even on the simplest issues could not be found if only because scholars find it sporting to disagree. That is, until the question was asked: What kind of world do we want for our children? In a time incredibly short for such conferences agreement was attained on far-reaching ends. But, of course, there was disagreement on the means; always there is disagreement on means.

A principle of minimum suffering requires agreement on *means and ends.* Humane purposes and human prospects deserve no less. Our science and technology must close with our moral imperatives. C. P. Snow has been one of the urgent voices to remind us that our wisdom is endangered because of our divisiveness: the gap between the two cultures, the culture of science and technology and the culture of the humanities. He reminds us:

Closing the gap between our cultures is a necessity in the most abstract intellectual sense, as well as in the most practical. When these two senses have grown apart, then no society is going to be able to think with wisdom. . . . Isn't

---

[10] Again, I am haunted by the thought that this phrase is not mine. It may have been stated by twice-Nobelist Linus Pauling in one of his speeches which I attended.

it time we began? The danger is, we have been brought up to think as though we had all the time in the world. We have very little time. So little that I dare not guess at it.[11]

And T. S. Eliot mourns, "Where is the wisdom we have lost in knowledge? Where is the knowledge we have lost in information?"

And so we turn to suggestions to ameliorate our condition of servitude to the terror of the future.

In short-term remedies we propose those which can be part and parcel of the present curriculum. The changes are almost imperceptible. Long-term remedies concern themselves with a perceptible and sustained change: the centrality of the humane to schooling and the marriage of the sciences, natural and social, with the humanities. The humanities impose humanity on us all—citizens, parents, teachers. We recognize, then, that the school is a place where a child should be encouraged to be right and wrong. A child expressing himself or herself is not necessarily right or wrong; she or he is engaged in growth.

Our conception of the child in schooling and education is of one who will in time grow to be as competent as compassionate, who will in time grow to the measures of civilized man, who will accept the Grail and the constraints of truth, beauty, justice, love, and faith as divined in the best of man's past and future—and live by them. In fact humanity has survived because it has upheld this Grail, these constraints, these measures. In spite of the contradictions, the absurdities, the comedy and tragedy of life, people generally have not lost sight of the possible. Thus humankind has survived terror.

For our part, we care only that the teacher care. As individual, a teacher is of supreme moral worth. So is any child. So is every child.

Short-term Remedies Through Science and Technology. Clearly we cannot go back to a primeval state; a remedy for the excesses of our technology is surely a better technology answerable to the needs of a modern society. Do we have remedies for shortage as a consequence of the limits of Planet Earth? We simply cannot continue the plunder of our resources. The factors of population, food, energy which we are examining form a network. They are intertwined because people and their needs in a "global village" are interdependent, as we can see from the following.

Population, Food, Energy: A Network of Interdependence. With resources of food and energy limited and an increasing population, the equation remains unbalanced. A reasonable conclusion would be admissible along lines somewhat like these. If we are to reach a satisfactory

[11] C. P. Snow. *The Two Cultures.* New York: Cambridge University Press, 1965. pp. 51, 52.

standard of living for the people of this globe *population should be equal to available resources*. Either global resources must be increased, or global population must be controlled.

Reason with us perhaps as follows: There are researches which are advancing food production. For example, new varieties of wheat and corn have greater yields, so too do varieties of rice, particularly IR-8 introduced into rice-growing countries. However, the increase in Asian, African, and South American populations has wiped out the gain in food energy—even assuming that Asian populations would change food habits.

Even assuming newer technologies in the production of food—chemical conversion of wood into carbohydrate; bacterial conversion of crude oils into protein; use of fish meals as protein adjuncts; use of plant protein in place of meat protein; reduced conversions of plant into animal (that is, a diet more vegetarian, such as cereal, than is now prevalent in DC's) —there is no present indication that for the next 30 years food production can outstrip a population growth of 2.8 percent in LDC's and UDC's. Result: extensive famine.

Even if we grant that in the long run science and technology do solve the problem of photosynthesis and invent devices by which food making is no longer dependent on the green plant, the process will not come soon enough to avert famine. Even if we grant food sharing by the United States and Canada with LDC's and UDC's, it is predictable that famines in UDC's may still occur—in the short run. In the long run, they certainly will unless population is controlled so that it approaches the one percent now characteristic of the highly industrialized nations and finally to zero population growth (zpg).

The conclusions with regard to energy are similar. It is predicted that by 1980, approximately nine percent of the electrical energy in the United States will be produced by nuclear fusion (using uranium and plutonium). Thus, it may well be that highly industrialized nations (DC's) and some high population centers in LDC's (Near East and Middle Eastern countries) will be utilizing some nuclear energy to equalize the reduction in fossil fuels; nuclear technology will not be advanced sufficiently for easy use by the majority of LDC's and UDC's. But fusion energy requires incredibly high temperatures exceeding that of the sun. A device using a hydrogen plasma (highly condensed hydrogen) enclosed and controlled by a magnetic field developed at the Massachusetts Institute of Technology has reached temperatures of $10,000,000°$ C. Ten times that is necessary; the scientist-technologist team at M.I.T. believes it can be done.

Nevertheless, for the next 30 years or so when world population may reach six to seven billion—unless controlled, the future looks grim for LDC's and UDC's—if not for DC's—unless policies of population control are instituted.

If a country wishes to institute a population control program, do we have the science and technology to institute educational programs which may accomplish the aim? Yes! In various countries sexual abstention, rhythm methods, medication (hormonal in nature—"the pill"), surgical devices—intrauterine devices (IUD's), vasectomies, tie-off of Fallopian tubes, and the like are utilized.[12]

Basic to all these approaches is a strong educational program not only based in sex education *per se* but in family planning with emphasis on psychosocial and economic factors.

Two pervasive factors need consideration. It seems clear that industrialized countries (DC's) in general have lower birthrates than do LDC's and UDC's. Further, it has been suggested that it is not industrialization *per se* that is the major underlying factor but the activity of women in industrialized societies demanding more satisfactory roles as individuals. It may well be that as women achieve social and economic equality with men a population growth will be achieved which harmonizes with the requirements of a planet plagued by limited resources.

Perhaps a policy of triage will be useful. Recall that triage refers to a military practice (of unknown origin) which dictated selection for medical and surgical treatment of those wounded with the greatest chance of survival over those with lesser chance. A policy of triage would suggest that we should selectively determine which UDC's the DC's would support with shipments of food and fossil fuels. Thus the poorest UDC's, in a state of famine, would take the incredible consequences of starvation and death. This writer, for one, considers this morally repugnant and not acceptable to civilized and humane peoples. Put otherwise, a nation that is determined to avoid annihilation through nuclear warfare cannot use other demolition tactics—such as withholding of food from starving populations. As a logical consequence of such action by DC's, the LDC's and UDC's would not forget. In a "global village" (Planet Earth) interdependence, and the socioeconomic policies consequent upon it, is no longer a luxury. Interdependence as fact and as policy is of first rank.

Well then, what of a drastic control of utilization of food, energy, by DC's? For example, the United States, with six percent of the population of the globe, uses some 35 to 40 percent of the world's energy and raw materials. True, it is experiencing a lowering of the population. Can we not do with less? Of course. But can we change our habits, through a change in values, within the next five years? Ten years? Thirty years?

[12] Recent reports indicate that such devices, particularly chemical interventions such as "the pill," should not be taken without medical advice.

Perhaps we can; there are some indications that we in the United States already have. For example, a recent Harris poll (given the assumption that the sampling is useful) report tells us that 53 percent of the population would favor environmental controls while 47 percent would consider increase of prices to achieve a healthful environment. For example, the birthrate has been reduced in recent years from 1.8 percent to .9 percent.[13] For example, "Environmental Protection Agencies" of one sort or another have multiplied in federal, regional, state, and city governing units. Note the decision of the governing bodies of the State of Delaware to limit further industrial growth and pollution. Likewise, note the growth of organizations of citizens devoted to protection of the environment—for example, class action suits against offshore drilling, against the Alaskan-Canadian pipeline, etc. But, as yet, policies of conservation of energy and food are not vigorous national policy and statute; certainly they are not universal.

We could by conservation policy, that is, change in fossil fuel consumption (reduction of car size, use of car pools, improved insulation, personal economies in utilization of energy and food, reduction of over eating, utilization of alcohol—the list is endless) reduce our demand by more than 20 percent. Some say 50 percent. The point: We are not yet serious about conservation practice. The "new" conservationists—Ehrlich, Commoner, *et al.*—deserve all the credit for the reforms they are attempting to initiate but they are not saying more than was said by organizations such as The Conservation Foundation, and the Council of Economic Education, or the Pinchot Institute for Conservation Studies some 25 to 30 years ago.

The foregoing—namely a *flat statement that we know much and can do much that can alleviate the situation for the short run*—applies to all the aspects we have arbitrarily subscribed under two major categories: *"Shortage for Life and Living"* and *"Quality for Life and Living."*

Further, the bibliography appended will support the foregoing statement. One major need, as this writer sees it, is a realization that the crisis is one of education: Once the public grasps it, internalizes it, mediates it, public policy will follow. At random, "the people" of San Francisco did save San Francisco Bay; Clear Lake in California, once on its way to "doom" because of indiscriminate use of DDT, is now thriving; the Thames has been restored to a clean, thriving river; the Hudson has far to go but citizens have taken the bit by the teeth; the Alaskan pipeline has been built with greater care of the environment. There are smog and clean air "watchers"; the Environmental Protection Agency is out of its swaddling clothes and is now a toddler; marketed foods are being

[13] Personal communication from Population Reference Bureau, Washington, D.C.

labeled as to their additives; government agencies, encouraged by their success in labeling cigarettes as dangerous (although it has not been as effective as one would like) are now "paying attention" to carcinogens; industrial plants are "paying attention" to health codes (note the Kepone controversy, asbestos and coal mining restrictions, etc.) ; car manufacturers are building smaller cars; our population growth is stabilizing; treatment of water supplies is under scrutiny; environmentalists are no longer the pariahs they once were; weight watching has become fashionable (even the French are now breaking tradition) ; penalties and judgments against polluters mount. The list grows.

At this writing, PCB's (polychlorinated biphenyls) have become the villain. If evidence continues to be adduced we predict that by the time this yearbook of ASCD is in print, PCB's will be recognized as harmful and controls will be instituted.

The issue is joined; the public is becoming aware. It remains for the schools to prepare present and future generations to recognize their obligation to defend the environment as a matter of ultimate survival. Defense of the environment, respect for life, has now become a moral imperative.

Short-term Remedies Through Schooling. When this writer was Director of Education for The Conservation Foundation and Co-Director of the Pinchot Institute for Conservation Studies, a study was made of more than 500 curriculums from a variety of schools in the United States and Italy, France, Germany, Great Britain. Even in the 1960's, more than 90 percent of all courses of study in the sciences and social sciences urged schools to deal with the "problems" and "content" of conservation. The following summary of these studies was made.

. . . Conservation is concerned, in good part at least, with fitness *to* the whole environment, socioeconomic and bioeconomic, and fitness *of* the whole environment, socioeconomic and bioeconomic. Education, definable as the conservation of man, also has its prime concern with the fitness of man to the environment.

We find, for instance, that practically every school system (elementary and secondary) has in its stated curriculum a series of activities under the rubric "conservation." These are generally conglomerates of readings (e.g., nature of soil, erosion, etc.) , some experiences (e.g., water-holding capacity of the soil), field trips (e.g., to fields), films (e.g., life in a forest) . But if one examines what actually goes on, one finds in about 50 percent of the cases that the topic is not considered—and this mostly in city schools. Reason: the teacher cannot "cover" the course as it is; he or she tends to gloss over, or neglect, an area which is not important or is thought to have little intellectual rigor. Particularly in city schools, conservation is thought to have little importance and no intellectual rigor. Besides, in a city, what fields or ponds or streams are available for that necessary field trip? In country schools, experiences in conservation are thought to be supererogatory. In any event, more than any other curricular area, conservation is honored in the breach. This would not be possible if the ecological, economic, and psychosocial concepts underlying practices in conservation ramified, or pervaded, the curriculum.

At other times, conservation education (truly a euphemism) is often a rubric for the occasional walk in the woods, or what is worse, a nature trail, for the trivial naming of specimens (rarely their study) ; for the remnant rules of an ancient agronomy, for a set of "don'ts." Too often, these "field trips" are conducted by agencies outside the school: that bus trip to a concentration camp for organisms which cannot otherwise survive. Almost never is conservation a study which combines the biological and the physical sciences, the behavioral sciences and the social sciences, in a conceptual structure, an art-science, which is relevant to the kind of world now in the making.[14]

A recent survey (1970-72) of practices in more than 200 schools— elementary and high schools—as well as their curriculums indicates that the situation has not measurably improved, for somewhat similar general reasons, plus:

1. Conservation *per se* is still not given over to the serious problem of shortage or quality of life but with the general problem of conserving the "green." This is laudable but markedly insufficient.

2. Because College Entrance Examinations and "standardized tests" do not emphasize conservation studies, particularly shortage, teachers tend not to emphasize them.

3. Because it is given some treatment—however glancing—in most curriculums; it is not given complete treatment in any one place.

4. Because the concept of conservation is not central to any one discipline, it is treated tangentially, or not "covered" because each course is "crowded with content."

In other words, conservation studies are not yet of sufficient concern to be given emphasis in a unified manner, that is, in a curriculum whose behavioral objectives are centrally concerned with modern problems of conservation: *shortage* (population, food, energy) and *quality* (industrial and agricultural pollution), annihilation and destruction, and the like.

Be that as it may, *short-term* solutions to be offered after certain other variables of the continuing crisis are discussed in the following.

14 Paul F-Brandwein. "Origins of Public Policy and Practice in Conservation: Early Education and the Conservation of Sanative Environments." F. Darling and J. Milton, editors. *Future Environments of North America*. New York: The Natural History Press, Doubleday & Company, Inc., 1966. pp. 629, 630.

1. Inclusion of serious treatment of the "continuing crisis" in sectors of the curriculum: For example, social science, economics, literature, mathematics. (See 1. following.) This for the short term.

2. Organization of a course (a domain of discourse and inquiry) in ekistics—defined as the science of human habitation. (See 2. following.)

For the short term, then, two thrusts—the reader will think of others. For the long term, see item 2.

1. *Introduction into existing curriculums.* (A "poor fit" is acceptable, of course, in first trials.)

a. *The Continuing Crisis: Shortage for Life and Living.* Suggested treatment:

(1) PROSPECT: POPULATION.
(2) PROSPECT: NUTRITION.
(3) PROSPECT: ENERGY.
(4) PROSPECT: INDUSTRIAL NUTRITION (MINERALS).

b. *The Continuing Crisis: Quality of Life and Living.* Suggested treatment:

(1) PROSPECT: PROLONGATION OF LIFE.
(2) ANNIHILATION.
(3) PURITY.
(4) PRIVACY.
(5) PSYCHOLOGICAL SAFETY AND PSYCHOLOGICAL FREEDOM.
(6) PURPOSELESSNESS.
(7) PRINCIPLE OF MINIMUM SUFFERING.

Thus "Population" might conceivably be introduced into "courses" on economics, problems of democracy, biology, government, etc.; "Energy" into the same, and into physics, chemistry, general science, etc. Similarly, "Purity" or "Pollution" into biology, social science, and the like. For reasons stated previously, it is the writer's opinion that this curricular thrust will not be effective. The curricular principle that is violated is this: *Responsibility for instruction in significant elements of curriculum which are stated and official policy is not discretionary.*

2. In the view of this writer, it is time to develop for the elementary and secondary school a curricular progression which treats concepts, values, and skills (capacities and attitudes) necessary to our survival as a planet.

It is the suggestion that such a domain of discourse (speaking in terms of discipline) or a life-affirming curriculum (speaking in terms of civilized in need) is now no longer a luxury but a commanding essential of highest priority. For reasons to follow, we suggest this curricular progression be titled: *Ekistics.*

When seen in the broader context of Ekistics, education about the environment takes on new dimensions and complexities, and the traditional terminology used to describe such a study appears inadequate.

Ekistics[15] is defined as that field of study, that area of knowledge, and the concepts and values through which humankind recognizes interdependence with the environment as well as responsibility for maintaining a culture that will sustain a healthy and sanative environment.

The discipline of ekistics, which delineates a host of experiences and a life-style as well, is now of consummate significance in the education of human beings and their young.

What constitutes the proper study of humans in their environment? Why not limit the study to science? To ecology? To social science? To economics? To engineering? To a variety of technologies? In analyzing the relationship of humans to their environment, the analysis has often been left to the specialist in a given field. Yet a serious study of the environment encompasses more than science, social science, or the humanities. Ekistics is essentially a study of choice, hence of values but based on what we know, on hard data; in short, on scholarship. Just as physicians are specialists yet generalists, so are ekisticians. But just as every man is responsible for his body, so every man is responsible for the environment. By analyzing some decisions that have been made to alter the environment, a more appropriate synthesis may be developed. In other words, ekistics develops a vocabulary and semantics, i.e., an *ekistician,* ekistically speaking. Further, it has a "hard tonality" such as physics, thereby implying a hard content (which ekistics has) and a discipline (which ekistics is). It is no more difficult to say ekistician than to say physician, or ekisticist than physicist.

What ingredients, concepts, generalizations, and principles make up the study of ekistics? What areas of content and what disciplines are involved? Does it have its own base, its own succession of problems, and its own solutions? (See footnote 15.)

Furthermore, it is clear that ekistics is more than science. An analysis of the individuals who banded together to save San Francisco Bay indicates that they were architects, economists, lawyers, legislators, resource-

15 A full discussion of a curriculum in Ekistics is offered in *Ekistics: A Guide for the Development of an Interdisciplinary Environmental Education Curriculum.* California State Department of Education, 1973 (permission granted). The publication (curriculum) can be ordered from Mr. Rudolph J. H. Schaefer, Consultant in Environmental Education, California State Department of Education, Sacramento, California.

use experts, land developers, city planners, historians, citizens in all their diversity—as well as scientists.

Ekistics draws then concepts and values from the social sciences, humanities, and sciences in an interdisciplinary way. It is a modern discipline created out of modern need. And it works.

Epilogue

We come then to a simple faith. Education is to make the child, born alien to his civilization and to the human quest, humane in purpose and human in prospect. The continuing crisis can then be put in all-pervasive terms. We are indeed, collectively, Noah. Planet Earth is our ark. What will we find after the symbolic 40 days?

Do we have time? Yes, if we work for it. Our history is long, whatever time scale we take. Suppose we take this drastically simplified one?

5,000,000 years ago—the "origins" of human life
500,000   —humans as food gatherers and food growers
50,000   —the human being—Cro-Magnon man—
                     as artist
5,000   —the first "true" city
500   —the first university (massive stirrings of
                     science and technics)
50   —beginning of universal education
5 (recent)   —humans in space

If we can buy time for another 50 to 100 years we may, if we wish, fashion a new striving, and a human path. Joshua Needham put it this way, as he spoke of our striving for a heaven:

Heaven, he said, is either

Here and now
Not here but now
Here but not now
Not here and not now

An earth, fit for the humane purpose and human prospect, is not here and not now. A nobler rendition of human values, of humane purpose, will ever bring those prospects "here" and in the "now."

Why should civilization, our humanity, die?

There is no need.

None whatever.

Selected Readings

Central aspects of curriculum dealing with environmental studies or ekistics have been treated within the body of this paper.

If one were to select works which would form the foundations of content (vis-à-vis subject matter), one might select the writings of Mumford, Dubos, Muir, the Ehrlichs, Commoner, and such general thrusts as "Beauty for America," and "The Future of North American Environments" (see below). The three faces of ekistics (science, social science, humanities) are treated by these authors and those whose works have been selected for the beginnings of a library in environmental studies—or ekistics. In many cases, the data within the body of this paper have been drawn from these publications, or have been checked against them. When the writer was successively Associate Director of the Joint Council of Economic Education, Director of Education for The Conservation Foundation, and Co-Director of the Pinchot Institute for Conservation Studies, the positions and researches presented in this paper were extant in some form. Now ekistics has matured, owing to the continuing work of activist groups like the Sierra Club, Friends of the Earth, The Conservation Foundation—but in the main to the massive contributions in this century of that firm but gentle philosopher of human humanity: Lewis Mumford.

Arthur B. Bronwell, editor. *Science and Technology in the World of the Future*. New York: John Wiley & Sons, 1970. (See particularly the chapter by Constantine Doxiadis, "Cities of the Future.")

Barry Commoner. *The Closing Circle: Nature, Man and Technology*. New York: Alfred A. Knopf, Inc., 1971.

Raymond F. Dasmann. *Planet in Peril: Man and the Biosphere Today*. New York: The World Publishing Company, 1972.

René Dubos. *Man Adapting*. New Haven, Connecticut: Yale University Press, 1965.

Paul R. Ehrlich and Anne H. Ehrlich. *Population, Resources, Environment: Issues in Human Ecology*. San Francisco: W. H. Freeman and Company, 1972. (A *must* for everyone.)

John Kenneth Galbraith. *The New Industrial State*. New York: The New American Library, Inc., 1967.

Carl B. Huffaker, editor. *Biological Control*. New York: Plenum Publishing Corporation, 1971.

N. Keyfitz and W. Flieger. *Population: Facts and Methods of Demography*. San Francisco: W. H. Freeman and Company, 1971.

Norman Landau and Paul Rheingold. *The Environmental Law Handbook*. New York: Ballantine Books, Inc., 1971.

D. L. Meadows *et al. The Limits to Growth: A Global Challenge*. New York: Universe Books, 1972.

128   IMPROVING THE HUMAN CONDITION

Lewis Mumford. *Technics and Human Development: The Myth of the Machine*. New York: Harcourt Brace Jovanovich, 1966.

Eugene P. Odum. *Fundamentals of Ecology*. Third Edition. Philadelphia: W. B. Saunders Company, 1971.

Population Reference Bureau, Inc., 1775 Massachusetts Avenue, N.W., Washington, D.C. 20036.

Stewart Udall. *Agenda for Tomorrow*. New York: Harcourt Brace Jovanovich, 1976.

5

Global and International Perspectives

Norman Abramowitz, Andrew J. Leighton,
Stephen Viederman

PERHAPS THE CENTRAL QUESTION confronting educators is: what do young people in the United States, today and in the immediate future, need to know, and what skills, attitudes, and values must they acquire in order to be responsible and effective citizens in the world of tomorrow? How, where, and when can and will they meet these needs?

In this chapter we will limit our attention to only one part of that question, namely, what is needed for the global dimension of citizenship. First, we will consider some of the substantive aspects of the issue: what are some of the questions confronting the United States in the world today that have meaning for life in the future? Second, we will consider some of the findings of research on young people's learning and socialization that have relevance for determining what to teach, when, and how. Finally, we will review what is happening in international and global education today.

Before beginning, we wish to make it explicit that our concern with international issues in the schools is not to develop a new orthodoxy, or "one worldism," but a strengthened understanding of our national interest within a global setting. With apologies to the Cambridge University economist Joan Robinson, the purpose of global education is not to acquire a set of ready-made answers to global questions, but rather to learn how to avoid being deceived by those who purport to be experts on global matters.

The Issues

Introduction. As we enter the fourth quarter of the twentieth century and the third century of our country's existence, we find a word cropping up with increasing frequency in both public and private discourse. The word is "interdependence" and seems to be used to signal some new state in our relations to others.

However, our lives in this country have always been intertwined with those of other countries. This is an indisputable fact. We have always been, and still are, a nation of immigrants. Even today, approximately one-fifth of the total annual population growth of the United States results from legal immigration to our shores. And added to this more than 350,000 annually, are the scores of illegal immigrants, estimated at up to one million annually. From our earliest times we have also relied upon others for staples and luxuries, and have looked upon others as markets for our goods.

What has changed has been the speed of communication. On July 4, 1776, George III was able to enter in his diary: "Nothing of importance happened today." In our times it is sometimes difficult to determine what was and was not of importance given the speed and ubiquity of the communication media, as we are constantly reminded in word and picture of what is happening elsewhere.

What has also changed is the number of actors involved in interactions. In the eighteenth century one could speak of the world as what we would today describe as the Western world. Africa, Asia, and Latin America were of little consequence to our concerns, despite the fact that then, as now, they represented between three-fourths and four-fifths of the world's population. Today, however, whether the terrain is the Olympic playing field or the halls of the United Nations, these new and sovereign nations are demanding to be heard and considered on a wide range of issues concerning both their futures and ours.

Finally, change has also occurred in the very speed with which change has itself occurred. Toffler has argued that "change is avalanching upon our heads," and C.P. Snow has observed that "until this century [social change was] so slow, that it would pass unnoticed in one person's lifetime. That is no longer so."[1]

Thus "interdependence" is not a new phenomenon. What is new is the frequency and number of interactions with others, as well as a heightened perception and awareness of these interactions. In addition, there is a growing recognition of the complexity of the relationships and the processes involved in them. Furthermore, there is growing sensitivity to the fact that decisions made today have important implications not only for our country in the present, but also for future generations here and in other parts of the world. In some very important respects, "the future is now," particularly in such areas as population change, resource use, environmental deterioration, and the like.

[1] Alvin Toffler. *Future Shock*. New York: Random House, Inc., 1970. pp. 14, 23.

What are some of the key concepts to which educators must direct their attention as they seek to define the global context of citizenship education for America's third century? Abraham Sirkin, recently a member of the Policy Planning Staff of the Department of State, writing for the National Commission on Coping with Interdependence, suggested the following about the United States:

1. *That we are no longer sufficient unto ourselves.* We are learning that our present state of interdependence is not merely the dependence of others on us (which is easy to take), but has in it a hard core of U.S. reliance on the outside world; decisions and developments that deeply affect our lives may take place, as has already happened, far from our own shores.

2. *That we cannot win 'em all.* We are still strong but we are not invincible. Besides being capable of losing Olympic games and withdrawing in exasperation from small wars, the dollar is most often not the strongest currency on the London and Zurich and Hong Kong exchanges. Our influence in world affairs remains enormous but it has declined somewhat from the halcyon days of World War II and its immediate aftermath when we did not have to accommodate our policies to anyone outside the Communist bloc.

3. *That we will have to cooperate with others to attain common objectives.* In major United States actions which affect other nations, we can no longer afford the luxury of acting unilaterally or consulting casually. Increasingly, as in the Law of the Sea Conference dealing, among other things, with mineral resources on the ocean floor, we may have to yield some of our independent freedom of action in order to achieve our own goals, which will have to mesh with those of our planetary neighbors.

4. *That we cannot remain forever a rich island in a sea of poverty.* Leaders of less-developed nations are beginning to insist on what they consider international "social justice" as a matter of right rather than charity. They are more interested in improved terms of trade than in further development aid programs of the "trickle down" variety. We, along with the other industrialized nations, are not likely to accept any substantial leveling-down process, but in our own interest we will need to make a major contribution to an effective leveling-up program. The continually growing gap between rich and poor nations is already becoming the centerpiece of multilateral politics.[2]

Other concepts, without his commentary, "with which we will have to refurbish our minds," in Sirkin's view, are shown in Table 1. They are offered not as a final list, but because they are suggestive of the range of matters to which educators will have to direct their attention. One might take issue with particular statements, for example, in terms of the directions they suggest. Thus, while there is little question that now, as in the

2 Abraham M. Sirkin. *Living with Interdependence: The Decades Ahead in America.* Interdependence Series No. 2. Princeton, New Jersey: Aspen Institute for Humanistic Studies, Program in International Affairs, 1975. p. 16. Reprinted by permission.

past, we, the people, have done harm to the biosphere, there is some evidence in some areas that things may be getting better rather than worse. The air in New York City in mid-1976 was reported to be better than it was a decade before. Similarly, the romantic image of the past as being pure and clean is called to question, as may be noted in the charming volume by Otto Bettmann, *The Good Old Days—They Were Terrible!*[3] Similarly, one's own political or ideological stance might suggest a different concern for cause and effect, as in the relationship between "the population explosion" and "unmanageable problems." There are those, for example, who would argue most strongly that rapid population growth is a symptom of problems, rather than a cause, as we shall see.

About the world:
    1. That nonrenewable resources will become more expensive and in some cases scarcer.
    2. That we are doing irreversible harm to the biosphere which sustains us.
    3. That the population explosion may cause unmanageable problems.

About ourselves:
    1. That our personal prospects of material advancement may be reduced.
    2. That we can no longer afford waste of energy and resources.
    3. That we will need to give greater attention to "fair shares" at home.
    4. That we may have to accept some further limitations on our freedom of action.
    5. That limits on the material side of things may lead, paradoxically, to some advances in the quality of life.

About the future:
    1. That we will be living increasingly with major uncertainties.
    2. That not every problem has a solution.
    3. That posterity has to enter all calculations.
    4. That indices of growth should include minuses as well as pluses and should measure quality as well as quantity.

Table 1. "Concepts To Refurbish Our Minds"[4]

What is clear in any review of the present world situation is the complexity of the issues. There is considerable room for honest disagreement on the nature of the problems that confront humanity today, their causes and their effects. Political disputes in these areas are reflective of the fact that scholars and scientists, the so-called experts, are also in disagreement. This in turn makes it more difficult to achieve a political consensus in our own democracy on what needs to be done, when, by whom, and to what ends. The fact that the issues are future-oriented, but

---

[3] Otto Bettman. *The Good Old Days—They Were Terrible!* New York: Random House, Inc., 1974.

[4] Abraham M. Sirkin, *op. cit.,* pp. 16-17.

necessitating action now, and long-term, requiring sustained interest and action, further complicates the problem.

There is general agreement on the "facts" that describe these problems. So too, usually, there is agreement on the severity of the issues, that things will be different (either better or worse) in the world of the future, and that decisions must be taken in order to most effectively cope with the future. The need to generate new "facts," new knowledge, is also not called to question. Nor is the role assigned to the schools to provide training in analytical modes of thinking so that children of today will be better able to deal with the different world of tomorrow.

Still, we are dealing with problems that are not clearly defined, applying intellectual and scientific tools that are primitive when viewed against the magnitude of the issues to be described and dealt with. The debate generated by the publication in 1972 of the Club of Rome's Report, *The Limits to Growth,* is a case in point. The Report, based upon a complex series of computer programs modeling a world system concluded:

> If the present growth trends in world population, industrialization, pollution, food production, and resource depletion continue unchanged, the limits to growth on this planet will be reached sometime within the next one hundred years. The most probable result will be rather sudden and uncontrollable decline in both population and industrial capacity.[5]

The Report received considerable reaction from the public, which was generally shaken by its gloomy conclusions. At the same time, scholars began to examine carefully the assumptions that generated the various models and to question the data base from which many of the projections of future trends were derived.

In 1976 another group of futurists published their forecasts, and these were much less gloomy than those of the original Club of Rome Report. The Hudson Institute's volume, *The Next 200 Years: A Scenario for America and the World,* authored by Herman Kahn and his colleagues, suggested that "200 years ago almost everywhere human beings were comparatively few, poor, and at the mercy of the forces of nature, and 200 years from now, we expect, almost everywhere they will be numerous, rich, and in control of the forces of nature."[6]

And in the intervening years since the publication of their first report, the Club of Rome itself seems to have reviewed and revised its position. Recognizing that the no-growth policies implied by the *Limits*

5 D. H. and D. L. Meadows *et al. The Limits to Growth. A Report for the Club of Rome's Project for the Predicament of Mankind.* New York: A Potomac Associates Book, Universe Books, 1972.

6 Herman Kahn *et al. The Next 200 Years: A Scenario for America and the World.* New York: William Morrow and Company, Inc., 1976.

study might have a negative effect on the drive for greater equity and social justice for the world's poor, it now appears to be urging carefully planned, conservation-oriented, selected growth policies that seek at the same time to redistribute global wealth.[7]

The debate will continue for some time to come. And unlike the physical sciences, where the laboratory may be used to test the validity of one's hypotheses, the futurist's laboratory is the world of the future itself. The study of the future is not, however, only "a pleasurable diversion for intellectuals." In the words of Tomás Frejka:

If behavior, decisions and actions—private and public—were not influenced, shaped, and modified by ideas, theories, and ideologies, then futurism might be an exclusively "academic" exercise. It may be difficult to quantify the extent of impact that the analyses and theories of scholars, be they Neo-Malthusians or Science and Technology advocates, have on human behavior and on institutional decision making, but the influence is not marginal.

This influence ranges over a wide spectrum of phenomena. It can influence personal decisions: whether to become a vegetarian, whether to buy a small or large car or none at all, whether to have a small or large family or no children at all. It can influence the decisions on all levels of government, industry, and academia: tax policies, price policies, research policies, educational policies, population policies, welfare policies, and investment policies. Even if this debate involved pure utopians and not serious scholars it would still be likely to have some impact.

The influence and impact of this debate is not marginal also because it is concerned with matters directly related to human survival, welfare and happiness; the debate is directly related to the most fundamental human needs and therefore attracts the concern and interest of many people. Which ideology will prevail will depend on the solidity of the arguments and evidence and on the persistence of their proponents. The more convincing, persuasive, credible, and widely acceptable particular ideas are, the greater influence they are likely to have by being internalized, consciously or subconsciously, by the public and by influential individuals in governmental, industrial, and scientific institutions.[8]

In a later section of this chapter we will return to some of the problems and possibilities that the schools face in these matters. Now we will turn to some of the substantive issues themselves.

Population. Most of the national concerns that may occupy the thoughts of the people of the United States—such as population, energy, food, the environment, and the economy—also have relevance for the rest of the earth's inhabitants. There are no single lines of causation connect-

[7] "Feeling Good About the Next 200 Years." *The Inter Dependent* 3 (7) :3; July/ August 1976.

[8] Tomás Frejka. Manuscript Review of Herman Kahn's *The Next 200 Years*. New York: The Population Council, July 1976. (Unpublished.)

ing any two of these phenomena; all are linked (inexplicably in some cases) to each other in an intricate web of causation and effect that is heatedly debated and seldom clearly resolved.

Consider population, for example. The "facts" are generally accepted; the debate arises from differing interpretation of the facts.

Facts. In 1790, the date of the first United States census, our country had about four million inhabitants. In 1976 our population stood at about 215 million, and was increasing by about 1.6 million annually. With one major exception—the post–World War II baby boom period 1947-62— measures of fertility have been declining consistently and have reached unprecedented low levels in the past several years, as illustrated in Figure 1.

Despite the fact that our birthrate is at or near an all-time low, below the number needed to replace parents in this generation, zero population growth (zpg) is still about a half-century away because of the "youth-heavy" character of our population. That is, despite the fact that couples are averaging fewer than two children each, there are more young potential parents in our population than ever before. Present low birthrates could be the harbinger of a long-term trend of lower fertility, or merely the postponement of childbearing which would cause birthrates to rise again in several years. We will have to wait a decade or two to be sure.

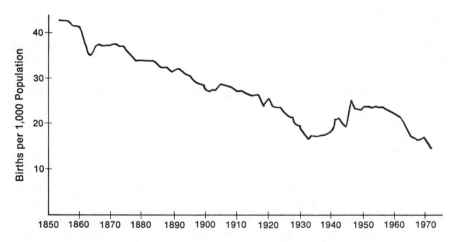

Figure 1. Estimated Crude Birthrate, United States, 1855-1970[9]

9 Source: U.S. Bureau of the Census and National Bureau of Vital Statistics, various publications. Appeared in: William Petersen. *Population.* New York: Macmillan Publishing Company, Inc., 1975. p. 558.

But there is more to the United States population story than just growth:

- There is distribution—the fact that according to the 1970 census more than three-quarters of our population lived on less than two percent of our land area. This phenomenon manifests itself almost entirely in urbanization. The findings from the 1980 census could verify indications from the mid-1970's that the trend toward urbanization has ended and that large numbers of the middle class are moving from central cities to suburbs and exurbs.

- There is composition—the sexual, racial, ethnic mix of our population and all the accompanying issues, from busing for racial integration to the Equal Rights Amendment.

- There is legal immigration—which because of our period of low fertility in the 1970's accounts for an increasing proportion of our annual population growth.

- There is illegal immigration—which may be adding more than a million people to our population annually.

The current world population situation is unique in history: the highest growth rate in human experience from the highest base in absolute numbers. While it took from the beginning of human history until about 1825 for our species to produce its first billion members, the fourth billion has been added between 1960 and 1976. World population of 4.1 billion is growing at slightly less than two percent annually— which indicates a doubling time of just over 35 years assuming present trends continue, which, of course, they never do. It should be noted that, because of the fact that fertility and mortality rates are constantly changing, concepts such as percentage growth rates and doubling times are *projections* rather than *predictions* of the future.

Population trends of developed nations (Europe, Japan, Australia, Canada, and the USSR) are roughly similar to those of the United States —post–World War II fertility increases followed by gradual declines. In the developing world (most of Latin America, Africa, and Asia) fertility rates have always been, and remain by developed standards, high. Technological advances—mainly in health care—have drastically lowered death rates and are the main causes of rapid population growth. As a result, although the present world population of 4.1 billion is divided about 70:30 between developing and developed peoples, approximately 65 million of the annual increment of 75 million people are accounted for by the developing world. In the coming decades, as shown in Figure 2, the population of the developing world is expected to increase even more disproportionately.

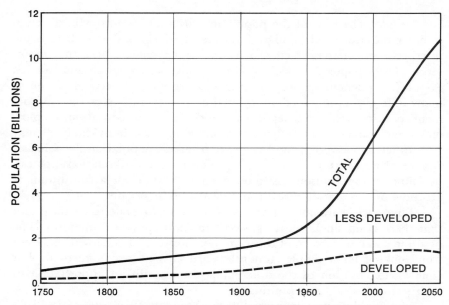

Figure 2. World Population Growth, By Developed and Less Developed Countries, from 1750, Projected to 2050[10]

Just as with the United States, world population issues involve more than growth. Migration, again in the form of urbanization, is a critical demographic variable, especially for the developing world. Although only about a third of the developing world's population was urban in 1975 (about three-quarters of the developed world was), the developing world's rate of urban growth was almost three times as high as the developed world;[11] its urban population is expected to more than double in the two decades between 1960 and 1980.[12] The implications of such migration are many: how can cities provide employment and housing for large numbers of unplanned migrants; what is to become of the teeming "squatter villages" that surround most cities in the developing world; what is to become of the economically and socially deprived people (usually the elderly and women) who are left behind in depopulated rural areas?

[10] Source: Nathan Keyfitz. "World Resources and the World Middle Class." *Scientific American* 235 (1):29; July 1976. Copyright © 1976 by Scientific American, Inc. All rights reserved.

[11] United Nations. *1974 Report on the World Social Situation.* E/CN.5/512/Rev./ ST/ESA/24. New York: U.N. Department of Economic and Social Affairs, 1975. p. 34.

[12] United Nations. *Urbanization in the Second United Nations Development Decade.* ST/ECA/132. New York: U.N. Department of Economic and Social Affairs, 1970. p. 8.

Debate. The facts of the population situation—on growth, distribution, composition, and immigration—are relatively undisputed. It is the interpretation of these facts that causes disagreements over the importance of the population variable in national and international affairs. Population phenomena are woven through so many aspects of life on so many different levels—food and nutrition, energy, resources, the environment, political relations, health care, social services, education, employment, and human rights—that nations, regions, and individuals all may have differing viewpoints and perceptions about population "problems." A general idea of the diversity of opinion on the interrelationships can be found in the Hudson Institute's volume,[13] while for a continuum of attitudes on population growth specifically see Berelson.[14]

That such a number of views exist serves to underscore the point that there is no single, neat "answer" to the population question. The best understanding, then, of this complex interrelated issue will come not from looking for a simple straightforward answer in our curricula but from an exploration of the different positions with an appreciation of their philosophical underpinnings.

The population-ecology revolution of the late 1960's and early 1970's prompted many in the United States to examine not only rapid rates of population growth in developing countries and levels of affluence and environmental deterioration in North America, but the interrelationship of these phenomena as well. Do Americans have a valid argument claiming that the population-ecology "problem" is caused by Asians breeding too rapidly? Do Asians have a valid argument contending that the population-ecology "problem" is due to smaller numbers of Americans living super-affluent life-styles that put too great a strain on the environment?

Naturally, there are elements of truth in both positions. But curricula emphasizing interdependence should stress not only the answers to major questions, but the search for other pertinent questions, possible responses to those questions, and an effort to see how all these issues fit together.

The first worldwide forum of countries convened to discuss population issues, the World Population Conference, was held in Bucharest, Romania, in August 1974. Latin American and African nations argued for increased emphasis on socioeconomic development which, they believed, would solve the problem of population growth. They also incor-

13 Herman Kahn *et al, op. cit.,* pp. 10-16.

14 Bernard Berelson. "World Population: Status Report 1974." *Reports on Population/Family Planning* (15) :18; January 1974. See also: Michael S. Teitelbaum. "Population and Development:Is a Consensus Possible?" *Foreign Affairs* 52 (4) ; July 1974; Bernard Berelson. *The Great Debate on Population Policy—An Instructive Entertainment.* New York: The Population Council, 1975.

porated the theme of a "new international economic order," which would among other things, involve a redistribution of wealth from rich to poor nations and an end to the exploitation of poor nations by the rich. Asia and the developed world contended that, while socioeconomic development policies were important, family planning and population policies should be strengthened in certain areas, because of sheer numbers alone.[15]

While the socioeconomic development or family planning discussion —a debate on the quickest route to lower population growth—that characterized the World Population Conference may seem somewhat abstract and distant in terms of our own government's affairs, the concepts hold definite implications for United States foreign policy, and thus form a potentially important element of citizenship education. For example, should our foreign aid to a country with a rapidly growing population such as Bangladesh be primarily in the area of family planning? Should our family planning aid be conditional—tied to specific demographic targets or social actions *our* government deems appropriate? Should our foreign aid emphasize broader areas of social and economic development? Should we apply great pressure to a small number of programs, or speed support across a wider range of possibilities? What are the chances of any of these strategies succeeding?

The only way we will gain answers to these questions is to have an understanding of the way that particular culture operates, and an awareness of the dynamics of change within that society. The success of foreign aid programs (and of a student's comprehension of world affairs) depends on a knowledge of the *substance* of that culture—of the importance of women's roles, employment, nonformal education, agricultural development, health care, and a range of other specific issues. Studying other societies is not just an interesting sidelight to American history, but a crucial part of it, and of our future as well.

Food. Just as there is a continuum of attitudes on the population growth issue, so too, could a continuum be produced to represent the range of opinion on the world food situation. It would be bounded on one end by those who contend that the earth's capacity to produce enough food for the present population is already oxerextended, to those who believe we have the potential to feed many more billions of people. How can such disparate views exist? Again, the facts are straightforward; it is their interpretation that causes disagreement.

[15] For a background on family planning and socioeconomic development, see the following: Ronald Freedman and Bernard Berelson. "The Record of Family Planning Programs." *Studies in Family Planning* 7 (1) ; January 1976; James E. Kocher. *Rural Development, Income Distribution and Fertility Decline.* New York: The Population Council, 1973; William Rich. *Smaller Families Through Social and Economic Progress.* Washington, D.C.: Overseas Development Council, January 1973.

Year	Reserve Stocks of Grain*	Grain Equivalent of Idled U.S. Cropland	Total Reserves	Reserves as Days of Annual Grain Consumption
		(Million Metric Tons)		
1961	163	68	231	105
1962	176	81	257	105
1963	149	70	219	95
1964	153	70	223	87
1965	147	71	218	91
1966	151	78	229	84
1967	115	51	166	59
1968	144	61	205	71
1969	159	73	232	85
1970	188	71	259	89
1971	168	41	209	71
1972	130	78	208	69
1973	148	24	172	55
1974	108	0	108	33
1975	111	0	111	35
1976**	100	0	100	31

* Based on carry-over stocks of grain at beginning of crop year in individual countries for year shown. The USDA has recently expanded the coverage of reserve stocks to include importing as well as exporting countries; thus the reserve levels are slightly higher than those heretofore published.
** Preliminary estimates by the USDA.

Table 2. Index of World Food Security, 1961-76[16]

Region	1934-38	1948-52	1960	1970	1976**
	(Million Metric Tons)				
North America	+ 5*	+23	+39	+56	+94
Latin America	+ 9	+ 1	0	+ 4	− 3
Western Europe	−24	−22	−25	−30	−17
E. Europe & USSR	+ 5	—	0	0	−27
Africa	+ 1	0	− 2	− 5	−10
Asia	+ 2	− 6	−17	−37	−47
Australia & N.Z.	+ 3	+ 3	+ 6	+12	+ 8

* Plus sign indicates net exports; minus sign, net imports.
** Preliminary estimates of fiscal year data.

Table 3. The Changing Pattern of World Grain Trade[17]

[16] Based on U.S. Department of Agriculture data and estimates of Lester R. Brown. Appeared in: Lester R. Brown. *The Politics and Responsibility of the North American Breadbasket*. Worldwatch Paper 2. October 1975. p. 17.

[17] Derived from U.N. Food and Agriculture Organization, U.S. Department of Agriculture data, and the estimates of Lester R. Brown. Appeared in: *Ibid.*, p. 11.

Facts. The decade of the 1950's marked the beginning of the period in developing countries when drastically lowered death rates caused sudden increases in population which contributed to an increased strain on world food production. In grain producing areas of the developed world, most notably Canada, Argentina, Australia, the U.S.S.R., and the United States, considerable surpluses were built.

The first half of the 1960's was characterized by higher rates of population growth in the developing world which increased demand for food and began to deplete grain stockpiles. In the mid-1960's research by agronomists begun 20 years earlier produced "miracle strains" of wheat and rice that drastically improved yields in the developing world. This "green revolution" caused widespread optimism (some would say complacency) that the food-population dilemma was solved. However, the new breeds of grain required more water, fertilizer, and special care than traditional crops. Some farmers were reluctant to change traditional patterns of life, others could not afford to, and many of those who did had difficulty keeping up with the expenses (both on their financial resources and on their land) .

In the early to mid-1970's production of grain in the developing world was erratic, while the few remaining developed nations producing reserves of any consequence (most notably the United States and Canada) had sold or donated much of their yield in advance. In the mid-1970's world grain reserves were at an all-time low, and North America had become the only region producing sizeable surpluses (Tables 2, 3) .

Debate. In 1976 the developing world had recovered from the crop failures of the early 1970's, due not only to good weather that aided their own harvests, but also to increased output from the chief grain-exporting nations, especially the United States. It has been estimated that population growth accounts for about 70 percent of the medium-term increase in total food demand in the developing countries.[18] However, in the developed world, affluence is the crucial factor in demand for food. While thousands starve to death daily in the developing world, American physicians caution their patients on the dangers of overeating and obesity. What are the implications of this situation?

[18] United Nations. *Population, Food Supply and Agricultural Development.* Rome: Food and Agriculture Organization of the United Nations, 1975, p. 2. Various interpretations of familiar issues serve to add confusion to an already multifaceted network of facts and interdependencies. In this case, for instance, what exactly does "food demand" mean? Does it refer to basic subsistence levels, healthy dietary levels, or consumption levels that parallel those of the United States? Actually, it refers to an FAO measure taken from the *FAO Agricultural Commodity Projections 1970-1980* (Rome, 1971) . Learners should develop the ability to discern and resolve these potentially confusing situations.

Our world has become separated into two worlds—rich and poor. Both groups share the same basic requirements for nourishment, but the rich have what economists term "effective" demand—they have the financial resources to afford choice foodstuffs. While Americans spend less than 20 percent of their incomes for food, it is not uncommon for inhabitants of the developing world to spend as much as 85 percent of their income on it. When prices jump, the rich can afford to spend more or to modify their diets by purchasing cheaper foods. But the poor, already spending most of their income for a meager subsistence diet, have neither alternative. The average daily consumption of protein per person in most cases bears a direct positive relationship to average annual per capita income, as shown in Figure 3.

In the developed world since 1945 levels of affluence have been rising in almost all aspects of life: automobiles capable of twice the speed limit, electric toothbrushes and carving knives, one-way cans and bottles for beer and soda, and especially the consumption of meat. In the period

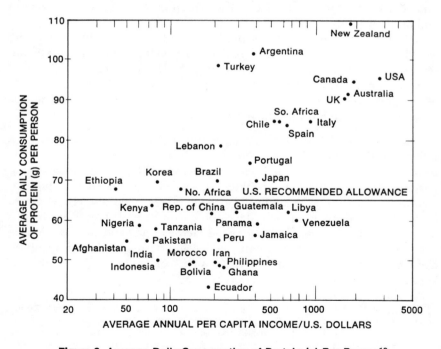

Figure 3. Average Daily Consumption of Protein (g) Per Person[19]

[19] Source: Stanford Research Institute. *Food Products and Processes.* September 1972. Appeared in: Douglas N. Ross. *Food and Population: The Next Crisis.* New York: The Conference Board, 1974. p. 9.

1960-1972 alone, meat consumption per capita rose more than 20 percent in the United States, and by considerably more in other developed countries (Table 4).

Higher United States meat consumption in a world of limited food supplies has direct implications for developing countries. It means that more grain is required to feed larger herds of livestock—grain that many argue could be more humanely used to prevent starvation in the developing world. It becomes easy to see how developing countries (indeed much of the developed world as well) is at least somewhat dependent on the United States for shipments of surplus food. At the same time, the United States is dependent on many developing nations whose demand for food creates markets for our surpluses. Without those markets we would be forced to fill our storehouses, and eventually begin paying farmers not to grow crops, as was the case in the 1950's. In addition, of course, the United States is also dependent on many developing nations for imports of special minerals and other raw materials that help keep our economy healthy. Any change in our food policy that certain developing countries considered not in their best interests could mean economic hardship for us.

Because so many variables are woven through the world food situation—population growth, affluence, weather, technology, economic trade

Country	1960 Meat Consumption* (pounds per year)	1972 Meat Consumption*	Increase (percent)
United States	208	254	22
Australia	234	235	0
France	168	212	26
Canada	167	211	26
United Kingdom	158	171	8
West Germany	144	192	33
Sweden	109	112	3
U.S.S.R.	80	104	30
Italy	70	136	94
Yugoslavia	62	75	21
Spain	51	96	88
Japan	14	51	364

* Includes beef, veal, pork, mutton, lamb, goat, horse, poultry, edible offals, other.

Table 4. Growth in Per Capita Meat Consumption in Selected Industrial Countries, 1960-72[20]

[20] Source: Organization for Economic Cooperation and Development. *Meat Balances in OECD Member Countries, 1959-1972.* Paris, January 1974. U.S.S.R. data from the U.S. Department of Agriculture. Appeared in: Lester R. Brown with Erik P. Eckholm. *By Bread Alone.* New York: Praeger Publishers, 1974. p. 201. Copyright © 1974 by the Overseas Development Council.

policy—reasonable individuals see varying implications for humanity and advocate different policies.

More than a decade ago two agronomists, William and Paul Paddock wrote a book titled *Famine 1975!* in which they predicted widespread food shortages.[21] They advocated a "triage" method for the United States to distribute scarce food reserves—give food only to those nations who could not survive without it, but withhold food from those nations judged in such serious condition that extra shipments would merely postpone eventual famine. In an article called "The Trouble with Triage" Alan Berg, another world food expert, argues that the main reasons for food shortages are high prices and inadequate distribution systems, and that there is still time to bring food and population into balance.[22]

Biologist Garrett Hardin favors what he calls "lifeboat ethics."[23] Methaphorically, he views each rich nation as a lifeboat full of comparatively rich people—with the poor of the world in much more crowded lifeboats or swimming in a stormy sea, attempting to gain admittance with the rich. Realistically, he favors a severe restriction on United States immigration, and opposes a world food bank, believing it would only postpone catastrophe. Daniel Callahan,[24] James Howe, and John Sewell[25] take issue with Hardin's lifeboat ethics. They believe that the rich are not self-sufficient in separate lifeboats, but that the world lives an interdependent existence together in a single craft. Furthermore, Howe and Sewell contend that with more efficient agricultural techniques greater food production is possible, especially in the developing world.

Hardin and the Paddocks would halt all grain shipments to India, for example, condemning millions to death for the long-term "benefit" of society. Their opponents would emphasize agricultural technology and distribution systems to help solve the world food problem. The existence of this range of views necessitates an understanding of how the United States food policy fits into the world food and population situation. Such an understanding is essential if we expect students to develop meaningful concepts about the interrelationships among nations.

21 William and Paul Paddock. *Famine 1975! America's Decision—Who Will Survive?* Boston: Little, Brown and Company, 1967. Reissued in 1976 with new introduction, postscript, and title: *Time of Famines—America and the World Food Crisis.*

22 Alan Berg. "The Trouble with Triage." *New York Times Magazine,* June 15, 1975.

23 Garrett Hardin. "Living on a Lifeboat." *Bioscience* 24 (10) :561-68; October 1974. A shorter version, "The Case Against Helping the Poor," appeared in *Psychology Today,* September 1974.

24 Daniel Callahan. "Doing Well by Doing Good—Garrett Hardin's 'Lifeboat Ethic'." *The Hastings Center Report* 4 (6) :1-4; December 1974.

25 James W. Howe and John W. Sewell. "Let's Sink the Lifeboat Ethics—An Alternative to 'Triage'." *Worldview.* October 1975, pp. 13-18.

Another relevant concept for the curriculum with respect to the food issue involves symbolic behavior. During the mid-1970's many advocated vegetarianism or cutting back meat (especially steak) consumption as a way of both saving money to be donated to needy countries and, more important, as a way of freeing quantities of grain to be shipped to needy countries. (One nutritionist wryly remarked that the only gains Americans would realize by cutting back on steak would be: (a) health savings from fewer heart attacks; (b) financial savings from purchasing cheaper substitutes; and (c) an easing of conscience.) Students should be taught to realize that unless large numbers of our population became involved and adequate methods of distribution were set up, that forgoing steak would be a symbolic rather than practically beneficial act. This is not to minimize the importance of symbolic action, which shows sincere concern and commitment—some of the greatest social movements in history began with symbolic acts—but simply to point out the difference between symbolic behavior and practical behavior that actually achieves program goals, and the fact that curricula should appropriately deal with this issue.

Clearly, it is impossible for students to gain even a rudimentary knowledge of the United States food situation without an understanding of the world food problem, and how the many pieces of the puzzle are dependent on each other to form a complete picture.

Energy. Just as the discussion of food led predictably to a number of intervening factors, so too, any examination of energy must focus on many of the same interrelated variables. In addition, as with the world food situation, changes in the availability of energy have different implications for developing and developed nations. As one might expect, there also exists a range of sentiment on energy: on the causes of the 1973-74 "crisis"; on our capacity to meet future energy demand; and on priorities for energy policy for both the United States and the rest of the world.

Facts. Every individual in the world, rich or poor, uses energy in some form to accomplish a range of objectives—from basic subsistence (fuel for cooking, warmth) to the most affluent pursuits (heat for swimming pools, electricity for pencil sharpeners, and so on). Developing nations consume traditional forms of energy that are usually available on a nonformal, individual basis (firewood, draft animals), while developed nations use commercial forms that are usually sold on a large scale by public or private entities (oil, gas, electricity).

The most startling energy development of modern times occurred in late 1973 when the Organization of Petroleum Exporting Countries (OPEC), who controlled the major share of the world's petroleum supply, quadrupled their prices for crude oil. OPEC members experienced what may be the most dramatic economic gain in history: in 1972 oil importers paid the exporting countries $15 billion; in 1973 the bill rose to $25 billion; in 1974 the figure was $80 billion. Experts project $650 billion in accrued funds for OPEC members by 1980, their cumulative assets increasing by at least $100 billion annually.[26]

OPEC's actions caused repercussions in every corner of the world. That economic event illustrated, far better than any curricula, the multitude of interrelationships between population, energy, technology and affluence, and the interdependent nature of our world.

The increase in oil prices caused individuals and institutions to scrutinize not only their oil-consuming activities, but also to look for oil substitutes as energy sources. Thus, OPEC's impact was not simply on oil, but on almost all forms of energy (and ultimately most economic activity as well). Few realized the pervasive nature of petroleum products in the United States as prices jumped on everything from gasoline to tennis balls.

The most visible short-term ramification in America was the long lines at gas stations. Millions of ration coupons were printed by the government, but never pressed into use. Individuals on fixed incomes, mostly the elderly, were particularly hard hit by higher prices. Car pooling and home insulation were urged as economy measures. On a longer-term scale, the oil shortage prompted the United States to form an official energy policy—Project Independence—that was supposed to make us energy self-sufficient by 1980. It wasn't long before government officials realized energy self-sufficiency was impossible by 1980 (or probably any other date); they quietly changed policy goals to make us "less dependent" on foreign sources of oil while at the same time encouraging work on the Alaska pipeline.

While most Americans were inconvenienced by the oil shortage, many developing nations were dealt a severe economic blow. For example, in the spring of 1975, the United States Department of Agriculture estimated that the Indian wheat crop was reduced by at least a million tons because of a shortage of fertilizer, and of fuel for irrigation pumps.[27] Because of the action of Middle Eastern countries, Indian farmers could no longer afford large amounts of fertilizer and fuel; consequently, India became more dependent on American grain. This, certainly, is a prime example of the international interrelationships among population, technology, energy, and food supply.

[26] Richard A. Falk *et al. State of the Globe Report 1974.* Amsterdam: North-Holland, 1975.

[27] Lester R. Brown, *op. cit.,* p. 16.

Debate. For a number of years before the OPEC oil embargo many had become concerned about the shortage of energy supplies in general. After extrapolating present rates of population growth and levels of consumption into the future some believed the United States would run out of most crucial resources (oil, coal, etc.) . Others contended that new supplies of resources would be discovered, and that new technology would give us an endless supply of cheap resources. As with the other population and food continua, the truth lies somewhere between the two extremes.

In the mid-1970's, debates raged on the future of United States energy policy. The expansion of peaceful nuclear power, seen as an obvious development in the previous two decades, was seriously questioned. Reactor orders went from 36 in 1973, to 27 in 1974, to 4 in 1975. Cancellations and deferrals outpaced new reactor orders by more than 25 to 1 in 1975, and there were similar reactions in a number of other developed countries.[28] The Faustian character of nuclear power—trading large amounts of energy for the possible safety of earth's present and future inhabitants—is another example of how the United States (in this instance) has been a prime factor in creating a more interdependent world.

The contention that Americans lead affluent lives is not a contention at all; it is fact. North Americans consume more than 30 times the energy per capita of Africans—and those U.N. figures are based on averages, so national variations can be even more disparate. On the average, energy consumption per capita in the industrialized world was 16 times that of the world's developing countries in 1976. In the past 25 years world energy output has tripled, with the developed world leading in production.[29] Some would claim that our affluence rests on a crumbling foundation, in view of the fact that we were dependent on foreign sources for a considerable number of important minerals in 1974, and our overall dependence has increased since then.

Another aspect of the energy debate in the United States relates to amounts of energy wasted. A strong case has been made that, besides wasting more fuel than was used by two-thirds of the world's population (in 1975) , Americans annually consume more than twice the fuel needed to maintain our current standard of living.[30] This argument, intriguing as it is, represents a different approach from the previous position. The former stressed a definite change in life-styles while the latter implies that

[28] Denis Hayes. *Nuclear Power: The Fifth Horseman.* Worldwatch Paper 6. May 1976. pp. 8, 9.

[29] Kathleen Teltsch. *New York Times,* July 30, 1976, p. D1.

[30] Denis Hayes. *Energy: The Case for Conservation.* Worldwatch Paper 4. January 1976. p. 7.

a change in life-styles may not be necessary if wastage is reduced. Curricula should enable students not only to explore separate positions, but also to understand the differences between them and to speculate on alternative future courses of action.

How would developing countries react if we: (a) decided to fast one day a week and eliminate steak consumption from our diet; (b) went on a campaign to reduce energy wastage while maintaining our early-1970's level of living; (c) decided to neither conserve energy nor modify our lifestyles? How would our own nation react to these possible futures: cattlemen in the Midwest; utility companies; oil producing companies; the Federal Energy Office? In pondering these possibilities it is not difficult to see how the actions of others (OPEC and mineral exporters) have and will affect our nation, and how we (energy conservation and life-style changes) have the power to affect others.

It would clearly take volumes to cover all the "facts," and all the issues in the debates surrounding the interrelationships among population, food, energy, technology, and how nations are dependent on one another. So it is that much more a difficult task to try to synthesize all these concepts and create a conceptual framework that fits all the issues together. Nonetheless, attempts are beginning to be made.[31]

The complexity of the issues, combined with the fact that a conceptual framework integrating those issues does not now exist, means that the attempts at conceptualization (for example, the Club of Rome Reports) themselves become part of the debate. That such a conceptual framework does not exist should not absolve us from further attempts at pulling the issues together to learn both how our lives affect the lives of people in this nation and other nations, and how the lives of people in other nations affect themselves and us.

Students' Current Levels of Global Civic Literacy

Over the last few years there has been an increasing effort to assess the knowledge, skills, and attitudes of young people.* Such assessments

31 See: Roger D. Hansen et al. The U.S. and World Development—Agenda for Action 1976. New York: Praeger Publishers, 1976; Herman Kahn et al., op. cit.; Richard A. Falk et al., op. cit.; Donella Meadows et al. The Limits to Growth: The Report for the Club of Rome's Project on the Predicament of Mankind. New York: Universe Books, 1972; Mihajl Mesarovic and Eduard Pestel. Mankind at the Turning Point—The Second Report to the Club of Rome. New York: E. P. Dutton & Co., 1974.

* This section has been reproduced with permission from Ward Morehouse, editor. Toward the Achievement of Global Literacy in American Schools. Preliminary report on the Wingspread Workshop on Problems of Definitions and Assessment of Global Education. Racine, Wisconsin, January 25-26, 1976. Convened under the auspices of the

have included the work of National Assessment of Educational Progress and the accountability efforts of state education departments and local school districts across the country. Recently, beginning with the California State Department, there has also been an interest in developing basic skills competency tests. Students of certain ages can attain the equivalent of a high school diploma, upon meeting certain test standards. While some of these assessments and basic skill examinations include questions dealing with citizenship and social science concepts, the greater emphasis has been on the knowledge and skills related to reading, mathematics, and writing. In addition, when questions measuring social science concepts have been included the issues dealt with have been largely national rather than international in character. There has been very little concern with measuring the ability of young people to understand global issues of population growth, famine, environmental pollution, cross-cultural conflict and communication, or depletion of natural resources.[32]

During the past 15 years, efforts aimed at educational evaluation as well as research by political scientists into the political information and attitudes of pre-adults have provided some information on levels of global civic literacy. A recent summary of major research in international socialization drew the following conclusions about American children:

1. International learning begins early in life.

2. International learning is cumulative . . . what children learn at one age builds upon and is influenced by what they have previously learned.

3. The time of middle childhood (grades three through eight) is an important period in international learning.

4. The beliefs, attitudes, values, and knowledge individuals develop about the world differ—each individual student brings his or her own particular configuration of orientations toward the world.

5. The mass media, especially television and newspapers, play an important role in children's international learning.[33]

The number of students who meet any specific criteria for global civic literacy was not determined by this review, however.

Council of Chief State School Officers Committee on International Education with the assistance of the Johnson Foundation, May 10, 1976.

[32] Nor, indeed, with their knowledge of human history which illuminates contemporary problems. We also need to recognize how seriously deficient we are in meeting one criterion accepted by most other societies throughout the world as a hallmark of the well-educated person, namely, working knowledge of at least one other language in addition to the mother tongue.

[33] Richard Remy, James Nathan, James Becker, and Judith Torney. *International Learning and International Education in a Global Age.* Bulletin 47. Washington, D.C.: National Council for the Social Studies, 1975. p. 40.

To be somewhat more specific, there is considerable evidence from early studies of socialization that a strongly positive attachment to the nation has been developed by second grade. Students may have misconceptions about geography and be naive with regard to the realities of politics; but this strong sense of national identity is present early.[34]

The IEA survey, conducted in 1971, of more than thirty thousand preadolescent and adolescent students in nine democratic nations demonstrates some variations between countries in the strength of this sense of support for the national government.[35] For example, students in Israel were very much like those in the United States in the strength of positive evaluations of their government. Students in the Federal Republic of Germany, Finland, and the Netherlands presented a contrasting almost anti-nationalistic position. In the IEA civic education survey, questions were asked about how frequently the students discussed different topics with parents, friends, and teachers.[36] Students in the United States ranked fairly high on total amount of discussion engaged in and on other aspects of active civic interest and participation. However, there was a difference in the topics that actually were of interest to students in different countries. Fourteen-year-old students in the Federal Republic of Germany, Finland, Italy, the Netherlands, and New Zealand on the average discussed "what is happening in other countries" more frequently with parents and friends than "what is going on in our country in government and politics." In Ireland and Israel, national politics were of slightly greater interest to students than events in other countries. The United States was the only country (of these eight) where there was substantially *less* interest among fourteen-year-olds in international political discussion than in national political discussion with friends and parents. Similar patterns characterized pre-university students.

The cognitive portion of the IEA questionnaire dealt with knowledge of domestic and international matters. The average American fourteen-year-old was more knowledgeable about domestic political institutions and processes than the average fourteen-year-old in any other country except Ireland. In other words, students in the United States scored relatively higher on cognitive items concerning domestic politics

---

[34] R. D. Hess and Judith Torney. *The Development of Political Attitudes in Children.* Chicago: Aldine Publishing Company, 1967.

[35] J. V. Torney, A. N. Oppenheim, and R. F. Farnen. *Civic Education in Ten Countries: An Empirical Study.* New York: Halsted Press, John Wiley & Sons, Inc., 1975.

[36] Material on the international orientations of students as revealed by the IEA study has been taken from: Judith Torney. "The International Knowledge and Attitudes of Adolescents in Nine Nations: The IEA Civic Education Survey." *International Journal of Political Learning,* 1976.

than on those concerning international politics. An opposite pattern, higher scores on knowledge of international processes, characterized students in the Netherlands and the Federal Republic of Germany at this age.

Other data collected by the IEA is helpful in attempting to understand the finding that adolescents in the United States seem to focus more on the national than on the international, while those in countries like the Netherlands tend to focus more on the international than on the national. An index of foreign contact for each nation in the IEA survey was formed. Of the countries testing in civic education, the Netherlands ranked the highest on percentage of the GNP which enters world trade (40 percent of GNP) and the United States ranked the lowest (6 percent). Similar indices of percentage of films imported, textbooks imported, international mail and telephone services, also placed the Netherlands as the highest and the United States as the lowest in foreign contact. Figures on television programs dealing with international topics also give the impression that U.S. students have relatively minimal exposure to international matters.

The questionnaire used in the IEA survey also included items relating to the United Nations. Seven out of 47 multiple choice cognitive questions administered to fourteen-year-olds dealt with the United Nations. To give an example of these findings, among students in the United States more than 65 percent knew that the Universal Declaration of Human Rights does *not* guarantee the right to disobey national laws if one's family is in danger. (The question, also administered to high school seniors, had a nearly equivalent percentage correct in that group.) Approximately 50 percent of the fourteen-year-olds knew that the Security Council (out of five listed U.N. units) is charged with major responsibility for the keeping of the peace.

The majority of both fourteen-year-olds and seniors in high school in the U.S. have accurate knowledge about the major activities of the U.N.; however, it is not an institution about which they have extensive knowledge, a clearly developed image, or strong positive attitudes. There is a very small change between the fourteen-year-old and the high school senior level with regard to knowledge and exposure to information about the U.N. or clarity of attitudes; this is in contrast to items with domestic political content which change considerably in this age period. Given the current situation in the U.N., however, it is difficult to define a desirable direction for student attitudes.[37]

There are a few sources of information about the existing attitudes of students toward the U.N.'s specialized agencies or toward U.N. activ-

[37] These results are all reported at greater length in Torney, *ibid.*

ities in the protection of human rights. Investigators concerned with political attitudes sometimes include questions about human rights in democratic society, but these usually focus on rights protected by the national constitution or laws. Since American civic education presents terms like "rights and freedoms" almost exclusively in the context of study of the U.S. Constitution and Bill of Rights, there is a tendency among American students to think only of those rights and freedoms guaranteed to citizens in those documents. This natio-centrism regarding human rights is reflected in the tendency of many young people to believe that ours is the only country which believes in protecting human rights. This may lead young people to the mistaken impression that people in other countries do not care about having such rights and freedoms. American students may have special difficulty in recognizing that they share a belief in human rights with people in underdeveloped countries who look and speak very differently. If one speaks a language which sounds strange to American ears, should one have the same right to freely express one's opinion as the speaker of English? Perhaps not for some Americans.[38] As Weissberg concluded after reviewing a number of socialization studies:

> For young children democracy is America and America is democracy . . . other countries may have this democracy but for a variety of inarticulable reasons, other people's democracy is not as good as the American version.[39]

The same may hold true for other people's human rights.

Many studies have noted the similar pattern of national groups which children seem to *dislike*. Young children tend to reject or see as dissimilar to themselves people from countries which are perceived either as having strange and exotic customs or as culturally backward (often Asian or African countries), are perceived as having recently been involved in a war (Vietnam, Germany), or are perceived as speaking a strange language. When asked how other countries differed from their own country, speaking a different language was mentioned spontaneously by more than 70 percent of a group of American six- through twelve-year-olds.[40]

[38] For a discussion of this problem see: Thomas Buergenthal and Judith Torney. *International Human Rights and International Education*. U.S. National Commission for UNESCO, Department of State, Washington, D.C.: U.S. Government Printing Office, 1976, which analyzes the 1974 UNESCO Recommendation on Education for International Understanding, Cooperation and Peace and Education Relating to Human Rights and Fundamental Freedoms, and presents materials to aid educators in its implementation.

[39] Robert Weissberg. *Political Learning, Political Choice, and Democratic Citizenship*. Englewood Cliffs, New Jersey: Prentice-Hall, Inc.. 1974.

[40] Judith Torney and Donald Morris. *Global Dimension of U.S. Education: The Elementary School*. New York: Center for War/Peace Studies, 1972.

International Education Today

In 1975 a survey, Civic Literacy for Global Interdependence, was prepared for the Council of Chief State School Officers Committee on International Education. Compared to a previous survey undertaken in 1969 we see some progress has been made in state education departments' attention to global issues.[41]

• Credit for overseas experience is now granted by many states, if the experience is related in general to the individual's teaching field. In some cases, this credit is only for renewal of teaching certificates; in others, it may be used instead of student teaching or other professional experience.

• Transfer of foreign credits is now allowed by more states and must in most cases be approved by a U.S. institution of higher education or by the U.S. Office of Education.

• Leave for foreign teaching is now available in many states. Generally it is not granted by the state education agency but by local school boards.

• In-service programs, continuing education programs, workshops dealing with international education and language education are sponsored by an increasing number of states.

• Citizenship requirements for teachers have become less stringent. Most of the states requiring citizenship or intent of citizenship grant waivers and give temporary professional permits and exchange teacher credentials.

• Efforts are expanding to meet the needs of students and adults whose primary language is other than English. Fourteen states mention specifically the introduction and expansion of bilingual, bicultural education.

• In the field of foreign languages not only Spanish, German, Latin and Russian are offered, but less-commonly-taught Western as well as Eastern languages, as for example: Portugese, Swedish, Greek, Hungarian, Polish, Hebrew, Chinese, Japanese, Arabic, and Swahili.

• Thirty-one states have some involvement in international exchange programs for teachers or students.

There is now the growing awareness of the concept of international education and the inclusion of more specific global and international

[41] Sigrid Juncker and Jo Ann Larson, editors. *Civic Literacy for Global Interdependence. New Challenge to State Leadership in Education.* Washington: Council of Chief State School Officers, 1976.

education courses, ethnic studies, population and world food crisis courses. There is an increase in the production of social studies and humanities materials dealing with the topic of international education. Thirty-five states claim involvement in this area of activity.

New York State was among the first to move in these directions. The Board of Regents as early as 1961 noted that "we daily bear witness to the emergence of non-Western nations into modern life. The imminent redistribution of world power—the rising aspirations of multitudes everywhere to share in human dignity and lessen the gap between rich and poor nations are certain to have an impact on education."[42]

Some school districts in the nation have through the years cultivated contacts with local university area study centers. These contacts frequently permit the use of university libraries by teachers and enable them to call on academic specialists for assistance in in-service training and in the scholarly evaluation of new curriculum materials. In 1976 the U.S. Office of Education mandated inclusion of a statement detailing the nature of projected "outreach" activities of university language and area centers desirous of receiving federal funding for the 1976-1979 phase of the NDEA Title VI. Thus, the trend toward involvement between school districts and universities should be accelerated.

Curriculum development projects are varied. Many are outgrowths of projects funded by the federal government in the 1960's. James Becker has summarized these earlier projects as follows:

> The most striking feature of the curriculum projects is their variety. They range from ambitious K-12 programs to intensive units of only a few weeks. Some stay rigorously within the bounds of a particular discipline while others make a point of borrowing freely from any of the social sciences—anthropology, history, economics, sociology, geography and political science. Their teaching procedures and materials go from the relatively traditional to the highly experimental, and include simulations and non-verbal games, artifacts, models and "original" documents, multimedia kits and audio visual resources, as well as pamphlets, source books and readings.

> Despite the diversity of their educational aims and methods, however, most of the curriculum projects share one common trait: a commitment to a new view of the social education in which students are encouraged to acquire skills and insights as well as information. Rote learning and expository teaching have been deemphasized. In their place has evolved an educational program based on teaching students how to learn, exposing them to general principles and concepts, and, above all, structuring the classroom experience in such a way that students are led to discover ideas for and by themselves.

Four general categories of curriculum projects can be distinguished: com-

---

42 Ward Morehouse. *State Leadership in International Education.* Report #14. Denver: Education Commission of the States, July 1969.

prehensive projects; projects structured around a specific discipline; area studies; and special purpose projects. Comprehensive projects aim at providing a complete social studies education for one or more grades.

What distinguishes these comprehensive programs from more traditional curriculum guides is their conscious attempt to produce intellectual consistency and coherence in the programs they develop and their explicit awareness of the academic disciplines within which they are operating.

The discipline-oriented projects tend to display a somewhat different emphasis. Although there are many points of similarity, projects fostered by economics, anthropology, geography or sociology are more likely to be preoccupied with the methods and problems peculiar to those disciplines.

Area studies, the third type of curriculum project, are generally distinguished by a wide-ranging multidisciplinary approach to their subject matter. The aim of these projects, such as Project Africa and the Asian Studies Inquiry Program, is to help students experience the totality of another culture by studying its social structure, religion, economic system, history and folklore.

A fourth category of curriculum projects includes all those which have some special aim or orientation not found in any of the other projects.[43]

A number of public and private educational agencies have worked in this area and some have developed materials for use in classrooms on a variety of grade levels.[44]

Some of these projects have not been unalloyed successes. Some were remote from the teacher's own knowledge; some were placed in "teacher-proof" packages and also became "student-proof"; some could not easily fit into standard curricula and so were not adopted; some remained experimental materials and were used in only selected schools briefly; some placed such emphasis on student creativity and ingenuity that few students could profit from their use; and some were so esoteric and remote from student interest and experience that they failed for this reason.

Some of the projects attempted to mold the insights of more than one discipline into a coherent and articulated "social science" program but foundered on the rock of teacher inflexibility or drifted in a sea of philosophical and methodological confusion. This was particularly the case in some programs which confused the terms cross-disciplinary and

43 James M. Becker. "A Background Paper Prepared for the Overseas Development Council Workshop on American High Schools and International Development." (December 1971, typescript.) pp. 7-10.

44 Listings of these agencies can be obtained from: The Interorganizational Commission on International Education, c/o Ms. Jayne Millar Wood, Overseas Development Council, 1717 Massachusetts Avenue, N.W., Washington, D.C. 20036; The Center for International Programs and Comparative Studies, New York State Education Department, Albany, New York 12230; The Social Studies Development Center, Indiana University, Bloomington, Indiana 47401.

inter-disciplinary. Conclusions drawn from deductions in one field did not necessarily carry over into another, particularly where these fields were psychology, sociology, and economics.

What we may learn from these programs is that raising the level of abstraction is not synonymous with valid extrapolation and generalization.

Developing an international perspective means different things to different people. The concept itself has undergone evolution.

In the past decade it meant encouraging the development of understanding and empathy for other countries and tolerance for other values. It meant broadening the traditional Western orientation of curricula and texts and increasing awareness of ethnocentric bias.

In the 1970's, the concept broadened as a result of the synergistic meshings of actors brought into the picture in the previous two decades. As a result there is now increased communication among research scholars, private nonprofit educational materials development agencies, innovative state education departments, and school districts. The focus in the mid-1970's is on the unity rather than on the diversity of humankind, on the awareness of the increasing global interdependence among peoples, on the fragility of the biosphere, and on the imperatives of international cooperation on crucial issues of transnational importance. There is, furthermore, an attempt in this Age of Aquarius to have students form their own values after due consideration of the variety of value systems extant in our world, and to develop the insight that there is more than one structural way of looking at the world around us, both philosophically and in social studies education.

The new trend follows several modes. The traditional one is to see the American nation as one among others and interacting with them. Another is to see the United States as one subgroup in a society of humankind; another is to view the earth as a unit much like a spaceship traveling through space in which obedience to physical principles and reactions to internal changes brought about by our own actions lead to evolutionary changes in governmental and societal actions both within nations and in relations between them. Roughly these ideas approximate those taken in the field of history, sociology, and the physical sciences. Whichever perspective one chooses, the point is that when the bells of war, of pestilence, poverty, and political tyranny toll for others we all hear the echoes.

Although this belief has gained currency in the United States since World War II, education agencies and textbook publishers still tend to give it low priority. Admittedly, adapting education to help Americans cope with global interdependency clashes with some of the traditional concepts regarding our own heritage.[45] Historically, one of the principle social purposes of the American common school was to fashion a national identity out of a population of diverse origins. The school was always a powerful force for cultural assimilation and linguistic homogeneity. Indeed, only within the past decade or two has recognition been given to the idea that America has not only blended diverse subcultures to its ultimate enrichment, but is also a place where there is significant leveling of culture differences and adaptation of the largely white, largely Anglo-Saxon, Protestant set of social values and norms. That schools accept society's beliefs and mores is a truism. There seems to be also little contact with foreign cultures. A UNESCO survey completed in 1973 revealed that only one to two percent of the average program weekend on commercial and public television in the United States was devoted to programs relating to international themes, and this is a figure lowest of all the other 100 countries surveyed.[46]

Even when other cultures are recognized they are frequently studied as a series of fragmented units, seen by both teachers and students as strange and esoteric aberrations of the general flow of history, which is toward progress, democratic norms, increasingly wealthy citizenries, and improved technology.

Recently the Asia Society surveyed 272 textbooks used in American classrooms.[47] The Report noted that teachers are frequently textbook bound, presumably because many do not have the independent knowledge of the subject they should. Many of the texts used provide no clue to the rich and enduring cultural heritage of Asia, to progress made in various areas of endeavor, or to the views of Asians themselves in interpreting their own society. Many texts discuss historical events in Asia primarily in terms of importance to American strategic, military, or economic interests. Clearly, a balanced grasp of the culture and aspirations of others, their relations to us, and their culture cannot emerge from the utilization of such textbooks. Even less so can the issues of interdependence be grasped.

A few weeks on Africa, Latin America, Asia, the Middle East, the United Nations, or, as is the case in several states, a brief study of the "evils of communism" can hardly prepare students to understand the present world situation much less cope with the emerging world in the next century. It is for these reasons that a number of curriculum agencies have embarked on projects designed to introduce global perspectives and

---

[45] Ward Morehouse. *A New Civic Literacy: American Education and Global Interdependence.* Aspen, Colorado: Aspen Institute for Humanistic Studies, 1975. p. 12.

[46] Thomas Buergenthal and Judith V. Torney, *op. cit.*

[47] The Asia Society. *Asia in American Textbooks: An Evaluation.* New York: The Society, March 1976.

the idea of global interdependence as recently expressed in scholarly research in the fields of ecology, social psychology, and the earth sciences.

The goals, though broad, are clear. James Becker has suggested that one of the major aims of global education is to provide a context that can encompass isolation and integration, diversity and unity, aggression and cooperation. Both visual and written materials for students, for example, have generally emphasized the differences within the human species rather than the commonalities: mankind has been depicted as racially, physically, culturally, and linguistically diverse. Education now needs to reassert the fact that mankind, while possessed of enormous diversity, is nonetheless a single species of life among multitudes of other forms. The heterogeneity of human behavior needs to be seen against a backdrop of shared traits: our common biological heritage as members of homo sapiens, our common habitat, and our common fate. He points out that education should not minimize the differences among peoples and cultures; but by the same token it should not ignore either the great variations within these cultures themselves or the similarities among all of them. "Students must be helped to form accurate perceptions of problems that transcend national boundaries. More importantly, they must be given a whole new map of the world—one that shows shared ethnic and cultural interests, ecological perspectives, overlapping social and economic concerns, as well as geopolitical configurations."[48]

Students should also be able to see the world as others see it and be made receptive to the idea that change in their own lives and in the world around them is inevitable and not necessarily evil. Moreover, an awareness that there is a pattern to change that is discernible is perhaps the major goal. Creating curriculum materials embodying the above concepts and avoiding the above-mentioned pitfalls is a formidable task.

A number of curriculum materials and readings designed to do so have already been created in specific subject areas for use in social studies and humanities classrooms. These are in the fields of "development," war-peace studies, future studies, and global perspectives, among others.

These curricular approaches, new as they are and frequently using different classes of information, have in common the fact that they foster global perspectives.[49] This is a concept more easily described than defined. Perhaps James Becker's thoughts are useful. "What kind of education will best prepare students to live in the world community of the future? In a specific sense it will have to embrace all of the interrelated issues mentioned above—war prevention, social justice, ecological balance,

[48] James Becker. "Perspectives of Global Education." (Unpublished 1976.) p. 3.
[49] See: "A Study of Secondary School Curricula and Student Views on Growth Implications and the Earth's Future." Cambridge, Massachusetts: Education Development Center, 1976.

world economic welfare, alternative futures, conflict management, social change, transnational institutions, global political development, and the need for international machinery to tackle these problems effectively. In a more general sense, it seems clear that global education should seek to connect rather than divide men, to make clear their common humanity, and to emphasize their common fate."[50]

How do we do all this within the standard curriculum and within the limits of current knowledge about these issues by teachers? The traditional methods of upgrading teacher knowledge, through in-service training, seminars and workshops, conferences, and overseas study tours have fallen on hard times.

What we have learned from the experience of federally sponsored curriculum projects funded in the 1960's, is that mere exposure to new information or to classroom materials is not enough to bring about curriculum change. Effective and lasting curriculum change occurs under certain conditions, innovations must be comprehensible and sensible to the managers of the school or district, teachers and administrators must be convinced of the need for change and the relevance and utility of the new methodologies used, the strategy for introducing the innovation must be consistent with the local reward system, and the innovations contemplated must be locally verifiable and modifiable on the classroom level.

Ideally, there should be community support, the ability to communicate with outside experimenters, sufficient finances to enable follow through activities and evaluation. Interestingly, one researcher discovered that in curriculum change the flexibility and attitudes of the staff were more significant than their strength of academic training. Of less significance is the history of innovation of the particular school or district. Some schools were willing to try something new for the first time and others were satiated with new experiments.[51] One significant characteristic affecting the rate of diffusion of new materials and methods after they have been developed and tested is the compatibility of these innovations with the values of the potential adapters and these values must perforce change at times if other changes are to come about.

There seems to be a growing receptivity on the part of teachers who teach about such issues. A survey conducted in 1971 by the Civic Education Project of the International Association for the Evaluation of Educational Achievement involved testing the international knowledge and attitudes of 30,000 ten- and fourteen-year-old students in European na-

[50] James Becker, op. cit., p. 12.

[51] National Seminar on the Diffusion of New Instructional Materials and Practices: Characteristics of the School. "What Are the Characteristics of Schools that Discourage or Encourage the Introduction and Use of New Ideas?" Boulder, Colorado: Social Science Education Consortium, June 1973.

tions, Israel, New Zealand, and the United States. Among teachers of pre-university students, international problems were regarded as equal in importance as national ones in the United States, although interestingly in the United States as in other nations surveyed, information on non-Western cultures was perceived as considerably less important than national and international problems.[52]

Student surveys showed different findings. In surveying the amount of discussion about "what is happening in other countries" with parents and with friends, there was substantially less interest among fourteen-year-olds in the United States than in the seven other nations surveyed. The lesser discussion is understandably congruent with lesser knowledge. The mean score of American fourteen-year-olds on knowledge of domestic institutions and processes was second highest among eight nations sampled and second lowest on knowledge of international institutions and processes.[53]

Parenthetically, a large majority of students in the United States and in all the eight nations surveyed on this issue rejected war as an instrument of national policy.[54]

Conclusion

Education and schooling are not synonymous. There is no denying that much learning takes place outside of the formal school system. Though data are not readily available, it is possible to hypothesize that young people's knowledge and attitudes about other lands and people, about global events and the whole range of "interdependence" issues derive more from the media than they do from the school day. But that is, perhaps, the heart of the problem of low levels of "global literacy."

As Hanvey[55] and others have noted, the media tend to be concerned with the event, rather than with the processes of change over reasonably long periods of time. Thus, we were besieged for years with information concerning Southeast Asia, when the American presence in Vietnam was so great. However, even a cursory review today of our leading "international" papers and magazines, let alone television, would indicate that little space or time is devoted to these regions now. Isolated facts about a given situation or event may be derived from a continuing review of the media, even a sense of the relationship of these facts and occurrences

[52] Judith V. Torney, "The International Attitudes and Knowledge of Adolescents in Nine Countries," *op. cit.*

[53] *Ibid.*, p. 13.

[54] The actual questions asked upon which this survey is based are: "War Is Sometimes the Only Way in Which a Nation Can Save Its Self Respect" and "Talking Things Over with Another Nation Is Better than Fighting."

[55] Robert G. Hanvey. *An Attainable Global Perspective*. New York: Center for Global Perspectives, 1976. pp. 2-3. Reprinted with permission.

one to the other, if the particular world situation is newsworthy over a reasonably long period of time. But the framework into which one might place these facts, the superstructure for understanding processes, is usually little covered, if at all.

Therein lies the role of the school in educating young citizens for their future roles in relation to international and global concerns. It is not simply a matter of increasing the number of "facts" which may characterize many efforts in these areas today. Instead, it is a matter of providing learners with the conceptual framework for analytical thinking about these myriad issues. It is to assist the learner in processing and organizing the information received from the whole range of sources in society—formal, nonformal, and informal.

Hanvey, recognizing the importance of "agencies of socialization" other than the school at the same time stresses the important role of the school in making a meaningful contribution to socialization and learning about global perspectives.

The schools must select a niche that complements the other educative agencies of the society. To the extent that those other agencies and influences work against a global perspective the schools can perform a corrective function; to the extent that the other agencies are glib and superficial the schools can seek to be more thorough; to the extent that the other agencies have blind spots the schools can work to supply the missing detail; to the extent that the other agencies direct attention to the short-term extraordinary event the schools can assert the value of examining the long-term situation or trend (which is sometimes extraordinary in its own right) .[56]

There are, however, formidable obstacles in attempting to introduce these perspectives into America's classrooms. These are of a scholarly as well as practical nature.

The basic problem is *not* to attempt to make public opinion agree on any particular perception of reality or on desirable solutions to the problems they suggest, but rather to reject and correct simplistic, emotional and uneducated stereotypes by the introduction of consequence laden insights and analysis.

Yet, as we have already observed, there is little agreement among scholars and experts on how to solve these problems or even on how critical such problems are alone, together, and through time. As a result, there is often reluctance on the part of school personnel to deal in areas which are characterized by such uncertainty. Yet this is the real challenge facing the educator. If there is true concern for educating young people for tomorrow, such education must deal with the uncertainties which characterize the future.

[56] *Ibid.*, p. 2.

Providing students with an opportunity to view the world with multifaceted (though not rose colored) lenses takes more than the development of effective teaching strategies through curriculum revision. It also requires teacher training, materials development, and the like.

It requires policy support and commitment by political and educational leaders at the national, state, and community levels to legitimize local initiatives in implementing instructional change by giving priority status to such initiatives and by allocating funds for it.

Also, only they can create a climate in which the results of recent scholarship on trans-national and transcending issues are given exposure and currency in the schools and in other public media.

The development of an international or global perspective is not the development of a new course, but rather represents a new way of looking at all education for citizenship. It involves the development of skills which have a high degree of transferability to other areas of responsible citizenship in a democratic, society. It can safely be asserted that this global perspective is not a frill, but an essential skill for life in the world of the future.

Selected Readings

American Council on Education. *Education for Global Interdependence: Report with Recommendations to the Government Academic Interface Committee*. Washington, D.C.: the Council, 1976.

The Asia Society. *Asia in American Textbooks: An Evaluation*. New York: the Society, 1976.

Otto Bettman. *The Good Old Days—They Were Terrible!* New York: Random House, Inc., 1974.

Lester R. Brown. *The Politics and Responsibility of the North American Breadbasket*. Worldwatch Paper 2. October 1975.

Thomas Buergenthal and Judith V. Torney. *International Human Rights and International Education*. Department of State. Washington, D.C.: Government Printing Office, 1976. U.S. National Commission for UNESCO.

Richard A. Falk *et al. State of the Globe Report*. Amsterdam: North-Holland, 1975.

Roger D. Hansen *et al. The United States and World Development—Agenda for Action*. New York: Praeger Publishers, 1976.

Herman Kahn *et al. The Next Two Hundred Years: A Scenario for America and the World*. New York: William Morrow and Company, Inc., 1976.

Social Science Education Consortium. *National Seminar on the Diffusion of New Instructional Materials and Practices: Characteristics of the School*. Boulder, Colorado: the Consortium, 1973.

Robert Weissberg. *Political Learning, Political Choice, and Democratic Citizenship*. Englewood Cliffs, New Jersey: Prentice-Hall, Inc., 1974.

6

Justice, Society, and the Individual

James Boyer, Rudolph E. Waters, Frederick M. Harris

CONCERN with the fulfillment of the American Dream of full and equal opportunity for all has led us to the realization that basic changes must occur in the direction of effort taken by society's leaders—and in the substance of activity sought by our major institutions. These institutions are numerous, but readers of this yearbook are among those who see the institution of the school as a major entity contributing to the quality of life. The culture of the school is always reflective of the culture of the society-at-large. Ideas about justice, about morality, about objectivity, and about human interaction are demonstrated daily through the substance of curriculum and through the processes by which curricular services are delivered.

Confusing perceptions of justice, of the nature of our society, and of the functions and needs of individuals are widespread. Curricular concerns with such issues are not as extensive as they might be—but observers of curriculum have not been able to escape the impact of the issues because of their pervasive character. The nature of our societal structure causes social and economic observers to suggest structural changes when discussions emerge that relate to resolving human problems. Because such structural modifications are generally measurable, generally easy to describe and frequently manageable, they tend to be embraced by the mass media, by the educator who depends on technique more than on ethical, philosophical analyses, and by those seeking easy answers to complex societal problems.

Before one can embrace the broad concepts associated with justice, society, and the individual, a review of the basic concepts associated with those terms seems appropriate. Additionally, one must raise questions about the human condition, about improving such a condition, and about the capacity of curriculum effort to respond to the critical issues and realities facing us as we approach the decade of the 1980's. Does the curriculum *predict* the realities? Or does it *reflect* the realities? Do curriculum workers have the capacity to construct and implement curriculum entities which respond to the combination of justice, society, and the individual?

Justice

When one begins to examine the concept of *justice,* it emerges as one of the most desirable of all entities associated with improved quality of life and with the improved human condition. The following are essential aspects of the notion of justice:

1. It is the impartial adjustment of conflicting claims;

2. It is the establishment or determination of rights according to the rules of law or equity;

3. It is the quality of being fair and impartial;

4. It is the quality of conforming to truth, fact, and reason;

5. It involves fair treatment, adequate consideration, and the display of due appreciation for an issue, an individual, or a group.

Despite the seemingly clear notions embodied in the aspects described above, it remains that justice is an emotional concept drawn from the capacity of human beings to think critically, to make decisions, and to systematically reach conclusions which affect human lives. Justice for one individual or group may appear to be blatant injustice for another. Descriptions of behavior, of policies, of programs often designed to lead to justice frequently appear to emerge underdeveloped and incomplete. Efforts to explain the concept frequently appear weak in their verbal form and character but the psychological and emotional impact of the concept tends to be consistently powerful. It is a desired element by practically every human being who understands its consequences, and its relationship to curricular responses in facing critical realities is rarely underestimated.

Additionally, justice is often discussed in the same context as equality, objectivity, freedom, and human value. Any efforts to clarify or define the quality of life must be executed within the framework of relationships based on the concept of justice. Human emotions will not permit (for very long) the existence of relationships which are not based on the concept of justice.

Justice is an ageless concept. Throughout the history of humankind it has had various connotations in the eyes of the beholder. In the great wars of recorded history, each side has given the impression that it would be victorious because its side was just—it was on the side of right.

There are many adjectives which have been used to describe justice —formal or abstract, commutative, distributive, social, religious, divine, universal, eschatological, and yes racial! Let us examine a few of these concepts.

Formal or abstract justice is a principle of action with which beings of one and the same category must be treated the same way. Commutative justice seeks to establish equality in each and every judicial act. It is the business of the judge. Distributive justice is concerned with the conferring of benefits—giving to each according to his/her own merits. Political rights and goods are meted by distributive justice while penalities are levied and fines paid according to commutative justice.

Justice has many facets. The principal who treats all students with equal harshness is considered just a bit cruel, while the judge who acquits a guilty man is considered unjust but charitable.

Let us return now, to several connotations of justice mentioned above. The connotations of justice of equality—*to each the same thing*— call for an equal proportion of whatever is to be divided. This concern makes no distinction between people. Regardless of a person's standing, he is entitled to an equal portion. Giving to each according to his merits, however, suggests that some characteristic must be possessed in the same degree. For two people to be treated in the same way, it is not enough that they should have merit but must have merit to the same degree.

Administering Justice. According to one's works suggests that persons are remunerated according to the quality of their performance. One who performs well is paid well. One who performs poorly is paid poorly. One's essential needs are considered in the administering of justice according to one's needs. In the application of this formula, a distinction between other needs and essential needs in an order of importance must be made.

The application of the formula "to each according to his rank" assumes the division of beings into classes, usually ranged in some hierarchical order. The formula "to each according to his legal entitlement" gives freedom to the judge responsible for applying it.

Society

Society is one of the most widely used concepts with varying interpretations but always associated with human composition. When one thinks of the society, it is usually in connection with the community of humankind and in connection with the norms, traditions, values, and styles of the majority of Americans in our times. The following are components of the concept of society:

1. Companionship or association with one's fellows;

2. Voluntary association of individuals for common ends;

3. Friendly and/or intimate associations;

4. Persons in contact with each other periodically because of common interests and beliefs;

5. Community, nation, or broad grouping of people having common traditions, institutions, and collective activities.

Further, the concept of society is characterized by social circles, by class distinctions, behaviors, manners, and the development of social units which endorse or reject behaviors based on the cultural orientation of group members. A society such as we know endorses and rejects behaviors with constant intensity. The society best known to us has become much smaller (an aspect of critical reality) due to the increased technology and to mass media communication practices. The Western tradition is so pervasive that we tend to think of society in Western terms. Such thinking is accompanied by the adoption of culturally oriented life styles and political philosophies on which individuals determine the degree and extent of justice exhibited, practiced, and adopted.

The society is composed of people. In the most basic understanding of people grouping, human beings emerge as powerful, significant, and worthy of preservation in every aspect. People are important to the maintenance of society and to the improvement of the human condition reflected in that society. To what extent do we relate the two? How extensively have we come to grips with the critical realities which threaten that societal composition? Are we willing to examine that set of concerns which could alert us to impending critical realities capable of decreasing the quality of life rather than improving it?

Societal Response to Realities. America is a complex country whose virtues have been extolled and upheld for centuries. While it is complex, it is also a powerful nation with the most advanced life-style known to humanity. Our technological advancement is, without question, the basis of our high standard of living and our technological and scientific approaches to critical realities appear to be increasing. Societal response to human problems has primarily been technical and scientific. The individual is complex, but not technical and scientific. For that reason, many of the societal responses to problems identified with human inter-action have been less rewarding than most of us would like. Secondly, societal responses to critical realities have tended to be remedial in total without any aspect of prevention being a part of resolution. Such efforts leave much to be desired. While mechanized transportation gets individuals to their places of employment and elsewhere, such transportation lacks the capacity to respond to anxiety, alienation, frustration, conflict, unhappiness, mental illness and scores of other societal ills. Concomitantly, increased technology, among other elements, has tended to change the styles of Americans to the extent that our "creations are controlling us" rather than our employing our creations. The society whose very composition is embedded in *companionship and voluntary association* cannot expect the resolution of critical problems to be forthcoming with increased technological advancement.

The society is also based on groups and grouping. It is expected that individuals will continue to migrate toward groups, to reject groups, and to adopt (sometimes at an alarming rate) group membership. Our organizational structure is staggering in its complexity and our need for acceptance by groups continues to be extremely strong. The society is a unique phenomenon. All of us are part of it—and few of us understand the dynamics of it as we close the decade of the seventies.

As far back as the earliest evolvement of our American society, a high premium was placed on such things as:

1. The dignity and worth of the individual;

2. His/her inalienable rights to pursue life, liberty, and happiness;

3. The duty and responsibility of society, institutions, and government to protect and nurture these rights; and

4. The belief that the people can only be assured such rights and conditions through a process whereby the governed are an integral and inseparable part of the governing process.

Even recently when the nation celebrated its bicentennial birthday, there were many Americans who pointed with pride to the accomplishments made in these and related areas.

There is little doubt that many criteria can be used as a yardstick to measure progress and accomplishments that this nation has witnessed during the past 200 years. Likewise, there is little doubt in some minds that the "tremendous" progress and the colossal accomplishments must be considered against a backdrop of annoying questions. How much of the progress and accomplishments are actually what they purport to be rather than delusions? Progress and accomplishments for whom and at what expense? To what extent has the American society actually realized progress when measured against its "rich" potential for progress?

Some doubt must be raised regarding the appropriateness of some of America's claim to fame in view of evidence that this society has sanctioned and supported a social and economic condition in which it is estimated that approximately five percent of the population controls 85 percent of the wealth. Thus, it can be said that within this socio-economic system, a small minority has been permitted to own and control the means of production and to utilize this process in the interest of personal profit. Because of this condition, a handful of persons have exercised (and continue to exercise) power in making decisions that determine to a greater extent the condition and fate of much of the remaining 95 percent of the population. Such decisions are naturally made in the interests of these persons and their particular class irrespective of the society as a whole, whose interests are usually sacrificed.

Some progress made within the American society has been realized only at the expense of an irresponsible assault on the environment. Today this assault threatens the very existence of life itself. More specifically, this assault has included:

1. The vulturous stripping and draining of our earth of its natural resources;

2. Using the atmosphere as a dumping ground for noxious chemicals;

3. Filling our oceans, rivers, lakes, and streams with detrimental waste materials.

Much of this assault can be traced to the selfish ventures of a minority in our society which possesses tremendous wealth and controlling power in America. A minority whose selfish profit producing activities are conducted without regard for their damaging effects to the existing population.

The Critical Realities. The continuance of America as a world leader in all aspects of human existence depends upon the establishment and maintenance of quality relationships. Which relationships? The list is endless, but we can start with: adult/child relationships; employer/employee relationships; older citizen/younger citizen relationships; male/female relationships; teacher/learner relationships; landlord/tenant relationships; salesperson/customer relationships; social worker/client relationships; physician/patient relationships; and attorney/client relationships.

The critical reality lies in the fact that the trust relationships in each of the above combinations have deteriorated to the point that it is almost impossible to conduct the service needed in those relationships. We have developed a sophistical legal system of reducing all contracts to written documents and—though this is very practical and feasible—we have permitted this legal style to permeate our entire lives. The trust relationship has been replaced with a legal relationship which deemphasizes voluntary societal associations of human beings. Thus, we have critical realities which are outgrowths of the first basic reality: *Lack of trust in other human beings.*

Critical Reality No. 2. A second critical reality is the realization of *population changes* and their accompanying impact on human perception. What are the moral implications of population change? In what way may we respond to growing world hunger and its relationship to population change? What about health care—both *preventive* health care and *remedial* health care? To what extent do we think of abortion at the same time that we think of adoption? What are the legal ramifications of population change? The critical reality occurs when we begin to examine the reaction of societal forces to human difference. We are well aware of the changes in socialization for our young (preschool age citizens) but we are unable to equate that socialization process to the changes in our ultimate population shifts. One of the reasons for this inability to face the critical reality resulting from population change is our lack of exposure to a philosophical base which *appreciates* rather than *tolerates* such changes.

Initially, the urban communities in America became crowded because more extensive technology was available there—among other conveniences, including greater employment. Large numbers of persons located geographically in the same place resulted in increased friction and conflict among human beings. The accompanying impact on human life has been widely documented and has advanced to our major concerns now about pollution and environmental defects.

Critical Reality No. 3. Critical reality No. 3 involves the continuing loss of *political integrity.* Some observers even speak of a "crisis in integrity" because the decade of the seventies was characterized by a tremendous loss of faith in the morality and the integrity of persons in whom the public had placed much trust. The visibility of persons whose personal weaknesses were so widely publicized resulted in limited participation in the democratic process (particularly the use of the ballot). This particular reality, perhaps more than others, threatens the very fiber of the quality of life in America. Our position is that the quality of life is the result of our political, economic, and social systems. The high quality of life which Americans have enjoyed has not been by accident, but rather by the deliberate design of specialists in the various systems. The general loss of integrity, however, cannot be experienced to the exclusion of its impact on curricular movement. The political structure on which we base our desires and exercise our best thinking for the good of the society has appeared in recent times to deteriorate before our very eyes. In order to improve the human condition and in order to increase the quality of life for all Americans we may need to begin a total restructuring of analysis related to the political behavior and political perceptions of Americans.

Alternatives to Societal Destruction. In this society, wealth and its concomitant power can and should be more equally distributed. Is there an arrangement in which our means of production and distribution can be owned more equitably by all people of this society? At any rate, such an equalization process could be successfully executed if given the necessary attention. The important consideration appears to be the inescapable demand for a more equitable distribution of wealth and power. For, until such a condition is realized, it is inevitable that certain individual and class interests will be enhanced at the expense of genuine humanity. Usually, it is the interest of the majority which is sacrificed.

Contrarily, the interests and the lives of each member within this society need not be sacrificed. No class or group need be the substance from which other classes or groups feed to sustain themselves. Each individual, in contrast, can be an essential force in this society and thus experience more completely the opportunities and resources therein.

A curtailment of the miserly assault on our precious natural resources and a *cessation* of the poisons we emit into the environment can change the course of societal direction. Failure to consider such curtailments in past societies has resulted in the inability of those societies to sustain human life. Is self-destruction inevitable for our society? Must we repeat the same societal mistakes?

We can continue utilizing the resources of our environment and advancing our technological efforts. However, we must do so within the constraints of ecological laws (laws which when viewed from any perspective should contain nothing new). For such have been the laws which have governed the natural existence of life throughout history. The ecology problem is one which is embedded in the economic, political, and social affairs of their society, solutions to which must find their counterparts in the solutions to those problems which prevent this society from reaching new levels of growth for all its constituents.

One such solution can reveal itself when government truly becomes more representative of all the people and of their best interests. The masses can become an essential and dynamic part of the governing process. In so becoming, the masses must, however, abandon their view of the state as some giant human entity and begin to see corrupt political behavior clearly. Elected officials are entrusted to balance the local interests of their constituency with the collective interests of the nation as a whole. Political officers supposedly have a commitment to the principles and ideals on which this society is based. A society dedicated to the belief that the only reason for government is to secure the rights, privileges, and protection of the governed is the only kind that can sustain itself in these times.

Each time that representative government acts, it implicates each member of this society into those acts. This means that we are no less than accomplices and fellow criminals in any detrimental acts of our elected officials. For this reason, literate societies that have adopted the general principles of survival—based on involvement of the governed—rely on the integrity levels of elected officials. Such reliance, then, has its direct relationship to the function of education—the development of human beings whose participation in that society is predicated on a practice of justice.

This requires a constant vigilance and monitoring of the behavior and affairs of our public office holders. It demands, based on past and current practices in government, that we critically approach each legislative act, rationale offered, and declamation made by these representatives.

Critical Reality No. 4. We are experiencing a tendency toward criminal behavior unprecedented in this century. Serious crime (both in the larger society and in the schools) continues to be a major problem. In a Report by the Senate Subcommittee To Investigate Juvenile Delinquency, it was indicated that in the first three years of this decade, the following crimes *increased* among juveniles: school-related homicides by 18.5 percent; rapes and attempted rapes by 40.1 percent; robberies by 36.7 percent; assaults on students by 85.3 percent; assaults on teachers by 77.4 percent; burglaries of school buildings by 11.8 percent; drug and alcohol offenses on school property by 37.5 percent; and number of weapons confiscated by school authorities by 54.5 percent.[1]

The increases during the early part of this decade have not yet reversed themselves. Secondly, these are just those acts of criminal behavior associated with school-age offenders. The pictures are not improved when we compile or list the adult offenders. Curricular alternatives to violence and vandalism are extremely limited. Most efforts, even by school specialists, have tended to be in the form of increased locks on buildings and *tightened security* rather than on the establishment of programmatic efforts to reach self-control levels.

[1] "Terror in Schools." *U.S. News and World Report*, January 1976.

Societal Injustice and American Minorities. Another form of injustice which has been historically perpetrated against a segment of this society is the perennial abuse of minorities. This has been indefensibly the case relative to the treatment of Mexican-Americans, Native American Indians, and blacks in this society. Of this group, the black American seems to have historically received the full force of these inequities. For, in addition to a background of slavery, skin color, texture of hair, and other distinguishing features have continually been used as bases for immediate exclusion.

Discrimination, segregation, and racism have been and are the manifestation of these exclusions. These are prevalent in all areas which are crucial and vital to the black person's survival, growth, and claim to the same quality of life in this society that others enjoy. Countless evidence will support this charge when considering:

1. The area of unemployment where the rate for blacks has been disproportionately high for decades;

2. Education where both overt and subtle racist practices have stifled the very raison d'être of this process;

3. Housing patterns for black families;

4. Health and medical care; and,

5. Equal protection under the law and the right of a fair and impartial trial when there is some question of law violations.

The psychological and social stress of such inequities leaves a wounded self-concept and sense of pride, dignity, and determination to succeed at given tasks which are crucial to a person in becoming all that he or she is capable of becoming.

Critical Reality No. 5. The decline in *authentic interpersonal relationships* between people who are different from each other results in a deterioration of the esteem in which we hold human life. The decade of the seventies has not, so far, brought us the solutions to human rejection based on ethnic, racial, economic, and political differences. Authenticity is crucial. Our lives have been bombarded with artificial factors and with "automatically conceived" solutions to the point that when this occurs in relationships across ethnic/racial identifications we are occasionally unable to distinguish the authentic from the imitative. Authentic interpersonal relationships with all people are critical—but those across ethnic/racial lines seem to take on even greater dimensions than others. To what extent are we prepared to respond to the loss of authenticity as described here? Are we psychologically educated and/or psychologically capable of responding to losses of this nature?

Formal Learning: A Societal Function. Education (formal learning) occupies an acute position in any attempt at refocusing the essentials in this society which will contribute to creating options to enhance life for all members. This is not, by any stretch of the imagination, an easy task especially in view of current educational conditions and practices. It is one, nonetheless, which should be approached as though the very survival of the society in question depended on it.

Many of the existing negative conditions in our society are permitted to exist through a process of mystification and distortion of reality. These are provided fertile soil in which to grow and consume the conscious awareness of the majority of people in this society. This fertility is *strengthened* by the mass media, "polished" tongues of politicians, and some of our institutions (particularly education), among others. This situation seems even more dismal when one considers the possibility that the whole process of deceit and the nurturing of half-truths appears to be a well-calculated effort to help maintain the unequal balance of power and wealth in our society as we now know it.

It is quite ironic that the one institution (education), which by its very nature should operate to counter such a process would be, at closer inspection, so intimately allied with it. For it is through this process that students become receptacles in which are poured these selected facts, data, and impressions that the society and its "appointed trustees" feel are indispensable. Deposited along with this conglomerate of "chosen knowledge" are biases, myths, and partial truths which assist in perpetuating the status quo.

The process is one in which the learner is deprived of any or given very little determination about what it is she should learn and the process through which she should learn it. These decisions are all made for her and supposedly in her behalf. The learner's roles then seem to be to remain passive and the learner accepts the dictates of her societal superiors.

Further, the educational setting (the school) is one in which students are rewarded for their docile acceptance of the process as is and others are reprimanded, sometimes severely, for their rejections of it. Complicating the procedure even more is the practice that certain students are rewarded and favored because of such extraneous factors as family status, income, and race. The other side of the coin is that other students are punished on the same grounds, thus being denied access to options which the favored groups enjoy.

In many instances, then, education in this society nurtures the growth of an end product which is other-directed and reliant, unquestioningly accepting of information (particularly when the source of that information can be traced to an "expert") , and void of creative inspiration. In other cases the end product is one whose face reflects dejection and broken promises. Products of such societal practices usually turn, in desperation, upon their societies because of feelings of oppression and exclusion.

First, what is the role of formalized education in any society? Has education assumed a more *initiative role* than a traditional *reactive role?* Our position is that education becomes attuned to the deeper pulsations of society in identifying the ramifications of its mission and the accomplishment thereof. *Deeper pulsations* is used here in contrast to such things as the flamboyance of political "double-talk," the shrewd manipulations of entrepreneurs, and the many deceptions transmitted through mass media. Once this awareness/realization has occurred, the education community must join hands with even more reflective elements of society in deciding what kind of improvements it would like to see emerge.

It is imperative that the analytical stage of this process not be treated lightly. In far too many instances, it becomes a common practice to center our analysis on the periphery of problems without penetrating their core. Thus the solutions which are offered are designed only to treat symptoms and leave the core of problems untouched.

A second major task of education is that it accepts a flexible and adaptive character. Can education eliminate the self-sustaining entity which is set apart from learners? If so, it must view one of its main functions as adapting to the various learning styles of its constituency. Learning must be viewed as a more dynamic change which evolves out of the student's interaction with the essential ingredients of the society's educational thrust and structure. When this change does not occur according to projections with *all* students, then it is time to cast a critical eye on the educational content, process, and structure and their implications for society. The intent of this is to make whatever alterations in these as may conduce to the desired development of all students.

Societal survival has historically been dependent on its ability to meet the expressed needs of its members. In much of the formal learning of present societies, the learner is seen as a "storage bank" into which regular deposits are made according to the perceptions of the educators. The ramification of this practice (and its ability to produce undesirable results) must be more clearly envisioned, not only in terms of its detrimental effects on individuals, but of its comprehensive impact on societal functions. What practices must be maintained and perpetuated? Which ones shall be discarded? And which shall be revised? Can our society develop a *diverse cultural pattern* of educating its young? Pupil demands for *acceptance of diversity of talent and skills* within the school's program suggest the need for reviews of much that we now demonstrate as sanctioned practice in schools.

The Individual

Our description of society was encompassed in terms denoting that two or more persons were involved. Voluntary associations implied that persons elected to function with each other. The concept of the *individual* embodies the notion that a single human being exists separate and apart from his/her associations. A single organism representing an indivisible entity comprises an *individual*. The implication is that an individual is a particular being as distinguished from a class, species, or collection. Individuality involves the total character distinguishing one from others. In relating the individual to the combined notion of justice, the society, and the individual, one becomes conscious of the interrelatedness of the three. Discussions attempting to separate the three have existed for years; however, our attempt here is to limit the discussion to the relationships peculiar to curricular responses.

The Association for Supervision and Curriculum Development was founded on the basic premise that *people are important*. Subscribers to ASCD's thrust are persons who share the belief in the significance of humankind. The individual, then, is in the center of the effort to describe or propose curricular responses. Pedagogical proficiency embracing the concept of individualized instruction has consistently supported the notion of human importance. Therefore, *individuals comprise the society and the society is the framework within which justice must be executed, analyzed, and practiced.*

Individuals, however, by their very nature represent *difference, diversity*, and *complexity*. Within the framework of human difference one must prepare for the ultimate quest of the good life.

Another View of Realities Regarding the School. While all these realities face us, there are those whose positions and visions have not permitted them to move (move within curriculum circles) in an effort to keep pace with the growing and changing realities. As we view the changing nature of schooling, of curriculum substance, or of procedural variations, can we continue to attempt functioning in traditional ways? The philosophical changes thrust upon the curriculum programs are moved away from (a) education for the selected few based on the caste system to (b) education for all, including changing the content and substance to confront new realities. Realities include war, sexual behavior, civil disorders, racial conflict—particularly in schools, poverty, the impact of television on our lives, and the continued awareness of "rights."

Within the past two decades we have moved through the following: civil rights; human rights (a broader concept) ; women's rights; children's rights.

Each of these new levels of awareness brought with it the accompanying necessity for curriculum response. We recognize that social attitudes are formed in relation to situations, persons, or groups with which the individual comes in contact in the course of his/her development. We all recognize that schools (and thus curriculum) touch the lives of more children in this country than any other institution. The feature that makes certain attitudes "social" is that they are formed in relation to social stimulus situations. Such is the case with concepts of justice and society. These stimuli result from contact with other persons, groups, or the products of human interaction—material and non-material.

Forming an attitude toward a group, an institution, a social issue, or the like is not an idle matter. It means one is no longer neutral to them; that they are value-laden in a positive or negative way. The end product of socialization at this level is embodied in the behaviors demonstrated by individuals as they function in societal frameworks.

Institutionalized inequality becomes part of the critical realities which support some of those cited earlier.

For example, justice rears its head when the following data are compiled:

Who goes to jail?

• 11 percent of the U.S. population is black, but 40 percent of U.S. prisoners are black.

• 14 percent more whites than blacks are paroled annually from federal prison.

• 97 percent of all prison administrators are white and 95 percent of all prison guards are white.

Average sentences:

• White Americans: 42.9 months; black Americans: 57.5 months.

Average sentences for income tax evasion:

• White Americans: 12.8 months; black Americans: 28.6 months.

Average sentences for drug-related cases:

• White Americans: 61.1 months; nonwhites: 81.1 months.[2]

---

[2] Source: Center for Urban Education, University of Nebraska, Omaha.

Lest the discussion of justice be limited to data such as those presented above (involving racial/ethnic inconsistencies), we share the following kinds of questions that are specifically school-related and deal with the *rights of students:*

1. What does the right to due process mean?

2. Do students have a right to a hearing each time a teacher or principal wants to punish them?

3. Can students be punished by being forbidden to participate in extracurricular activities without a hearing?

4. Does the student have a right to bring witnesses to a disciplinary hearing?

5. Can a student challenge his/her placement in a special school for disturbed or retarded children, or exclusion from regular school?

6. At what age may students rather than their parents have access to and control over the release of their school records?[3]

Answers to questions like those above could be very useful to a school administrator or curriculum worker who was in quest of justice for individuals entrusted to them.

The Capacity for Curricular Response. Whenever one begins to think of curricular response, the basic function of the curriculum arises as a question. Historically, the public school curriculum in America has been a *responder* rather than an *initiator.* At the same time, curriculum specialists have been called on to respond to pressing human problems. Substantive requirements within the school program of studies are frequently established in response to some pressing need (for example, heavy traffic casualties resulted in driver training classes and safety education). Because of this, it is no wonder that curriculum specialists are now working toward avenues through which responses might be forthcoming.

Our position is that curriculum substance and curriculum implementers both have the capacity to respond to the critical realities. Prior to the specifics of that response, however, must come a review of the philosophical bases. In a chapter on "Preserving the Dignity of Children in a Desegregated Society," the following is offered:

But before we can preserve it (dignity), we must assume that it exists. We must re-declare our belief in the dignity of children and youth. To what extent do I (the teacher) really believe in such ideas? Preservation of it involves other subsequent notions:

[3] Alan H. Levine *et al. The Rights of Students.* New York: Avon Books, 1973.

1. The way in which a teacher talks with learners

2. The territorial rights assumed by educators and others

3. The assumptions made about social class and economic class

4. The selection of instructional content which creates images

5. The analysis of decision-making practices and policies in adult/child relationships

6. The ability to share the power of decision making

7. The ability *to be assessed* by children and youth as well as to assess. (Assessing human behavior.) [4]

If such preservation is part of the philosophical base, then it is difficult to explain the following data regarding dropouts:

Who graduates from high school?

- 90 percent of all whites (enrolled)
- 65 percent of all blacks
- 27 percent of all Mexican Americans
- 26 percent of all Puerto Ricans.[5]

Our assumption is that affective concerns which embrace curricular response to essentially human problems are, in some instances, inconsistent with the extent of the problem. Of course, dropping out of secondary school is a complex entity which involves many variables, but the affective response must be part of that complexity.

When we recognize that interaction comprises the basic foundation upon which perceptions of life will rest (particularly among secondary learners), then our assessment of relationships within the curriculum/ school program begins to take on new significance. Justice is or has been too narrowly defined. Its application has been too limited. Its implications have not been disseminated widely enough. Confronting the nature of the realities also means confronting the nature of our personal styles, our pedagogical styles, and the manner in which we enhance and develop curriculum for responsive action.

Does the School Have the Power To Confront Realities? Power is also a complex word. Its basic notion implies control over variables, over others, or over other things. When we ask if the school has the power to confront realities, we are also asking if the school is free to find solutions to human problems through curricular effort. Indeed it is, and we urge school people to accept the challenge.

---

[4] James Boyer. "Preserving the Dignity of Children in a Desegregated Society." In: James and Joe L. Boyer, editors. *Curriculum and Instruction After Desegregation.* Manhattan, Kansas: AG Press Publishers, 1975. p. 14.

[5] Source: Center for Urban Education, University of Nebraska, Omaha.

Without any reservation, we take the position that real curricular response to critical realities must be one that is designed toward the elimination of several ills. Chief among these ills to be eliminated are racism, sexism, and elitism.

Curricular Efforts To Eliminate Racism, Sexism, Elitism. Curricular response which fails to embrace multicultural curriculum as one avenue toward facing critical realities is basically inadequate for the times. In other words, to acknowledge that a society is composed of many cultural and ethnic groups, of many economic groups, and of two sexual groups is to *expose a basic contradiction* in the concept of improving the human condition. The reduction of racism involves decreasing the belief that race is the primary determinant of human traits and capacities. It further involves decreasing the belief that racial differences produce the inherent superiority or inferiority of a particular race. The reduction of institutional racism involves the operation of those entities (the school is an example) which directly affect the lives of people and the philosophies on which their operations are based.

Sexism is the belief that one sex (male or female) is inherently superior to the other. Such belief manifests itself in behaviors which restrict one sex from opportunities, activities, and privileges normally granted to the other sex. Sexism is also demonstrated in the substance of curricular materials and in policies made within schools. (Both the material's substance and the discriminatory policies preclude justice for individuals.) In recent times, the ideas of sexism have referred primarily to discriminatory behavior against females, but it is not limited to this. Reduction of this belief would constitute one approach of curricular response.

Elitism is the idea that one group (usually an economic group) is better than another based on the value judgments of that group regarding their attributes and characteristics. Elitism involves the concept of social superiority because of economic advancement. Further, it incorporates the idea that one group in society is better able to govern and, therefore, should hold the political power. Elitism, however, may be practiced on several economic levels and may reflect a number of contributing factors. Vigorous curriculum response includes attempts to reduce the concept and practice of elitism by substantively declaring a notion of the *dispersal of power* in all its dimensions.

Justice Withheld. When individuals feel restricted in opportunities for participating in the full spectrum of American life, the behavioral response is often violence and vandalism—among other societal liabilities. Persons with experiences that are characterized by the withholding of justice (in classrooms, in courtrooms, on playgrounds, in business/indus-try, etc.) tend to develop a view of life whose attitude toward death, violence, and other similar ills is weakened. Limited opportunity to feel that objectivity characterizes your personal experiences results in human destruction at several levels.

We know that most violent crimes do not result in material gain for the offenders. Many are just demonstrating the degree of their frustra-tions. Our response to increased undesirable behavior has been increased codes and raised penalties. Curricular response requires that we work from a *preventive base* so that we commit equally as many resources to the prevention of crime, to "self-control" efforts, as we do through remediation efforts. Crime, incidentally, is not the only indication of the lack of justice in our society.

We call for the review of punitive personnel policies in schools, business, and in other organizations that have control over their own policies. We call for the review of procedures which, by their very nature, do not permit objectivity and full opportunity. We call for the dissemina-tion of information in a manner that *includes* rather than *excludes*.

We call for an analysis of instructional materials for their substance and their capacity for confronting some of the critical realities cited earlier. Our removal of chronic offenders has far surpassed our critical efforts toward regeneration. (Regeneration is preferred over rehabilita-tion.)

Curricular response will also involve increased pupil/consumer choice in policy, procedure, and evaluation and review of the extent to which our curricular programs fail the "perpetual losers." Everybody needs to win. All human beings respond to praise and encouragement. Continuous receipt of punishment teaches the systematic exclusion from the reward system. Curricular *exclusion* also contributes to human offenses and to the realities themselves.

We repeat that the institution of the school is a reflection of the larger society. Whenever justice is withheld in the larger society, it begins to be withheld in the school. Curriculum specialists work very hard at remaining aware of the total context in which behaviors and decisions emerge, but because of the rapidity with which current change emerges, it has sometimes forged ahead of us. Learners within the American school are primarily individually oriented, particularly at the younger ages. Their quest for justice is frequently encompassed in the resolution of conflict with other individuals within the school setting (playground fights, disagreement with teacher directives, etc.) .

As we analyze the delivery of justice within the context of the school, we must remember that the curriculum is composed of a variety of elements: program of academic studies, program of student activities, program of guidance—among others. This delivery system transcends the classroom and expands into the various activities in which learners participate. What behaviors are exhibited by the teacher that would be objectionable if demonstrated by the learner? (For example, teachers who sit on the desk in class would probably not endorse that same behavior in learners.) Do learners see that behavior—and some call it a freedom—as a withdrawal of justice because most learners are not free to sit on their desks? It is very possible. A further analysis of the display of justice in relation to the individual and the society (the school is its own micro-society) involves the following:

Crisis and Conflict Resolution. This dimension suggests that many interactions within the school emerge from direct conflict of ideas or perceptions. This occurs at every level of human interaction within the micro-society of the school. Administrators disagree and experience unhappiness with the declaration of certain decisions. Teachers and supervisors disagree, and learners disagree. Depending on the age level, many of these disagreements result in physical confrontation (fights). To what extent are these dealt with in light of a micro-judicial system? Are all of the curricular responses of short-range duration? Do they solve problems except for the minute?

Consciousness Raising. At another level, curricular response must be in relation to larger, more comprehensive issues and realities. To what extent does the curricular substance incorporate the consciousness raising with regard to pollution and environmental disorder? Are these consciousness-raising efforts *limited to a course* on environmental education? Is consciousness raising a regular part of the curricular thrust? Are procedures generated for teacher behavior which is designed to diminish erratic decision making? Are our efforts still considerably limited to *legal* consciousness raising? Or have we begun to consider *moral* consciousness raising? Do we really involve learners in the awareness training of self-and-others? To what extent do we study the dynamics of a particular school, community, region? Part of this must also include pedagogical consciousness raising.

Long-Range Curricular Response. The task at hand is one of ultimately improving the totality of instruction through the use of curricular substance of extended duration. The human quality is still extremely complex. The values extolled have not changed radically where human life is concerned. Long-range curricular response, however, involves serious study of the *impact of curricular response.* To what extent will learners be affected by today's schooling in the process of choosing a basic behavioral pattern for adulthood? How seriously do they take the substance (content) of literary assignments, student activities? Long-range response suggests that increased professional attention must be given to the changes in curriculum which will yield the kind of interaction among *justice, the society, and the individual* that would be operable decades from now.

Can the study of these entities continue to be ignored? Human dignity—as a characteristic of civilized societies—must be nurtured if the society is to avoid self-destruction. At what cost is the enhancement of human dignity for all societal members?

Selected Readings

R. W. Baldwin. *Social Justice.* Long Island City, New York: Pergamon Press, 1966.

Benjamin N. Cardozo. *Paradoxes of Legal Science.* Westport, Connecticut: Greenwood, 1928.

Thomas Fenton. *Education for Justice: A Resource Manual.* Maryknoll, New York: Obris Books, 1975.

A. V. Freeman. *International Responsibility of States for Denial of Justice.* Millwood, New York: Kraus, 1938.

Carl J. Friedrich, editor. *Justice.* New York: Lieber-Atherton, 1974.

Howard Kiefer and Milton Munitz, editors. *Ethics and Social Justice.* Albany: State University of New York Press, 1970.

N. M. Nathan. *The Concept of Justice.* Atlantic Highlands, New Jersey: Humanities Press, Inc., 1972.

John Rawls. *Theory of Justice.* Cambridge, Massachusetts: Harvard University Press, 1971.

Whitney N. Seymour, Jr. *Why Justice Fails.* New York: William Morrow and Company, Inc., 1974.

Andrew Von Hirsch. *Doing Justice.* New York: Hill and Wang, Inc., 1976.

7 The Learning of Values

James John Jelinek

ON THE BASIS of the work of Wilhelm Wundt, Emil Kraeplin, Alfred Binet, Lewis Terman, Charles Spearman, Cyril Burt, Karl Pearson, and others in intelligence testing, teachers of previous generations had serious concerns about the educability of their individual students— about the capacity of their students to learn. As an aftermath of the present era of operant conditioning in education, teachers of the future might very well have a different kind of concern about the educability of their students, especially in terms of what I identify as the arrestment paradox.[1]

The Arrestment Paradox in the Learning of Values

The history of education highlights basic disagreements of pioneer investigators in the field of scientific learning theory: William James, the first great American writer in the area of learning, posited the hypothesis that repetition is "the great law of habit." His student, E. L. Thorndike, found it impossible to make the law of repetition ("use") account for all his experimental findings and formulated the "law of effect." John B. Watson, by way of his affinity for Pavlovian thought, concluded that the conditioned response is "the fundamental unit of habit." Within the last four decades many investigators have vigorously pursued the implications and the relationships of these various fundamental concepts which were formulated during the first decades of the century. The result has been an ambitious attempt by psychologists, among the first of whom was E. B. Holt[2] in 1931, to base the psychology of learning exclusively upon the principle of conditioning.

[1] James John Jelinek. *Principles and Values in School and Society.* Tempe, Arizona: Far Western Philosophy of Education Society, 1976.
[2] E. B. Holt. *Animal Drive and the Learning Process.* New York: Henry Holt and Company, Inc., 1931.

183

Foremost among the early critics of the single principle theory of conditioning was O. Hobart Mowrer who stated, "there are two basic learning processes: the process whereby the solutions to problems, that is, ordinary 'habits' are acquired, and the process whereby emotional learning, or 'conditioning,' takes place." "Similarly," he stated, "in the field of education it is useful to differentiate between teaching and training" to help decide "the oft-debated question as to whether 'indoctrination' is a legitimate function of education." A distinction between teaching and training, he said, also was "relevant to the issues which have arisen between progressive education and more traditional educational philosophies."[3]

Today, what light can an intensive examination of these critical analyses of pioneer investigators of 25 to 75 years ago bring to bear on the effects of training on learning as contrasted with the effects of teaching on learning?

Pavlov's experiment of the dog, the meat, and the bell is too well known to require retelling here, but it is important to reconstruct the main point of the experiment, that point being that artificial stimuli can become incorporated into the makeup of an individual. For a dog to salivate when meat was brought to it was to be expected, but no one in Pavlov's time would have supposed that a dog would salivate when a bell was rung. Yet by ringing a bell every time meat was brought, Pavlov was able to "condition" dog nature so salivation took place merely at the ringing of the bell, without the presence of meat. Out of this and subsequent experiments the idea of the "conditioned response" entered the thinking of our century.

In these experiments what was found to be true of the dog was easily shown to be true of a human being. A person can be conditioned to be a creature that he or she otherwise is not. The act of conditioning is the act of training—the mode by which an artificial stimulus becomes built into the structure of any living organism, including, of course, a human being. By way of training a person can be conditioned to eat an olive and like it, to kill another person and feel proud of it, to insult a minority race and feel justified in doing so.[4] The eating of the olive is accompanied by approving smiles; the killing of a fellow human being is accompanied by citations, medals, and praise; the insult to a minority race is accompanied by praise for the concern of the majority. In each

---

3 O. H. Mowrer. "On the Dual Nature of Learning: A Reinterpretation of 'Conditioning' and 'Problem-Solving'." *Harvard Educational Review* 17:102-48; 1947. Copyright © 1947 by President and Fellows of Harvard College.

4 George G. Nathan. *The New American Credo: A Contribution Toward the Interpretation of the American Mind.* New York: Alfred A. Knopf, Inc., 1927. passim.

case the artificial stimulus is so closely tied up with the satisfaction of a particular want that the response to the stimulus is felt to be "natural."

Yet what seems to be "natural" turns out to be grossly "unnatural." It would seem to be likely that a person, or even an animal, would be alert to the consequences of his or her acts: if the consequence is favorable, the action producing it would be perpetuated; if the consequence is unfavorable, the action producing it would be abandoned. However, in a state of arrestment, "negative disintegrationism,"[5] there is a paradox of behavior that is at the same time self-perpetuating and self-defeating. In this arrestment paradox, actions which have predominantly unfavorable consequences persist over a period of months, years, or even a lifetime. The actions in such instances are self-perpetuating and self-defeating.

Having observed the arrestment paradox in his experimental subjects, Pavlov concluded that it was a "chronic pathological state" caused (a) by a "clashing of excitatory and inhibitory processes" and (b) by "overexcitation." In both instances he conceived of the arrestment paradox as the resulting "disturbance of the higher nervous activity involving definite injury of or damage to the brain cells."[6] He regarded it as a "pathological" state involving structural or physiochemical derangement of cortical mechanisms. Because he felt the arrestment paradox to be a matter of brain damage, he thought therapy should follow traditional medical practices—sedation, rest, diet, and the like. These observations led Pavlov to an elaborate classification of constitutional, temperament types of dogs to the exclusive neglect of life-history factors. He had no conception of the extent to which what happens in one situation is influenced by what has been learned in past situations.

The fact of the matter is that the arrestment paradox is caused by the conditioning, the training process, itself. How to produce the arrestment paradox, or "vicious circle" or "psychopathic upset,"[7] as it is sometimes called, is a simple matter for the research physiologist: The animal is trained to react in certain ways to certain stimuli, and then is placed into a situation in which these responses are impossible. Although each of its attempts is blocked, the animal continues to go on responding as it has been trained to do, caught in the grips of the arrestment paradox, until it finally breaks down. Its actions become abnormal, quite different from what is natural to it in health. The sheep, normally gregarious, becomes solitary and morose, neither mingling with other sheep nor

5 James John Jelinek. "A Reconstructed Epistemology for Philosophy of Education." *Philosophy of Education: 1969.* Tempe, Arizona: Far Western Philosophy of Education Society, 1969.

6 I. P. Pavlov. *Conditioned Reflexes.* G. V. Anrep, translator. London: Oxford University Press, 1927. pp. 284, 318.

7 O. H. Mowrer, *op. cit.*

eating nor drinking nor responding even to the simplest and most familiar circumstances. Likewise the rat in the arrestment paradox continues responses that are self-perpetuating and self-defeating, continuing trained responses by dashing its head against a locked door until, bruised and bleeding, it batters itself to exhaustion.

Again, what is found to be true of animals is easily shown to be true of people. For example, the research studies on the condition of American youth completed by a staff of specialists for the National Youth Commission reveal that being a black youth means living in an intimate culture whose incentives, rewards, and punishments prevent the development of those types of personal standards, attitudes, and habits the general community deems desirable.[8] The society trains youth to live up to the ideals of the country—to cringe to no one, to choose one's own life work, to resist affronts to human dignity, to work toward honestly earned success—but the society puts black youth into the situation of the animal in the psychological laboratory in which the arrestment paradox is to be caused by making it impossible to live up to those national ideals as other youth in America do. There are indeed among our students those whose behavior patterns give evidence of the arrestment paradox, those who give evidence of self-perpetuating, self-defeating behavior characterized by the same bewildered, senseless tangle of abnormal nerve reactions studied in animals by psychologists in laboratory experiments.

The basic assumption of training is that one's behavior can be conditioned effectively through external stimuli—by grades, money, or other rewards. This assumption postulates a certain view of the nature of human beings and of society that is saturated with materialism, bred in mechanism, and steeped in empiricism. The consequences of this mode are identifiable: The person (a) does not think and is characterized by mindlessness, (b) becomes the prey of those who do the conditioning, (c) loses the desire to find out the "why" of life, (d) loses the ability to formulate ideals and to bring them to fruition, (e) becomes a passive individual upon whom habits are impressed by the trainer, (f) becomes anti-intellectual, (g) relinquishes responsibility for his or her own actions, (h) turns to violence when rewards are withheld, (i) loses the freedom to infinite individuality,[9] (j) becomes limited in perspective, (k) is law-abiding only when being observed, (l) learns gamesmanship, especially the game of revenge.

Until recently there has been little evidence to show how the twelve

---

[8] Winfield H. Rogers *et al. Explorations in Living: A Record of the Democratic Spirit.* New York: Reynal and Hitchcock, 1941. p. 198.

[9] B. F. Skinner. *Beyond Freedom and Dignity.* New York: Alfred A. Knopf, Inc., 1971.

billion cells within the brain store memory. The most noted explorer in this field has been Wilder Penfield who has conducted a series of experiments during which he has touched the temporal cortex of the brain of a patient with a weak electric current transmitted through a galvanic probe.[10] On the basis of this research it was concluded (a) that the electrode evokes a single recollection, not a mixture of memories or generalization, (b) that not only past events are recorded in detail but also the feelings that were associated with those events, (c) that the brain functions as a high-fidelity recorder of every experience from birth, and (d) that the person exists in two states at the same time—that is, is at the same time *in* the experience and *outside* of it, observing it.

The Development of Central Value-Learning Ego States

A significant extension of the research by Penfield came from Lawrence S. Kubie during the course of which he concluded "that early in life, sometimes within the earliest months, a central value position is established. . . . The clinical fact which is already evident is that once a central value position is established it becomes the affective position to which that individual will return automatically for the rest of his days."[11]

There are three basic conceptualizations of self (central value positions or ego states) that can be developed—that of the Trainee, that of the Trainer, and that of the Teacher/Learner.

The Trainee Ego State: Characteristics. In the Trainee ego state the individual feels at the mercy of others. As a child one lacks the equipment and experience necessary to form a different conceptualization of self, so one's only guide is the reactions of others. There is little cause for questioning these appraisals, and in any case one is far too helpless to challenge them or to rebel against them. One passively accepts the judgments which are communicated empathetically at first, and by words, gestures, and deeds in this period. . . . Thus the self-attitudes (conceptualizations of self) are carried forever by the individual, with some allowance for the influence of extraordinary environmental circumstances and modification through later experiences.[12] Thus, basic to the development of the Trainee ego state (conceptualization of self) is the mode of manipulation, the mode of reward and punishment, by the trainer.

10 Wilder Penfield. "Memory Mechanisms." *American Medical Association Archives of Neurology and Psychiatry* 67:178-98; 1952.

11 Lawrence S. Kubie. "The Neurotic Process as the Focus of Physiological and Psychoanalytic Research." *The Journal of Mental Science* 104 (435) ; 1958.

12 Harry Stack Sullivan. *Psychoanalytic Theories of Personality.* G. S. Blum, editor. New York: McGraw-Hill Book Company, 1953.

Submission to authority, desire for a strong leader to tell in behavioristic terms what to do, when to do it, how to do it, and even how to feel about it, all characterize the Trainee ego state. Authoritarian submission is evoked in relation to a variety of authoritarian figures—parents, older people, political leaders, academic trainers, supernatural power, and the like. The Trainee ego state is characterized by an exaggerated, all-out emotional need to submit. This would be indicated by agreement that obedience and respect are the most important virtues children should learn, and that a person should obey without question the decisions of the trainer. In this sense there is a certain masochistic component to the Trainee ego state.

The Trainer Ego State: Characteristics. The Trainer ego state, on the other hand, is essentially made up of behavior copied from parents or authority figures. A person in the Trainer ego state is a playback of the trainer. Thus, in this state the person is essentially nonperceptive and noncognitive. He employs a constant and arbitrary basis for decisions, and serves as a repository of traditions and values of his or her own trainers.

The Trainer ego state is developed at a time when the individual lives under a system of rigid restraints and for this reason feels put upon and is likely not only to seek a person to "take it out on" but also be particularly annoyed at the idea that that person as an object is "getting away with something." There is a sadistic component to the Trainer ego state, just as there is the masochistic component to the Trainee ego state.

The person in a Trainee ego state who cannot bring himself to criticize his trainers has a desire to condemn, reject, and punish those who violate these values. Once the individual is convinced there are people who ought to be trained, he has the mode through which his impulses may be expressed, even while thinking of himself as thoroughly moral.

The Teacher/Learner Ego State: Characteristics. When a person is in a Teacher/Learner ego state she regards herself and others as subjects, a subject being one who knows and acts, rather than as objects, an object being one who is known and is acted upon. She is inner, rather than outer, directed. She invokes modes of inquiring, hypothesizing, problem-solving, and reconstructing experience. Growth for her is a matter of rethinking an experience, thus facing each subsequent situation a different person.[13]

In these terms, the philosophical implications of training as con-

---

[13] James John Jelinek. "Presidential Address." *Philosophy of Education: 1972-1973.* Tempe, Arizona: Far Western Philosophy of Education Society, 1973.

trasted with teaching can be stated by way of principles, the independent variables of which identify the behaviors inherent in the ego state and the dependent variables of which identify the consequences of those actions:

The Trainee Ego State: Behaviors and Consequences. The basic principles of the Trainee ego state include the following:

Necrophileticism. If individuals are alienated from their own decision making, then they change into objects.

Passivism. If students (trainees) accept the passive role imposed upon them by their trainers, they adapt to the world as it is and to the fragmented view of reality deposited in them.

Action. If persons are frustrated in their efforts to act responsibly, if they find themselves unable to use their faculties, then they experience a sense of anguish which causes them to reject their impotence by submitting to and identifying with a charismatic person, a benevolent trainer, or a group having power, thus by this symbolic participation in another's life having the illusion of acting, when in reality they are only submitting to and becoming a part of those who act.

Essentialism. If trainees work at storing deposits entrusted to them, then they do not develop the critical approaches necessary for the reconstruction of their experience.

Exploitation. If the oppressed remain unaware of the causes of their condition, then they fatalistically accept their exploitation.

Self. If the oppressed is at the same time himself and the oppressor whose will he has internalized, then he is confronted over and over again with the choice between being a whole self or a divided self, between following another's prescriptions or his own values, between speaking out or being silent, between experiencing respect or alienation, between being a spectator or an actor, between being a phony person or an authentic person.

The Trainer Ego State: Behaviors and Consequences. The basic principles of the Trainer ego state are as follows:

Conditioning. If a trainer sets up environmental situations that force trainees to make those responses desired by her, if she reinforces those responses when they occur, if she creates an emotional response of acceptance of both herself and those competencies that are to be learned, if she presents problem-solving situations in this context of acceptance, if she extinguishes largely through nonreinforcement and partly through mildly punishing contingencies behavior that interferes with the trainees' learning the competencies she wants them to learn, if she presents situations in which the trainees know in strict behavioristic terms what they are to learn to do, if the trainees receive immediate feedback from their trainer concerning responses they make and they compare their progress with their past performance to see if they are doing what they are supposed to do, then the trainer changes the behavior of the trainees, individually and in groups, so that they behave in ways she wants them to behave and they do not behave in ways she does not want them to behave.

Democracy. If a society and its institutions, especially educational institutions, preach about democracy as a philosophy to the exclusion of implementing it as a technique, then its young are easy marks for any dictator who sets his sights upon them and manipulates them—their thoughts, feelings, and actions—for his personal aggrandizement.

Didacticism. If the trainer and trainee relationship at any level, inside or outside the school, is narrative in character, if it involves a narrating subject (the trainer) and patient listening objects (the trainees), then (a) education becomes the act of depositing in which trainees are the depositories and the trainers are the depositors, (b) the content of instruction, whether it be descriptive or valuational, is lifeless, petrified, motionless, static, compartmentalized—alien to the existential experience of the trainees, detached from the meaning and the totality that engendered it and could give it significance, (c) the narration leads the students to memorize mechanically the narrated content, turns them into containers to be filled by the trainer—thus the more completely the container is filled the better the trainer; the more meekly the containers permit themselves to be filled, the better trainees they are, (d) the approach is irrelevant to the reconstruction of experience of the trainee, (e) knowledge is a gift bestowed by those who consider themselves knowledgeable to those whom they consider to know nothing, (f) the approach minimizes and annuls the creative power of the trainees and encourages their credulity in such a way as to serve the interests of the oppressors who care neither to have the world nor the experience of the trainees reconstructed, (g) the interests of the oppressors lie in changing the consciousness of the oppressed, not the situation which oppresses them, for the more the oppressed can be led to adapt to the situation the more easily they can be dominated, (h) the approach masks the effort to turn humans into automatons and thereby negates their efforts at humanization, (i) the oppressors react forcefully against any action in the educational situation which stimulates the critical faculties of the trainees who seek to solve the problems of their own lives, (j) the oppressed are regarded as pathological cases of a healthy society, marginal individuals who deviate from the general configuration of a good society, and who must be trained to adapt to the world as it is and to the fragmented view of reality deposited in them, (k) the educated person is the adapted person because he/she is better fit for the world as it is.

Doublemindedness. If in a pedagogical encounter there is extrinsic motivation, divided attention, doublemindedness, that is, if the goals of the trainer are different from the goals of the trainee, if the demands of the trainer forbid the direct expression of the purposes of the learner, if the entire surrender and wholehearted adoption of the course of action demanded of the trainee by the trainer is impossible, if there is so-called "stern discipline"—external coercive pressure—if there is motivation through rewards extraneous to the thing to be done, if there is schooling that is merely preparatory, schooling with ends beyond the student's present grasp, if there is exaggerated emphasis upon drill exercise designed to produce skill in action independently of thought—exercises having no purpose but the production of automatic skill—if what is spontaneous and vital in mental action and reaction goes unused and untested, then (a) the trainee deliberately revolts or deliberately attempts to deceive others, (b) the outcome is a confused and divided state of interest in which the trainee is fooled as to his own real intent, (c) the trainee tries to serve two masters at once—on the one hand, he wants to do what is expected of him, to please others, to get their approval, to be apprehensive of penalty, to "pay attention to the lesson" or whatever the requirement is; but on the other hand, he wants to pursue his own purposes since the evident suppression of their exhibition does not abolish them, he finds irksome the strain of attention to what is hostile to desire, his underlying desires determine the main course of his thought and his deeper emotional responses in spite of his outward behavior, his mind wanders from the nominal subject and devotes itself to what is intrinsically more desirable, (d) there is an obvious loss of energy of thought immediately available when one is consciously trying to seem attentive to one matter while his imagination is spontaneously going out to more congenial affairs, (e) there is a subtle and permanent crippling of intelligent activity based upon the fostering of habitual self-deception inherent in the doublemindedness that hampers integrity and completeness of mental action, (f) a split is developed between conscious thought and attention and impulsive emotion and desire, (g) reflective dealings with the content of instruction are constrained and halfhearted attention wanders, (h) dealings with the interests of the student by the student become illicit; transactions with the student are furtive; the discipline that comes from regulating response by deliberate inquiry having a purpose fails; the deepest concern and most congenial enterprises of the imagination (since they center about the things dearest to desire) are casual and concealed; they enter into action in ways which are unacknowledged; and they are demoralizing because they are not subject to rectification by consideration of consequences.

Dehumanization. If teachers are well-intentioned trainers who do not realize they are serving only to dehumanize their students, if they fail to perceive their efforts to train are themselves contradictions about reality, then, sooner or later, these processes of dehumanization lead even passive students to turn against their trainers and to discover through existential experience that their present way of life is irreconcilable with their becoming fully human, and that, through their relations with others, reality is basically a process, undergoing constant transformation.

Domination. If there is domination of one person over another, if a person manipulates another to gain his or her own ends, then there is pathology of love—sadism in the dominator and masochism in the dominated.

The Teacher/Learner Ego State: Behaviors and Consequences. The basic principles of the Teacher/Learner ego state include the following:

Heurism. If the teacher and student relationship at any level, inside or outside the school, is heuristic in nature, if it involves modes of inquiring, hypothesizing, problem solving, if teachers and students are both subjects (a subject being one who knows and acts) rather than subjects and objects (an object being one who is known and is acted upon), then (a) education becomes a matter of responding to the intentionalities of the participants, (b) languaging replaces narrating, (c) acts of cognition replace transferrals of information, (d) cognizable objects (referents) intermediate cognitive individuals (the subjects—the teachers and the students), (e) dialogical relations are used to the fullest capacity of the cognitive actors (teachers and students) to cooperate in perceiving the same cognizable objects (referents), (f) the term subject or teacher/student replaces trainer-of-the-trainees and subjects or students/teachers replaces trainees-of-the-trainer, (g) the teacher is no longer merely the one-who-teaches, but one who is herself taught in dialogue with students, who, in turn, while being taught also teach; all become jointly responsible for the process in which they all grow, (h) no one teaches another, nor is anyone "self-trained"; individuals teach each other, mediated by the referents of their world, (i) the teacher/student is not cognitive in her preparation and narrative in her presentation, (j) the teacher/student does not regard cognizable objects (referents) as her private property but as the objects of reflection by herself and her students, (k) the teacher/student reconstructs her reflections in the reflections of students, (l) the students are critical coinvestigators in dialogue with the teacher, (m) the teacher/student studies reality with students and reconstructs her earlier reflections and considerations as the students express their own, (n) education involves a constant unveiling of reality, (o) education strives for the emergence of consciousness and critical intervention in reality, (p) teachers and students pursue problems relating to themselves *in* the world and *with* the world and feel increasingly more challenged and obliged to respond to that challenge, (q) authentic reflection considers persons in their reactions with the world, (r) students, simultaneously reflecting on themselves and on the world, increase the scope of their perception and begin to direct their observations toward previously inconspicuous phenomena, (s) students develop their power to perceive critically the way they exist in the world with which and in which they find themselves; they come to see the world not as a static reality, but as a reality in process, in reconstruction.

Dialogue. If individuals speak their word, name the world, and reconstruct it in thought and/or action, then their dialogue becomes the way in which they attain significance as persons: (a) the dialogue is not reduced to the act of one individual's depositing ideas into another, (b) it is not a simple exchange of ideas to be consumed by discussants, (c) it is not a hostile, polemical argument between individuals who are committed not to the search for truth and meaning but rather to the imposition of their own truth and meaning, (d) it is not a situation in which some individuals name the world on behalf of others, (e) it is not a crafty instrument for the domination of one individual by another.

Education. If education is carried on by "A" for "B" or by "A" about "B," if oppressors act upon people to indoctrinate them and adjust them to a reality which must remain unreconstructed, then the ensuing behaviors are training behaviors that are, in themselves, acts of violence; if, on the other hand, education is carried on by "A" with "B," if the participants ask themselves what they will dialogue about, then the preoccupation with the content of the dialogue is a preoccupation with curriculum in authentic education, mediated by the world, a world which impresses and challenges both teacher and student, giving rise to descriptions and valuations about it impregnated with hopes, anxieties, doubts, and the like.

Interactionism. If an individual perceives content as instrumental toward eliminating a factor that disintegrates his dynamic equilibrium, then (a) he pursues that content with a discipline, even if it is at first unpleasant to him, (b) he considers it a means to an end, (c) he learns it, (d) he builds it into structure so that he can use it whenever the disintegrative factor reappears, and (e) he develops pleasure in it.

Conscientiatization. If human beings gain inner freedom, then they learn conscientiatization—to perceive social, political, sexual, religious, and economic contradictions and to take action against the oppressive elements of the society that create these contradictions.

Reconstructionism. If a person rethinks his experience, then he faces each subsequent situation a different person.

Disintegrationism. If the dynamic equilibrium of the individual is disintegrated, then (a) he responds to remove the disintegrative factor, (b) his responses continue if his first response is not instrumental in the removal, (c) his responses vary, and (d) he builds into structure the response that effectively removes the disintegrative factor.

Epistemology in the Learning of Values

Epistemology is basically concerned with those principles upon which an individual can rely when going about the crucial business of developing that most precious of possessions—human knowledge, values, and effective intelligence. On these grounds a theory of epistemology sets forth principles of how a person knows what she knows. Such a theory is the theory of Positive and Negative Disintegrationism.

According to this theory an individual is always a part of an environment. Within that environment she is self-regulative. If anything occurs within the person or within the environment to disintegrate her dynamic equilibrium, she responds to that disintegrative factor. Her responses *continue* and they *vary* until her dynamic equilibrium is restored.

In other words, if old responses are inadequate to eliminating a factor that disintegrates a person's dynamic equilibrium, the person contrives different responses that *are* adequate to eliminating it. Thereafter, she uses these newly contrived, effectively established responses whenever that factor again disintegrates her dynamic equilibrium.

In this sense the newly contrived response brings a change, an increment, to the structure of the person herself. She is not now exactly the same person she was before she contrived the response that eliminated the factor that disintegrated her dynamic equilibrium.

If a factor inside or outside the individual disintegrates her dynamic equilibrium, if the person contrives a response new to her that discombobulates that disintegrative factor and restores her dynamic equilibrium, if she builds that response into structure for future use, and if she can reconstruct it when circumstances and contingencies seem to warrant such reconstruction, positive disintegrationism prevails. Clearly the individual by way of positive disintegrationism develops effective intelligence: She develops behavior which is guided by an anticipation of consequences.

She makes it possible for herself to rethink her behavior and to face subsequent situations a different person.

If, however, an individual contrives a response to a disintegrative factor that cuts off further growth and is not amenable to reconstruction, negative disintegrationism prevails. Negative disintegrationism is adevelopmental and is characterized by (a) a stabilization or involution of primitive impulses, (b) a clear lack of symbolization and creativity, (c) a feeble growth pattern and retarded realization of goals, and (d) a lack of tendency to transformation of structure.

Positive disintegrationism can be distinguished from negative disintegrationism by the prevalence of multilevel actions over unilevel actions. Multilevel actions, for example, are largely conscious, independent, and influential in determining personality structure. They include such actions as arousal of shame, feeling of discontent, and sense of guilt with respect to the person's concept of self. Unilevel actions, on the other hand, are largely characterized by a compact and automatic structure of impulses to which intelligence is a completely subordinated entity. They include actions that are limited to direct, uninhibited, and immediate satisfaction of primitive impulses. Individuals characterized by such actions are not able to understand the meaning of time; they cannot postpone immediate gratification; and they cannot follow long-range plans. They are limited to the reality of immediate, passing feelings. They are not capable of evaluating, selecting, or rejecting environmental influences or of changing their typological attitudes.

The following statement written by a student is an example of multilevel, positive disintegrationism:

For several years, I have observed in myself obsessions with thinking, experiencing and acting. These obsessions involve my better and worse, higher and lower character. My ideals, my future vocation, my faith in my friends and family seem to be high. Everything that leads me to a better understanding of myself and my environment also seems high, although I am aware of an increased susceptibility for other people's concerns which cause me to neglect or abandon "my own business." I see the lower aspects of my character constantly in my everyday experiences: in decreased alertness to my own thoughts and actions, a selfish preference for my own affairs to the exclusion of other people's, in states of self-satisfaction and complacency . . .

Also, I see my lower nature expressed in a wish for stereotyped attitudes, particularly in regards to my present and future duties. Whenever I become worse, I try to limit all my duties to the purely formal and to shut myself away from responsibilities in relation to what goes on about me. This pattern of behavior makes me dejected. I am ashamed of myself; I scold myself. But I am most deeply worried by the fact that all these experiences do not seem to bring about any sufficient consolidation of my higher attitudes, do not influence my "self" to become my "only self." I remain at once both higher and lower. I often fear that I lack sufficient force to change permanently to a real, higher man.[14]

Disintegrationism, then, is positive when it enriches life, opens vistas, and brings forth hypothesizing; it is negative when it cuts off growth or causes involution or regression.

The following statement written by a young man characterized by affective and cognitive excitability in a period of emotionally retarded puberty is an example of unilevel, negative disintegrationism:

I cannot understand what has recently happened to me. I have periods of strength and weakness. Sometimes I think I am able to handle everything and at others a feeling of complete helplessness. It seems to me at some hours or days that I am intelligent, gifted, and subtle. But then, I see myself as a fool.

Yesterday, I felt very hostile toward my father and mother, toward my whole family. Their movements and gestures, even the tones of their voices struck me as unpleasant. But today, away from them, I feel they are the only people I know intimately.

I often have sensations of actual fear when watching tragic plays and movies; yet, at the same time, I weep for joy or sorrow at what I see and hear, especially when the heroes mostly lose in their struggles or die.

I often have thoughts full of misgivings, anxiety, and fear. I feel that I am persecuted, that I am fated. I have a trick of repeating phrases, like a magic formula, which drives out these obsessive thoughts. At other times, I merely laugh at such notions; everything seems simple and easy.

I idealize women, my girl friends, mostly. I have feelings of exclusiveness and fidelity toward them, but at other times I feel dominated by primitive impulses.

I hate being directed by others, but often I feel no force within me capable of directing my actions.[15]

Clearly evident here is instability of structure and attitude, lack of an articulated value structure, and absence of a meaningful concept of self.

Positive disintegrationism thus can be differentiated from negative disintegrationism in various ways: The presence of consciousness, self-control, and self-consciousness; the predominance of global forms of disintegrationism over narrow, partial ones; the flexibility of cognitive and affective transformations; the prevalence of multilevel actions over uni-level actions; the presence of tendencies to hypothesize; and the absence of automatic and stereotyped responses all characterize the disintegrative process to be positive rather than negative.

[14] Kazimierz Dabrowski. *Positive Disintegrationism*. Boston: Little, Brown and Company, 1964. p. 9.
[15] *Ibid.*, pp. 7-8.

The implications of positive and negative disintegrationism for education are of far-reaching significance. While most lay and professional persons regard the broad range of processes from emotional disharmony to complete fragmentation of the personality as harmful to the person and to the society of which he or she is a part, those disruptive factors, according to disintegrationism, are generally positive developmental processes, their negative aspects being only marginal, a small part, and a relatively unimportant part, in the evolutionary development of the person.

More specifically, the present prevalent view is that disintegrative factors such as disquietude, shame, discontentment, guilt, inferiority, anxiety, and nervousness and factors that characterize hysterics, psychasthenics, paranoics, and schizophrenics, factors that discombobulate the dynamic equilibrium, are disorders that are psychopathological in nature. According to the theory of disintegrationism, however, they are not only not psychopathological disorders but rather profound expressions of developmental continuity—they are behavioral examples of positive disintegrationism at work. Perhaps a specific example can clarify the point:

On the basis of her admission examination Jane Doe, seven and one-half years old, is admitted to the second grade of a public school. In this situation she has many difficulties: She is overexcitable. She has trouble eating. She cannot sleep. She cries at night. She experiences a rapid loss of weight. She shows signs of sporadic anxiety and transient depression. Under these circumstances she asks her parents to have her transferred to the first grade.

Jane's mother is a harmonious person, rather introverted, and systematic in her work. She is concerned about the long-range implications of Jane's difficulties. Jane's father is dynamic, self-conscious, and self-controlled. He is characterized by cyclic and schizothymic traits. Both the mother and the father feel Jane is obedient, overexcitable, ambitious, independent, and sensitive in her own private way. Both consent to the administration of medical and psychological examinations to Jane, all of which thus far have been negative.

What would be the effect if these symptoms were considered to be psychopathological and treated by intensive psychotherapy? To begin with, the emotional, introverted, and self-conscious child could be deeply injured. Identifying the behaviors of Jane as pathological, thus making intensive psychotherapy necessary, would in itself have negative effects, not the least of which would be that those with whom Jane associates would consider her to be mentally disturbed, her parents would treat her with increasingly greater apprehension and perhaps artificiality, her teacher would consider her to be abnormal and behave accordingly, and

Jane herself, with the focus of pathology upon her, would accentuate her anxiety, inhibition, and flight into sickness, into negative disintegrationism.

What, on the other hand, would be the effect if the symptoms were considered to be those of a child with a high potential for development, a development that could be enhanced by a crisis precipitated by a new and different situation? One of the discernible effects would be the building into structure of the results of her continued and varied responses to the disintegrative factor—the crisis—hindered, it is true, by her inhibition, but supported by her obligations, her ambitions, and her determination to handle new situations despite her anxiety. Another effect would be the increased awareness on her part of the positive rather than the negative function of her symptoms. Still another effect would be that she would decrease her inhibition, strengthen her ability to hypothesize, and open vistas for her further development.[16]

In summary, then, the theory of positive and negative disintegrationism is basically concerned with the formulation of those principles of epistemology upon which individuals can rely when, first, they develop human knowledge, values, and effective intelligence for themselves, and second, they attempt to determine how they know what they know. Stated in terms of "If . . . , then . . ." relationships, these principles include the following: (a) If the dynamic equilibrium of an individual is disintegrated, he responds to that disintegrative factor on a continued and varied basis until the disintegrative factor is eliminated. (b) If the individual contrives a response that eliminates a factor that disintegrates his dynamic equilibrium, he builds that response into structure for future use. (c) If the individual rethinks his response to a factor that disintegrates his dynamic equilibrium, he faces each subsequent situation a different person. (d) If the individual in confronting a factor that disintegrates his dynamic equilibrium develops a response that cannot be changed, he adds an increment to his structure that stultifies further growth. It is on the basis of these foundational principles, then, that individuals do or do not develop values that serve them as guides to conduct.

The Nature of Human Values

In his colossal study on *The Nature of Human Values* sponsored by the National Science Foundation and the Center for Advanced Study in the Behavioral Sciences, Milton Rokeach analyzes huge collections of statistical data purporting to identify (a) the values of American society

16 *Ibid.*, pp. 23-27.

by sex, income, education, race, age, religion, and politics and (b) the values of certain substrata in American society—counselors, hippies, non-hippies, homosexuals, professors, police, priests, seminarians, lay persons, students, scientists, writers, artists, business executives, small entrepreneurs, salespeople, and the like.[17] The report is written with two audiences in mind: first, it is written for professionals in all the social science disciplines and in philosophy and religion as well; second, it is written for college students as a textbook in courses on human values. It is on these grounds that a basic, critical, and philosophical analysis of the assumptions foundational to the Rokeach study is warranted.

On the basis of his study of A. O. Lovejoy,[18] Robin Williams,[19] Clyde Kluckhohn,[20] M. Brewster Smith,[21] and Fred Strodtbeck,[22] Rokeach identifies eight assumptions upon which his study is based: (a) The total number of values that a person possesses is relatively small—18 terminal values and 18 instrumental values. (b) All people everywhere possess the same values to different degrees. (c) Values are organized into value systems. (d) The antecedents of human values can be traced to culture, society and its institutions, and personality. (e) The consequences of human values will be manifested in virtually all phenomena that social scientists might consider worth investigating and understanding. (f) Values are enduring mainly because they are initially taught and learned in isolation from other values in an all-or-none manner, such-and-such a mode of behavior or end-state always being desirable. (g) A value is a mode of conduct (an instrumental value) *or* an end-state of existence (a terminal value) . (h) "Every human value is a 'social product' that has been transmitted and preserved in successive generations through one or more of society's institutions."[23]

On the basis of these assumptions Rokeach presents to each of his respondents two lists of 18 alphabetically arranged instrumental values

[17] Milton Rokeach. *The Nature of Human Values.* New York: Free Press, 1973. passim.

[18] A. O. Lovejoy. "Terminal and Adjectival Values." *Journal of Philosophy* 47:593-608; 1950.

[19] Robin Williams. In: E. Shils, editor. *International Encyclopedia of the Social Sciences.* New York: Macmillan Publishing Co., Inc., 1968.

[20] Clyde Kluckhohn. "Values and Value Orientations in the Theory of Action." In: T. Parsons and E. A. Shils, editors. *Toward a General Theory of Action.* Cambridge, Massachusetts: Harvard University Press, 1952.

[21] M. Brewster Smith. *Social Psychology and Human Values.* Chicago: Aldine Publishing Company, 1969.

[22] Fred Strodtbeck and Clyde Kluckhohn. *Variations in Value Orientation.* Evanston, Illinois: Row, Peterson and Company, 1961.

[23] Milton Rokeach, *op. cit.,* pp. 3.

and 18 terminal values, each value being presented along with a brief definition in parentheses. Each respondent is instructed to arrange the values "in order of importance to *you*, as guiding principles in *your* life."[24]

By way of this approach he establishes frequency distributions of rankings obtained for each of the 18 terminal values and the 18 instrumental values separately for American men and women and separately for subgroups varying in income, education, race, age, religion. How the rank orders of the respondents are analyzed by Rokeach is shown in Tables 1 and 2.[25]

In a most impressive array of statistical analyses, Rokeach uses the nonparametric median test as the main test of statistical significance of his data, but no amount of statistical significance covers the inadequacy of the basic assumptions upon which the entire study is founded. As Dewey pointed out more than three decades ago, what is a value—end-state of existence—is "determined in its concrete makeup by appraisal of existing conditions as means." "The assumption of a separation between things useful as means and things intrinsically good in themselves," says Dewey, "is foolish to the point of irrationality." As a matter of fact, he

	Male	Female
A comfortable life	7.8(4)	10.0(13)
An exciting life	14.6(18)	15.8(18)
A sense of accomplishment	8.3(7)	9.4(10)
A world at peace	3.8(1)	3.0(1)
A world of beauty	13.6(15)	13.5(15)
Equality	8.9(9)	8.3(8)
Family security	3.8(2)	3.8(2)
Freedom	4.9(3)	6.1(3)
Happiness	7.9(5)	7.4(5)
Inner harmony	11.1(13)	9.8(12)
Mature love	12.6(14)	12.3(14)
National security	9.2(10)	9.8(11)
Pleasure	14.1(17)	15.0(16)
Salvation	9.9(12)	7.3(4)
Self-respect	8.2(6)	7.4(6)
Social recognition	13.8(16)	15.0(17)
True friendship	9.6(11)	9.1(9)
Wisdom	8.5(8)	7.7(7)

Figures shown are median rankings and, in parentheses, composite rank orders.

Table 1. Terminal Value Medians of Ranks of Respondents and Composite Rank Orders for American Men and Women

24 *Ibid.*, p. 27.
25 *Ibid.*, p. 57.

	Male	Female
Ambitious	5.6(2)	7.4(4)
Broadminded	7.2(4)	7.7(5)
Capable	8.9(8)	10.1(12)
Cheerful	10.4(12)	9.4(10)
Clean	9.4(9)	8.1(8)
Courageous	7.5(5)	8.1(6)
Forgiving	8.2(6)	6.4(2)
Helpful	8.3(7)	8.1(7)
Honest	3.4(1)	3.2(1)
Imaginative	14.3(18)	16.1(18)
Independent	10.2(11)	10.7(14)
Intellectual	12.8(15)	13.2(16)
Logical	13.5(16)	14.7(17)
Loving	10.9(14)	8.6(9)
Obedient	13.5(17)	13.1(15)
Polite	10.9(13)	10.7(13)
Responsible	6.6(3)	6.8(3)
Self-controlled	9.7(10)	9.5(11)

Figures shown are median rankings and, in parentheses, composite rank orders.

Table 2. Instrumental Value Medians of Ranks for Respondents and Composite Rank Orders for American Men and Women

continues, "the measure of the value a person attaches to a given end is . . . the care he devotes to obtaining and using the *means* without which it cannot be attained."[26]

The key to any meaningful general theory of value, a key that Rokeach does not take into account, is that values always emerge within a prior pattern of actions. More specifically, they are contrived by the individual when his/her dynamic equilibrium is disintegrated.[27]

The restoration of the dynamic equilibrium, then, constitutes the need of the person. Where there is no need, there is no desire, and, therefore, no valuation. Value formulation is thus dependent upon our ability to analyze our needs, to anticipate what, under certain circumstances, will satisfy those needs, and to decide upon a course of action that tends to realize the projected end.

Rokeach states, "It is difficult for me to conceive of any problem social scientists might be interested in that would not deeply implicate human values." The concept of values, he says, "is the main dependent

26 John Dewey. *Theory of Valuation.* Chicago: The University of Chicago Press, 1939. pp. 26, 27. Copyright © 1939 by the University of Chicago.

27 James John Jelinek. "A Reconstructed Epistemology for Philosophy of Education." In: James John Jelinek, editor. *Philosophy of Education: 1969.* Tempe, Arizona: Far Western Philosophy of Education Society, 1969.

variable in the study of social attitudes and behavior."[28] There is no argument on this point except perhaps to refine the statement by saying that value theory starts from the premise that all deliberate, all planned human conduct, personal and collective, is influenced, if not controlled, by estimates of value or worth of ends to be attained. Even among lay persons good sense in practical affairs is generally identified with a sense of relative values. It is clear that the problem of value, of valuation, is one of crucial significance in human affairs.

The difficulty, however, is that Rokeach muddies the waters of valuational analysis by identifying interjections, ejaculations, as values. To evince one's feelings is not quite the same thing as to express one's values. Interjections of feeling such as "hideous," "beautiful," "a world of beauty," "happiness," and such, are like the first cries of a baby or his early cooings, gurglings, and squeals. They are sounds *involuntarily* uttered. They are part of a larger organic condition and are not in any sense whatever value expressions. They are in point of fact hypostatizations, words without referents, maps for territories that do not exist.

When a cry, gesture, or posture is *purposely* made, it is not a feeling that is evinced. It is a communicatory act undertaken to obtain a change in a condition or situation. It is not a hypostatization but rather a proposition. Even exclamations like "Fire" or "Help" are implicit propositions because they refer directly to an existing situation and indirectly to a future situation which they are intended to produce. The expressions are used to bring about an intended change. Involved in a value situation, then, is, first, the disintegration of the dynamic equilibrium of the person—a dissatisfaction with an existing situation—and an attempted restoration of the equilibrium—an attraction toward a prospective possible situation, and, second, there is involved in a value situation a specifiable and testable relationship between the end-in-view and the activities that are to serve as the means of accomplishing it.

The main point, a point which the Rokeach theory of values does not take into account, is that valuations occur in concrete situations in which the individual has his dynamic equilibrium disintegrated, situations in which the individual finds it necessary to bring into existence something that is lacking, or situations in which it is necessary to conserve in existence something that is being threatened.

In these terms the adequacy of a given value of a person depends upon its adaptation to the demands imposed by the situation, and this adequacy, statable in proposition form, is empirically testable.

In a very specific sense each individual lives in a unique world, seeing things not as they are but as he or she is. A person's values thus

28 Milton Rokeach, *op. cit.*, p. ix.

are a very personal thing, in many respects quite unlike the values of her or his fellows, Rokeach to the contrary.

Before a person acts, his dynamic equilibrium is disintegrated. He experiences a need or deficiency that suggests a goal for action that will alleviate the felt need and restore the lost equilibrium. In the light of this projected goal, the individual then examines, reexamines, and examines again the means that lead to the attainment of the goal. By way of this process or reexamination the goal itself might become a matter of deliberation and in the course of the reexamination, might become clearer and more detailed. The situation as a whole takes on more and more the aspects of an orderly consideration of the conditions and things, useful or otherwise, by means of which the goal in greater or less degree is attained or not attained. The evaluation of the value inherent in the situation thus culminates in the functional unity of a finished plan of action in which all the available means are effectively coordinated and the value realized.

Value making, then, includes the universe of goals, the means of action, and the conditions that make the ends and means possible. To ignore any one of these phases of the value-making process, as indeed Rokeach does, is to come up with one sweeping hypostatization—a generalization for which there is no referent in the real world.

Examples of our theme abide in the affairs of the day: Before Richard Nixon became president he frequently expressed the value of taking a job, but never oneself, seriously, but when the means of power, fueled as they were by anxiety, were in his grasp, the neurotic need to deny his own human limitations led to failures that perverted the political process and gave us the Watergate phenomenon. In Watergate as in all human affairs it is folly to separate values from means. Values have a way of changing their complexions, depending upon the means at hand for the value maker.[29]

During the past year I visited, on the basis of a grant from the Ford Foundation, more than one hundred schools and school communities in the Soviet Union. I watched with fascinated horror the gap between professed values and the use of the means of power and saw with greater clarity than ever that real as opposed to professed values emerge within prior patterns of actions. While, for example, the Soviet Union by way of its various media professes values of freedom and equality, these values, even identified as rights by Soviet law, are denied in practice and have provoked thousands of arrests and some of the harshest repression in the history of the world, the acts of oppression being committed by the

29 Eli S. Chesen. *President Nixon's Psychiatric Profile: A Psychodynamic Genetic Interpretation.* New York: Peter H. Wyden, 1974.

Komitet Gosudarstvennoy Bezopasnosti, the KGB, the powerful clandestine apparatus of the Communist Party known as the Committee for State Security: Y. M. Suslensky, a teacher of foreign language, imprisoned for protesting the invasion of Czechoslovakia; Valentin Moroz, professor of history, imprisoned for writing that some of the same men who ran concentration camps under Stalin continue to run them under Brezhnev; Lev Ubozhko, a student, imprisoned in a concentration camp for possessing writings of Amalrik, Sakharov, and Solzhenitsyn; M. Bartoshuck, Baptist minister, imprisoned for instructing children in religion; V. Diemlyuga, imprisoned in a concentration camp for stating there is no freedom of speech in the Union of Soviet Socialist Republics.[30]

But even more impressive, perhaps because they involve individuals more like ourselves, are the recent experiments conducted by Dr. Stanley Milgram in the United States.[31] In these experiments, states Milgram, two people come to a psychological laboratory to take part in a study of memory and learning. One of them is designated as a "teacher" and the other a "learner." The experimenter explains that the study is concerned with the effects of punishment on learning. The "learner" is conducted into a room, seated in a chair, his arms strapped to prevent excessive movement, and an electrode attached to his wrist. He is told that he is to learn a list of pair words; whenever he makes an error, he will receive electric shocks of increasing intensity.

The real focus of the experiment is the "teacher." After watching the learner being strapped into place, he is taken into the main experimental room and seated before an impressive shock generator. Its main feature is a horizontal line of 30 switches, ranging from 15 volts to 450 volts, in 15-volt increments. There are also verbal designations which range from "Slight Shock" to "Danger—Severe Shock." The "teacher" is told that he is to administer the learning test to the person in the other room. When the "learner" responds correctly, the "teacher" moves on to the next item; when the other person gives an incorrect answer, the "teacher" is to give him an electric shock. He is to start at the lowest level (15 volts) and to increase the level each time the "learner" makes an error, going through 30 volts, 45 volts, and so on.

The "teacher" is simply a person who has answered a newspaper advertisement requesting individuals to come to the laboratory to participate in an experiment. On the other hand, the "learner," or victim, is a person deliberately selected to serve as an actor. The actor plays the role

[30] Cf., John Barron. *KGB: The Secret Work of Soviet Secret Agents.* New York: Bantam Books, Inc., 1974.

[31] Stanley Milgram. *Obedience to Authority: An Experimental View.* New York: Harper & Row, Publishers, 1969. passim.

of a protesting victim receiving the increasingly greater electrical shocks, but actually he receives no shocks at any time. Thus the experiment makes it possible for the experimenter to measure how far each person will go as he is ordered to inflict pain upon a victim, to measure at what point the person will refuse to obey the authority figure—the experimenter.

As the experiment proceeds the "teacher" experiences responses from the "learner"—the actor—and from the authority figure—the experimenter. As he increases the shocks the "learner" first grunts, then complains verbally, then demands to be released from the experiment, until at 285 volts and beyond he responds with agonized screams. If the "teacher" hesitates to administer the shocks, the authority figure, the experimenter, orders him to continue. Thus, by his actions, the "teacher" identifies if, when, and how he would defy authority on the basis of a moral imperative—a value—to the effect that it is wrong to inflict pain upon another.

Says Milgram, "Despite the fact that many subjects ("teachers") experience stress, despite the fact that many protest to the experimenter, a substantial proportion continue to the last shock on the generator. Many subjects will obey the experimenter no matter how vehement the pleading of the person being shocked, no matter how painful the shocks seem to be, and no matter how much the victim pleads to be let out. It is the extreme willingness of adults to go almost to any lengths on the command of authority that constitutes one of the chief findings of this study and one of the facts most urgently demanding explanation."[32]

Importantly inherent in such an explanation is the concept of freedom, a concept of critical concern in the field of education. There are basically two phases of freedom—inner freedom and outer freedom. Of the two, the most difficult to identify and sustain is inner freedom.

Inner freedom is the absence of mental restraint. An individual who has been trained or conditioned to believe a certain idea and on the basis of that training or conditioning is not free to examine alternative ideas lacks inner freedom. For example, an individual who has been conditioned or trained to be obedient to authority in terms of what to do, when to do it, how to do it, and how to feel about it is not free to examine alternative ideas about how to solve the problems of people and is lacking in inner freedom. The person with inner freedom is characterized by the use of inner direction, inquiry, induction, hypothesis generation, principle formulation.

Outer freedom is the absence of physical restraint. Limitations to

[32] *Ibid.*, p. 5.

outer freedom are readily observable and sometimes combatable. An individual readily substantiates the absence or presence of physical restraint. A person who is bound, gagged, and kidnapped, for example, does not have outer freedom in that situation.

Be that as it may, it is also important to note that both types of freedom—inner and outer—have an impact on each other. Such is the case, for example, in Pavlovian conditioning and Skinnerian conditioning. B. F. Skinner discusses this at length as being beyond "freedom and dignity."[33]

Given freedom, a person is intrinsically alert to the consequences of his action: if the consequence is favorable, he is free to and likely to perpetuate the action producing it; if the consequence is unfavorable, he is free to and likely to abandon or reconstruct the action producing it. In a state of freedom, man rethinks his experience and faces subsequent situations a different person. Freedom, then, is the basic critical variable in the educative process. The difficulty has been that this independent variable has been imperfectly known and largely ignored by experimenters doing so-called "scientific educational research." These experimenters, groping in the dark, arrange investigations that might invoke one of the forces of freedom but fail to deal with others. Or a single innovation might engage one force so as to facilitate growth in achievement but inadvertently act on another unknown force to inhibit growth.

As a consequence of this experimenters have seemingly tried to investigate the impact on pupil achievement of every conceivable independent variable under the sun in lieu of freedom. The profession now has mountains of research on pupil achievement as correlated with such widely diverse independent variables as administrative factors, attendance, television, independent study courses, class size, individual consultations, counseling, teacher effort, homework, student involvement, study time, distraction, school size, teacher selection, teacher education, teaching load, ability grouping, policy differences, general approach, discussion method, group-centered techniques, frequency of quizzes, programmed instruction, and the like. Anyone familiar with the literature admits the vast number of negative results in the data from the experiments.

On the basic of the so-called "scientific investigations" we have a vast preponderance of negative results which in the words of the investigators themselves identify that "no significant differences exist at levels of confidence based on odds of 1 to 100, 3 to 1000" or whatever. These investigations completed by the following experimenters are classic in the field of

[33] B. F. Skinner. *Beyond Freedom and Dignity*. New York: Alfred A. Knopf, Inc., 1971. 225 pp.

educational research: Peters and Voorhis,[34] Nachman and Opochinsky,[35] Harris,[36] Eaton,[37] Ellis,[38] Hatch and Bennett,[39] Herrick,[40] Heck,[41] Finch and Nemzek,[42] Schramm,[43] Barrington,[44] Bittner and Mallory,[45] Childs,[46] Dysinger and Bridgman,[47] Parsons,[48] Jensen,[49] Milton,[50] Bent,[51] Leton,[52] Marr,[53] McKenna,[54] Fleming,[55] Kidd,[56] Powell,[57] DeCecco,[58] Marklund,[59] Eash and Bennett,[60] Giffen and Bowers,[61] Hoehn and Salz,[62] Greene,[63] Hartmann,[64] Callis,[65] Shouksmith and Taylor,[66] Winborn and Schmidt,[67] Tilton,[68] Schoenhard,[69] Jacobs,[70] Gropper and Lumsdaine,[71] Strang,[72] Newman and Mooney,[73] Trueblood,[74] Brambaugh and Maddox,[75] Remmers,[76] Heisler,[77] Rieciuti,[78] Thompson,[79] Douglas,[80] Garrett,[81] Hoyt,[82] Lathrop,[83] Kemp,[84] Wiseman,[85] Ryans,[86] Medley and Mitzel,[87] Adams,[88] Kight,[89] Stephens and Lichtenstein,[90] Hopkins,[91] Shaplin and Olds,[92] Ginther and Shrayer,[93] White,[94] Zweibelson,[95] Lambert,[96] Ekstrom,[97] Pattison,[98] Svensson,[99] Borg,[100] Cremin,[101] Boss,[102] Caldwell and Courtis,[103] Gerberich,[104] Gray,[105] Harding,[106] Leonard and Eurich,[107] Muir,[108] Wrightstone,[109] Wallen and Travers,[110] Brown and Abell,[111] Burns and Dessart,[112] Rainey,[113] Lisonbee and Fullerton,[114] Stovall,[115] McKeachie,[116] Anderson,[117] Sears and Hilgard,[118] Stein,[119] Selakovich,[120] Standlee and Popham,[121] Lumsdaine,[122] Poppleton and Austwick,[123] Owen,[124] Feldhusen,[125] and Feldman,[126]

[34] C. C. Peters and W. R. Van Voorhis. *Statistical Procedures and Their Mathematical Bases*. New York: McGraw-Hill Book Company, 1940. p. 476.

[35] M. Nachman and S. Opochinsky. "The Effects of Different Teaching Methods: A Methodological Study." *The Journal of Educational Psychology* 49:345-49; 1958.

[36] D. Harris. "Factors Affecting College Grades: A Review of the Literature." *Psychological Bulletin* 37:125-66; 1940.

[37] M. T. Eaton. "A Survey of the Achievement in Social Studies of 10,220 Sixth Grade Pupils in 464 Schools in Indiana." *Bulletin, School of Education, Indiana University* 20 (3) ; 1944.

[38] J. R. Ellis. "The School Program: General Instructional Procedure." *Review of Educational Research* 30:49-56; 1960.

[39] W. B. Hatch and Ann Bennett. "Effectiveness in Teaching." *New Dimensions in Higher Education*. Washington, D.C.: United States Office of Education, 1960.

[40] V. E. Herrick. "Administrative Structure and Processes in Curriculum Development." *Review of Educational Research* 30:258-74; 1960.

[41] A. O. Heck. "Pupil Personnel Work, II. School Attendance." *Encyclopedia of Educational Research*. New York: Macmillan Publishing Co., Inc., 1950.

[42] F. H. Finch and C. L. Nemzek. "Attendance and Achievement in Secondary Schools." *Journal of Educational Research* 34:119-26; 1940.

[43] W. Schramm. "Learning from Instructional Television." *Review of Educational Research* 32:156-67; 1962.

[44] H. Barrington. "A Survey of Instructional Television Researchers." *Educational Research* 8:8-25; 1965.

[45] W. S. Bittner and H. F. Mallory. *University Teaching by Mail*. New York: Macmillan Publishing Co., Inc., 1933. passim.

46 G. B. Childs. "A Comparison of Supervised Correspondence Study Pupils and Classroom Pupils in Achievement in School Subjects." *Journal of Educational Research* 47:537-43; 1954.

47 D. W. Dysinger and C. S. Bridgman. "Performance of Correspondence Study Students." *Journal of Higher Education* 28:387-88; 1957.

48 T. W. Parsons. "A Comparison of Instruction by Kinescope, Correspondence Study and Customary Classroom Procedures." *Journal of Educational Psychology* 48:27-40; 1957.

49 B. T. Jensen. "Instruction and Personality Factors in Student Performance." *Journal of Educational Research* 47:529-35; 1954.

50 O. Milton. "Two Year Follow-up: Objective Data after Learning Without Class Attendance." *Psychological Review* 11:833-36; 1962.

51 R. K. Bent. "Scholastic Records of Non-High School Graduates Entering the University of Arkansas." *Journal of Educational Research* 40:108-15; 1946.

52 D. A. Leton. "An Analysis of High School General Educational Development Test Scores." *California Journal of Educational Research* 8:214-18; 1957.

53 J. N. Marr and others. "The Contribution of the Lecture to College Teaching." *Journal of Educational Psychology* 51:277-84; 1960.

54 B. H. McKenna. "Greater Learning in Smaller Classes." *NEA Journal* 46:437-38; 1957.

55 Charlotte M. Fleming. "Class Size as a Variable in the Teaching Situation." *Educational Research* 1:35-48; 1959.

56 J. W. Kidd. "The Question of Class Size." *Journal of Higher Education* 23:440-44; 1952.

57 J. P. Powell. "Experimentation and Teaching in Higher Education." *Educational Research* 6:179-91; 1964.

58 J. P. DeCecco. "Class Size and Coordinated Instruction." *British Journal of Educational Psychology* 34:65-74; 1964.

59 S. Marklund. "Scholastic Attainments as Related to Size and Homogeneity of Classes." *Educational Research* 6:63-67; 1963.

60 M. J. Eash and C. M. Bennett. "The Effect of Class Size on Achievement and Attitudes." *American Educational Research Journal* 1:229-39; 1964.

61 Kim Giffen and J. W. Bowers. "An Experimental Study of the Use of Lectures to Large Groups of Students in Teaching the Fundamentals of Speech." *Journal of Educational Research* 55:383-85; 1962.

62 A. J. Hoehn and E. Salz. "Effect of Teacher-student Interviews on Classroom Achievement." *Journal of Educational Psychology* 47:424-35; 1956.

63 E. B. Greene. "Certain Aspects of Lecture, Reading, and Guided Reading." *School of Society* 39:619-24; 1934.

64 G. W. Hartmann. "Comparative Pupil Gains under Individual Conferences and Classroom Instruction." *Journal of Educational Psychology* 26:367-72; 1935.

65 R. Callis. "Counseling." *Review of Educational Research* 33:179-87; 1963.

66 G. Shouksmith and J. W. Taylor. "The Effects of Counseling on the Achievement of High Ability Pupils." *British Journal of Educational Psychology* 34:51-57; 1964.

67 B. Winborn and L. G. Schmidt. "The Effectiveness of Short-term Counseling upon the Academic Achievement of Potentially Superior but Underachieving Freshmen." *Journal of Educational Research* 55:167-73; 1962.

68 J. W. Tilton. "An Experimental Effort To Change the Achievement Test Profile." *Journal of Experimental Education* 15:318-22; 1947.

69 G. H. Schoenhard. "Home Visitation Put to a Test." *Personnel Guidance Journal* 36:480-85; 1958.

70 J. N. Jacobs, J. H. Grate, and Ullainee M. Downing. "Do Methods Make a Difference in Television Education?" *Elementary School Journal* 63:248-54; 1963.

71 G. L. Gropper and A. A. Lumsdaine. *Studies in Television Instruction: The Use of Student Response To Improve Televised Instruction.* Pittsburgh: American Institute of Research, 1962.

72 Ruth Strang. *Behavior and Background of Students in College and Secondary School.* New York: Harper & Row, Publishers, 1937.

73 S. C. Newman and R. L. Mooney. "Effects of Student Self Help." *Journal of Higher Education* 11:435-42; 1940.

74 D. L. Trueblood. "Effects of Employment on Academic Achievement." *Personnel Guidance Journal* 36:112-15; 1957.

75 A. J. Brambaugh and C. Maddox. "Extra-curricular Activities: Higher Education." *Review of Educational Research* 6:212-17; 1936.

76 H. H. Remmers, editor. "Studies in Extra-curricular Activities." *Purdue University Studies in Higher Education* 39:16-30; 1940.

77 Florence Heisler. "A Comparison between Those Elementary School Children who Attend Moving Pictures, Read Comic Books, and Listen to Serial Radio Programs to an Excess with Those Who Indulge in These Activities Seldom or not at All." *Journal of Educational Research* 42:182-90; 1948.

78 E. A. Rieciuti. "Children and Radio: A Study of Listeners and Non-listeners to Various Types of Programs in Terms of Selected Ability, Attitude, and Behavior Measures." *Genetic Psychological Monographs* 44:69-143; 1951.

79 G. W. Thompson. "Children's Acceptance of Television Advertising and the Relation of Televiewing to School Achievement." *Journal of Educational Research* 58:171-74; 1964.

80 H. R. Douglas. "The Relation of High School Preparation and Certain Other Factors to Academic Success at the University of Oregon." *University of Oregon Public Education Series*, 3 (1) ; 1931.

81 H. F. Garrett. "A Review and Interpretation of Investigations of Factors Related to Scholastic Success in Colleges of Arts and Sciences and Teachers Colleges." *Journal of Experimental Education* 18:91-138; 1949.

82 D. P. Hoyt. "Size of High School and College Grades." *Personnel Guidance Journal* 37:569-73; 1959.

83 I. I. Lathrop. "Scholastic Achievement at Iowa State College Associated with High School Size and Course Pattern." *Journal of Experimental Education* 29:37-48; 1960.

84 L. C. D. Kemp. "Environmental and Other Characteristics Determining Attainment in Primary Schools." *British Journal of Educational Psychology* 25:67-77; 1955.

85 S. Wiseman. *Education and Environment.* Manchester, England: University of Manchester, 1964.

86 D. G. Ryans. "The Prediction of Teacher Effectiveness." *Encyclopedia of Educational Research.* New York: Macmillan Publishing Co., Inc., 1969. pp. 1486-91.

87 D. M. Medley and H. E. Mitzel. "Measuring Classroom Behavior by Systematic Observations." In: N. L. Gage, editor. *Handbook of Research on Teaching.* Skokie, Illinois: Rand McNally & Company, 1963. pp. 247-328.

88 J. J. Adams. "Achievement and Social Adjustment of Pupils in Combination Classes Enrolling Pupils of More than One Grade Level." *Journal of Educational Research* 47:151-55; 1953.

89 E. E. Kight. "A Study of Double Grades in New Haven Schools." *Journal of Experimental Education* 7:11-18; 1938.

90 J. M. Stephens and A. Lichtenstein. "Factors Associated with Success in Teaching Grade Five Arithmetic." *Journal of Educational Research* 40:683-84; 1947; and J. M. Stephens. *The Influence of the School on the Individual.* Ann Arbor, Michigan: Edwards Brothers, 1933.

91 K. D. Hopkins, A. Oldridge, and M. Williamson. "An Empirical Comparison of Pupil Achievement and Other Variables in Graded and Ungraded Classes." *American Educational Research Journal* 2:207-15; 1965.

92 J. T. Shaplin and H. F. Olds, Jr., editors. *Team Teaching.* New York: Harper & Row, Publishers, 1964.

93 J. B. Ginther and W. A. Shrayer. "Team Teaching in English and History at the Eleventh Grade Level." *School Review* 70:303-13; 1962.

94 R. W. White. "How Successful Is Team Teaching." *Science Teacher* 31 (6) :34-37; October 1964.

95 I. M. Zweibelson and L. Lyman. "Team Teaching and Flexible Grouping in the Junior High School Social Studies." *Journal of Experimental Education* 34:20-32; 1965.

96 P. Lambert and others. "A Comparison of Pupil Achievement in Team and Self-contained Organizations." *Journal of Experimental Education* 33:217-24; 1965.

97 Ruth B. Ekstrom. "Experimental Studies of Homgeneous Grouping: A Critical Review." *School Review* 69:216-26; 1961.

98 W. Pattison. "Streaming in the Schools." *Educational Research* 5:229-35; 1963.

99 N. E. Svensson. "Ability Grouping and Scholastic Achievement: Five Year Followup Study in Stockholm." *Educational Research* 5:53-56; 1962.

100 W. R. Borg. "Ability Grouping in the Public Schools." *Journal of Experimental Education* 34, 2:1-97; 1965.

101 L. A. Cremin. *The Transformation of the Schools: Progressivism in American Education, 1876-1957.* New York: Alfred A. Knopf, Inc., 1961. passim.

102 Mabel E. Boss. "Arithmetic, Then and Now." *School and Society* 51:62-64; 1940.

103 O. W. Caldwell and S. A. Courtis. *Then and Now in Education: 1845-1923.* New York: Harcourt Brace Jovanovich, Inc., 1924.

104 J. R. Gerberich. "The First of the Three R's." *Phi Delta Kappan* 33:345-49; 1952.

105 W. S. Gray. "What Is the Evidence Concerning Reading?" *Progressive Education* 29:105-10; 1952.

106 L. W. Harding. "How Well Are the Schools Now Teaching Skills?" *Progressive Education* 29:7-14, 32; 1951.

107 J. P. Leonard and A. C. Eurich. *An Evaluation of Modern Education.* New York: Appleton-Century-Crofts, 1942. passim.

108 N. D. Muir. "A Comparison of the Competence in Algebra of the Grade IX Students of the Edmonton Public Schools in 1938 and 1939." *Alberta Journal of Educational Research* 7:175-84; 1961.

109 J. W. Wrightstone. *Evaluating Achievement in Basic Skills in Newer Versus Conventional Schools: A Summary of Major Research Studies.* A Report to the Childhood Education Committee of the Governor's Fact-finding Commission on Education, 1951. 13 pp.

110 N. E. Wallen and R. M. W. Travers. "Analysis and Investigation of Teaching Methods." In: N. L. Gage, editor. *Handbook of Research on Teaching.* Skokie, Illinois: Rand McNally & Company, 1963. pp. 448-505.

111 K. S. Brown and T. L. Abell. "Research in the Teaching of High School Mathematics." *Mathematics Teacher* 59:53-57; 1966.

112 P. C. Burns and D. J. Dessart. "A Summary of Investigations Relating to Mathematics in Secondary Education." *School Science and Mathematics* 66:73-80; 1966.

The fact of the matter is that the time is right for us to philosophize about a single coherent approach to freedom to explain some of the positive accomplishments of the school and the flood of negative results as well. It is possible that this approach accounts for the surprising constancy of the school's achievements in the face of stupendous efforts to modify those achievements.

An individual who does not have inner freedom in a given situation is in a state of arrestment in that situation. In this state of arrestment there is a paradox of behavior that is at the same time self-perpetuating and self-defeating. Actions which have predominantly unfavorable consequences persist over a period of days, months, years, or even a lifetime.[127]

---

[113] R. G. Rainey. "A Comparison of the CHEM Study Curriculum and a Conventional Approach in Teaching High School Chemistry." *School Science and Mathematics* 64:539-44; 1964.

[114] L. Lisonbee and B. J. Fullerton. "The Comparative Effect of B. S. C. S. and Traditional Biology on Student Achievement." *School Science and Mathematics* 64:594-98; 1964.

[115] T. F. Stovall. "Classroom Methods: Lecture versus Discussion." *Phi Delta Kappan* 39:255-58; 1958.

[116] W. J. McKeachie and others. "Individualized Teaching in Elementary Psychology." *Journal of Educational Psychology* 51:285-91; 1960.

[117] R. C. Anderson. "Learning in Discussion: A Résumé of Authoritarian-Democratic Studies." *Harvard Educational Review* 29:201-15; 1959.

[118] Pauline S. Sears and E. R. Hilgard. "The Teacher's Role in the Motivation of the Learner." *Yearbook of the National Social Studies Education* 63:182-209, Part I; 1964.

[119] G. G. Stein. "Measuring Noncognitive Variables in Research on Teaching." In: N. L. Gage, editor. *Handbook of Research on Teaching.* Skokie, Illinois: Rand McNally & Company, 1963. pp. 398-447.

[120] D. Selakovich. "An Experiment Attempting to Determine the Effectiveness of Frequent Testing as an Aid to Learning to Beginning Courses in American Government." *Journal of Educational Research* 55:178-80; 1962.

[121] L. W. Standlee and W. J. Popham. "Quizzes' Contribution to Learning." *Journal of Educational Psychology* 51:322-25; 1960.

[122] A. A. Lumsdaine. "Educational Technology, Programmed Learning, and Instructional Science." *Yearbook of National Social Studies Education* 63:371-401, Part I; 1964.

[123] Pamela K. Poppleton and K. Austwick. "A Comparison of Programmed Learning and Note-Taking at Two Age Levels." *British Journal of Educational Psychology* 34:43-50; 1964.

[124] S. G. Owen and others. "Programmed Learning in Medical Education." *Postgraduate Medical Journal* 41:201; 1965.

[125] J. F. Feldhusen. "Taps for Teaching Machines." *Phi Delta Kappan* 44:265-67; 1963.

[126] Margaret E. Feldman. "Learning by Programmed and Text Format at Three Levels of Difficulty." *Journal of Educational Psychology* 56:133-39; 1965.

[127] O. H. Mowrer. "On the Dual Nature of Learning: A Reinterpretation of Conditioning' and 'Problem Solving'." *Harvard Educational Review* 17:102-48; 1947.

The arrestment paradox, the absence of inner freedom, is caused by conditioning. The conditioned person is not a free person. In the language of freedom, then, conditioners or trainers are the oppressors and the trainees or conditionees are the oppressed. If action is required and individuals are frustrated in their efforts to act responsibly, if they find themselves unable to use their faculties, then they experience a sense of anguish that sometimes causes them to reject their impotence by submitting to and identifying with a charismatic person, a benevolent dictator, a trainer/conditioner, an oppressor, or a group having power, thus by this symbolic participation in another's life having the illusion of acting, when in reality they are turning away from becoming authentic persons to become phonies submitting to and becoming part of those who act. Because the oppressed consider themselves to be individuals of action they consider themselves to be free. Thus it is easy for them to have the illusion of freedom, when in point of fact they are programmed, conditioned "Manchurian Candidates."

Perhaps the most fundamental lesson to be learned from the Milgram research on obedience to authority is that ordinary people representing working, managerial and professional classes, simply doing their jobs and without any hostility on their part can become participants in a terribly destructive process. Even when they are asked to carry out actions at odds with fundamentals of morality, with values they profess to have and believe, few people have the inner freedom to resist the means of authority.[128]

In summary, then, I emphasize again my main theme that value making includes the universe of goals, the means of action, and the conditions that make the ends and means possible. To ignore any one of these phases of the value-making process, as indeed Rokeach does, is to come up with one sweeping hypostatization—a generalization for which there is no referent in the real world.

An Example of a Value Crisis in a Technological Culture

Not all educators are philosophers, but all educators, no matter what their level of sophistication in philosophy, deal in one way or another with the enduring issues with which systematic philosophy deals—absolutism and/or relativism, matter and/or vacuum, time and/or eternity, good and/or evil, unity and/or variety, one and/or many, mechanism and/or vitalism, determinism and/or freedom, mindlessness and/or meaningfulness.[129]

128 Stanley Milgram, *op. cit.*, p. 5.
129 Frank Barron. *Creativity and Personal Freedom*. Princeton: Van Nostrand Company, 1968.

The decisions educators make in their resolution of these enduring issues, the emotions they harbor, and the passions that sway them are of much less significance at any given moment than the assumptions and values upon which those decisions, actions, and passions are founded, for assumptions and values, left unexamined and unchanged not only have consequences as of the moment, but consequences that extend as far into the future as the assumptions and values upon which they are built all thrive and endure.

The enduring issues and the role of assumptions and values in the resolution of those issues have a special significance in the valuational analyses of cultural phenomena, especially of modern technology, by present-day educators. They lay bare certain basic relationships between futurology, philosophy, and education.

The Assumptions and Values Inherent in Neexosomaticism. On the one hand, for example, there are the assumptions and values inherent in neexosomaticism (neergomonicism). Basic among these assumptions and values is the belief that advances in the technologizing of culture more and more deprive the individual of choice. Marcuse,[130] Ellul,[131] Whyte,[132] Kafka,[133] Toynbee,[134] and Orwell,[135] expostulate this assumption and value with force and clarity. Maximum individual development, according to neexosomaticism, is the democratic ideal. Technological advances make of people mindless consumer creatures, surrounded by standardized goods and educated in standardized schools. Being fed a diet of standardized mass culture the people are compelled to adopt standardized life styles.

More specifically, the assumption is that technological advances cause bureaucratization, alienation, helplessness, and dehumanization among people: Marx, for example, states the artifacts produced by man become an independent power ruling over him "as something alien, as a power independent of the producer." Furthermore, he says, "The worker puts

---

130 See the following by Herbert Marcuse: *Eros and Civilization.* Boston: Beacon Press, 1955; *Essay on Liberation.* Boston: Beacon Press, 1969; *One Dimensional Man.* Boston: Beacon Press, 1964; *Negations: Essays in Critical Theory.* Boston: Beacon Press, 1969; *Reason and Revolution.* Boston: Beacon Press, 1963.

131 Jacques Ellul. *The Technological Society.* New York: Vintage Books, 1967.

132 William H. Whyte. *The Organization Man.* New York: Simon & Schuster, Inc., 1956.

133 Franz Kafka. *Diaries of Franz Kafka.* Volumes I and II. New York: Shocken Books, Inc., 1948.

134 Arnold Toynbee. "Why I Dislike Western Civilization." *The New York Times Magazine,* May 10, 1964.

135 Sonia and Angus Orwell. *The Collected Essays, Journalism, and Letters of George Orwell.* Volume I-IV. New York: Harcourt Brace Jovanovich, 1968.

his life into the object; but then his life no longer belongs to him but to the object."[136]

"The industrial society," states Etzioni, "is the archetype of an alienating society . . . and in effect led to a society that stood between its members and the service of their basic needs." He states, "The postmodern society inherited from its predecessor an alienating structure: the product of modernity—industrialization, bureaucratization, and the like."[137]

Roszak likewise identifies the prime force of alienation to be technocracy. "The great secret of technocracy," he says, "lies in its capacity to convince us . . . that the vital needs of man are (contrary to everything the great souls of history have told us) purely technical in character."[138]

Humankind, according to Ellul, was far freer in the past when "choice was a real possibility." Today "the human being is no longer in any sense the agent of choice." In the future "man will apparently be confined to the role of a recording device." He will be acted upon, but he will not be active. He will be robbed of choice.[139]

"Whatever the gains of our technological age," says Keniston, ". . . many Americans are left with an inarticulate sense of loss, of unrelatedness and lack of connection."[140] With this Fromm agrees. Industrialization, he says, must give way to humanization.[141]

The Assumptions and Values Inherent in Exosomaticism. On the other hand there are the assumptions and values inherent in exosomaticism (ergomonicism). Basic among these assumptions and values is the belief that transience, novelty, and diversity become increasingly greater for individuals in a society as the culture of that society becomes increasingly more technological. The writings of Malinowski,[142] Boas,[143]

136 See the following by Karl Marx: *Economic and Philosophical Manuscripts of 1844.* In: Dirk J. Struik, editor. Martin Milligan, translator. New York: International Publishing Company, 1963; *Early Writings.* New York: McGraw-Hill Book Company, 1963.

137 Amitai Etzioni. *The Active Society.* New York: Free Press, 1968.

138 Theodore Roszak. *The Making of a Counter Culture.* New York: Doubleday & Company, Inc., 1964. Copyright © 1968, 1969 by T. Roszak. Reprinted by permission.

139 Jacques Ellul, *op. cit.*

140 Kenneth Keniston. "Youth: A 'New' Stage of Life." *The American Scholar;* Autumn 1970.

141 Erich Fromm. *The Sane Society.* New York: Holt, Rinehart and Winston, Inc., 1955.

142 See the following by Bronislaw Malinowski: *Freedom and Civilization.* Bloomington: Indiana University Press, 1960; *Scientific Theory of Culture.* Chapel Hill: University of North Carolina Press, 1944; "Magic, Science, and Religion." In: Joseph Needham, editor. *Science, Religion, and Reality.* London, 1925. pp. 19-84.

143 See the following by Franz Boas: *Anthropology and Modern Life.* New York: W. W. Norton & Company, Inc., 1962; *Race, Language, and Culture.* New York: Free Press, 1965.

Lederer,[144] Ogburn,[145] Medawar,[146] Chase,[147] and Toffler,[148] provide vigorous and powerful elaborations of this assumption. The consequence of advanced technology, according to exosomaticism, is not a deprivation of individual choice but rather a plenitude, a complexity, a surfeit of individual *over*choice. The consequence is a matter of ergonomics—the extension of certain relationships between human beings and machines, especially in terms of their physiological, psychological and technological components.

Medawar, for example, states that, "What is human about Man in his technology. . . . The assimilation of technological to ordinary organic evolution [has] substance because all instruments are functionally parts of ourselves. Some instruments like spectrophotometers, microscopes, and radio telescopes are sensory accessories inasmuch as they enormously increase sensibility and the range of quality of the sensory input. Other instruments like cutlery, hammers, guns, and automobiles are accessories of our effector organs; they are not sensory but motor accessories. A property that all these instruments have in common is that they make no functional sense except as external organs of our own. All sensory instruments report back at some stage or by some route through our ordinary senses. All motor instruments receive their instructions from ourselves. . . . We are integrated psychologically with the instruments that serve us."[149]

Likewise Malinowski points out, "Man in order to live continually alters his surroundings. On all points of contact with the outer world he creates an artificial, secondary environment. . . . Were man to rely on his anatomical equipment exclusively, he would soon be destroyed or perish from hunger and exposure. . . . The man of nature, the Naturmensch, does not exist."[150]

The contrasting views of the exosomaticists (ergomonicists) and the neexosomaticists (neergomonicists) are clear indeed. While, for example, Ellul states, "Enclosed within his artificial creation man finds that there is no exit, that he cannot pierce the shell of technology to find again the ancient milieu to which he was adapted for hundreds of thousands of

---

[144] Emil Lederer. "Technology." In: Edwin R. A. Seligman and Alvin Johnson, editors. *Encyclopedia of Social Sciences*. Volume XIV. New York: Macmillan Publishing Co., Inc., 1937.

[145] W. F. Ogburn. *Social Change*. New York: Macmillan Publishing Co., Inc., 1922.

[146] Sir Peter Medawar. "What's Human about Man Is His Technology." *Smithsonian* 2 (2) :22-28; May 1973. Copyright © 1973 Smithsonian Institution.

[147] Stuart Chase. "Two Cheers for Technology." *Saturday Review;* February 20, 1971, pp. 20-21, 76-77. Copyright © 1971 Stuart Chase and *Saturday Review*.

[148] Alvin Toffler. *Future Shock*. New York: Bantam Books, Inc., 1970.

[149] Sir Peter Medawar, *op. cit.*

[150] Bronislaw Malinowski, *op. cit.*

years."[151] Chase is saying, "This would seem to indicate that we did better in the Stone Age. . . . The philosophy of retreat to a simpler era may have had some validity two hundred years ago when Rousseau was celebrating the virtues of Cro-Magnon Man, but too much water has gone through the turbines. The growth curves of science and technology have profoundly changed (our) cultural habits. . . ."[152]

If, as we stated at the outset, the decisions educators make in their resolution of enduring socio-philosophical issues in general and enduring socio-technological issues in particular continue to be based upon assumptions and values of exosomaticism (ergomonicism) or neexosomaticism (neergomonicism), what in the Wellsian sense of futurology can we now establish as hypotheses in the teaching of creative philosophical thinking that are likely to become principles of education in the future?

"Futurology is so new that to many persons it still seems clumsy," says Williamson, "but the probing of possible futures has lately become a full-time profession. There is a World Future Society open even to amateurs, and an Institute of the Future, which produces forecasts under contract. A staff of futurologists is now as essential to any large military or governmental or commercial establishment as a coterie of soothsayers used to be to a barbarian emperor. Those older forecasters tried hard enough, often with their lives at stake; however, their methods were based on theology or magic or sheer opportunism. But it was Wells, to quote his own *Experiment in Autobiography,* who made the first attempt to forecast the human future as a whole and to estimate the relative power of this and that great system of influence."[153]

Hypotheses for the Testing of Exosomaticism/Neexosomaticism. It is in this sense of Wellsian futurology that the following hypotheses are presented to anticipate the independent variables and the dependent variables inherent in a value crisis of our time—the value crisis of exosomaticism (ergomonicism) versus neexosomaticism (neergomonicism). Parallel hypotheses extrapolated from the basic value of exosomaticism and neexosomaticism are as follows:[154, 155, 156, 157, 158, 159, 160, 161, 162, 163, 164.]

[151] Jacques Ellul, *op. cit.*

[152] Stuart Chase, *op. cit.*

[153] Jack Williamson. "H. G. Wells: The Man Who Discovered Tomorrow." *Saturday Review;* January 1, 1972, pp. 12-15. Copyright © 1972 Jack Williamson and *Saturday Review.*

[154] Frank Barron, *op. cit.*, passim.

[155] A. J. Cropley. *Creativity.* London: Longmans, Green and Company, 1967.

[156] Paul R. Ehrlich and John P. Holdren. "Technology for the Poor: We Cannot Abandon Technology, But It Must Be Focused on Human Needs with a Minimum of Adverse Side Effects." *Saturday Review* July 3, 1971, pp. 46-47.

Freedom. If a person espouses exosomaticism, rejects the notion that each artifact in the environment has an independent reality, dissolves that which separates what she is from what she thinks she should be, then there is personified meaning—the word made referent, alive and changing, taking its chances, open to beauty and decay; if on the other hand she espouses neexosomaticism, internalizes the impact of artifacts in the environment (in the sense of things being in the saddle and riding humankind), then she is not free to act according to her deepest inclinations and develops stultified meanings—the ancient, rigid laws and lawgivers, fixed, abstract, decided.[165, 166]

Self. If the individual's perception of himself as he relates to the artifacts of his culture is exosomatic, if he feels he is characterized by (a) a certain positive valuation of intellect and cognitive originality, as well as a spirit of open-mindedness (logical, rational, original, idealistic, fair-minded), (b) a high degree of personal involvement and emotional reactivity (emotional, excitable, moody), and (c) a lack of social ease,

---

157 William J. J. Gordon. *Synectics: The Development of Creative Capacity.* London: Collier-Macmillan, 1968.

158 See the following by James John Jelinek: "Competency-Based Education: Consensus Cognoscenti Versus Reconstructio Experientiae." In: James John Jelinek, editor. *Philosophy of Education: 1972-1973.* Tempe, Arizona: Far Western Philosophy of Education Society, 1973. pp. 1-11; "A Reconstructed Epistemology for Education." In: James John Jelinek, editor. *Philosophy of Education: 1969.* Tempe, Arizona: Far Western Philosophy of Education Society, 1969. pp. 17-24; "The Identification and Modification of Philosophies of Education Held by Graduate Students in Teacher Education Programs." In: John Schulte, editor. *Proceedings of the Annual Meeting of the Far Western Philosophy of Education Society, 1967.* Santa Barbara: Far Western Philosophy of Education Society, 1967; "The Governance of Colleges in a Democracy." *Philosophy of Education: 1970-1971.* In: James John Jelinek, editor. Tempe, Arizona: Far Western Philosophy of Education Society, 1972; "The Influence of the Teaching of Certain Elementary Principles of Philosophy Upon Modification of Basic Aspects of the Concept of Self Held by College Students." In: James John Jelinek, editor. *Philosophy of Education: 1968.* Tempe, Arizona: Far Western Philosophy of Education Society, 1968.

159 Harold H. Anderson, editor. *Creativity.* New York: Harper & Row, Publishers, 1959.

160 E. Paul and J. Pansy Torrance. *Is Creativity Teachable?* Bloomington, Indiana: Phi Delta Kappa Educational Foundation, 1973.

161 Charles S. Whiting. *Creative Thinking.* New York: Reinhold Publishing Corporation, 1958.

162 Arlene Metha. "Existential Frustration and Psychological Anomie within Select College Student Subcultures." In: James John Jelinek, editor. *Philosophy of Education: 1972-1973.* Tempe, Arizona: Far Western Philosophy of Education Society, 1973.

163 Calvin W. Taylor. *Creativity: Progress and Potential.* New York: McGraw-Hill Book Company, 1964.

164 B. F. Skinner. *Beyond Freedom and Dignity.* New York: Alfred A. Knopf, Inc., 1971.

165 Cf. Frank Barron, *op. cit.*

166 Cf. James John Jelinek, *op. cit.*

or an absence of commonly valued social virtues (tactless, reckless, forgetful, mischievous), then he is inner directed and self-actualizing and he exercises independence of judgment; if, however, the individual's perception of himself as he relates to the artifacts of his culture is neexosomatic, if he feels he is characterized by (a) ease and helpfulness in interpersonal relations (kind, obliging, appreciative, considerate, enthusiastic, friendly, helpful, tactful), (b) personal effectiveness and planfulness in achieving some goal (determined, efficient, patient, wise), and (c) personal stability and healthy-mindedness (stable, optimistic, humorous, modest, dignified), then he is outer directed and not self-actualizing and yields to the judgments of others.[167, 168]

Morality. If a person is exosomatic, if her awareness includes the broadest possible aspects of the artifacts in her culture and the deepest possible comprehension of them, while at the same time, she is most simple and direct in her feelings, thoughts, and actions concerning those artifacts, then she rebels, resists acculturation, refuses to adjust, is adamant in her insistence on the importance of self and individuality and actions, is usually virtuous in the simple moral sense of the term, does what she thinks is right and what she thinks is right is that people should not lie to one another or to themselves, that they should not steal, slander, persecute, intrude, do damage willfully, go back on their word, fail a friend, or do any of the things that put them on the side of death as against life, and she lives and functions in such a way that she knows who she is and you know who she is, she is aware of both herself and

The Learning of Values in Teacher Education Programs

Thus far in our discourse on the learning of values we have pointed out among other things that the substance of operant conditioning can be stated in the form of a principle: If a trainer sets up environmental situations that force trainees to make those responses desired by her, if she reinforces those responses when they occur, if she creates an emotional climate that those competencies and those responses are to

That this principle has wide appeal in teacher education is clearly ... the implementation of the principle is the ... which the elite in the

certain relationships between values and the human condition.

involved in improving the human condition.

—monicism). As such the extrapolation attempts to lay bare ... inherent in a value crisis of our time—exosoma-tic ... versus exosoma-somatic (intergomonicism) ... monicism). As such the extrapolation attempts to lay bare ... -logical extrapolation of inde-...[171, 172]

Freedom. If a person espouses exosomaticism, rejects the notion that each artifact in the environment has an independent reality, dissolves that which separates what she is from what she thinks she should be, then there is personified meaning—the word made referent, alive and changing, taking its chances, open to beauty and decay; if on the other hand she espouses neexosomaticism, internalizes the impact of artifacts in the environment (in the sense of things being in the saddle and riding humankind) , then she is not free to act according to her deepest inclinations and develops stultified meanings—the ancient, rigid laws and lawgivers, fixed, abstract, decided.[165, 166]

Self. If the individual's perception of himself as he relates to the artifacts of his culture is exosomatic, if he feels he is characterized by (a) a certain positive valuation of intellect and cognitive originality, as well as a spirit of open-mindedness (logical, rational, original, idealistic, fair-minded) , (b) a high degree of personal involvement and emotional reactivity (emotional, excitable, moody) , and (c) a lack of social ease,

[157] William J. J. Gordon. *Synectics: The Development of Creative Capacity.* London: Collier-Macmillan, 1968.

[158] See the following by James John Jelinek: "Competency-Based Education: Consensus Cognoscenti Versus Reconstructio Experientiae." In: James John Jelinek, editor. *Philosophy of Education: 1972-1973.* Tempe, Arizona: Far Western Philosophy of Education Society, 1973. pp. 1-11; "A Reconstructed Epistemology for Education." In: James John Jelinek, editor. *Philosophy of Education: 1969.* Tempe, Arizona: Far Western Philosophy of Education Society, 1969. pp. 17-24; "The Identification and Modification of Philosophies of Education Held by Graduate Students in Teacher Education Programs." In: John Schulte, editor. *Proceedings of the Annual Meeting of the Far Western Philosophy of Education Society, 1967.* Santa Barbara: Far Western Philosophy of Education Society, 1967; "The Governance of Colleges in a Democracy." *Philosophy of Education: 1970-1971.* In: James John Jelinek, editor. Tempe, Arizona: Far Western Philosophy of Education Society, 1972; "The Influence of the Teaching of Certain Elementary Principles of Philosophy Upon Modification of Basic Aspects of the Concept of Self Held by College Students." In: James John Jelinek, editor. *Philosophy of Education: 1968.* Tempe, Arizona: Far Western Philosophy of Education Society, 1968.

[159] Harold H. Anderson, editor. *Creativity.* New York: Harper & Row, Publishers, 1959.

[160] E. Paul and J. Pansy Torrance. *Is Creativity Teachable?* Bloomington, Indiana: Phi Delta Kappa Educational Foundation, 1973.

[161] Charles S. Whiting. *Creative Thinking.* New York: Reinhold Publishing Corporation, 1958.

[162] Arlene Metha. "Existential Frustration and Psychological Anomie within Select College Student Subcultures." In: James John Jelinek, editor. *Philosophy of Education: 1972-1973.* Tempe, Arizona: Far Western Philosophy of Education Society, 1973.

[163] Calvin W. Taylor. *Creativity: Progress and Potential.* New York: McGraw-Hill Book Company, 1964.

[164] B. F. Skinner. *Beyond Freedom and Dignity.* New York: Alfred A. Knopf, Inc., 1971.

[165] Cf. Frank Barron, *op. cit.*

[166] Cf. James John Jelinek, *op. cit.*

or an absence of commonly valued social virtues (tactless, reckless, forget-ful, mischievous), then he is inner directed and self-actualizing and he exercises independence of judgment; if, however, the individual's percep-tion of himself as he relates to the artifacts of his culture is neexosomatic, if he feels he is characterized by (a) ease and helpfulness in interpersonal relations (kind, obliging, appreciative, considerate, enthusiastic, friendly, helpful, tactful), (b) personal effectiveness and planfulness in achieving some goal (determined, efficient, patient, wise), and (c) personal stability and healthy-mindedness (stable, optimistic, humorous, modest, dignified), then he is outer directed and not self-actualizing and yields to the judg-ments of others.[167, 168]

Morality. If a person is exosomatic, if her awareness includes the broadest possible aspects of the artifacts in her culture and the deepest possible comprehension of them, while at the same time, she is most simple and direct in her feelings, thoughts, and actions concerning those artifacts, then she rebels, resists acculturation, refuses to adjust, is ada-mant in her insistence on the importance of self and individuality and actions, is usually virtuous in the simple moral sense of the term, does what she thinks is right and what she thinks is right is that people should not lie to one another or to themselves, that they should not steal, slander, persecute, intrude, do damage willfully, go back on their word, fail a friend, or do any of the things that put them on the side of death as against life, and she lives and functions in such a way that she knows who she is and you know who she is and she knows who you are when her thoughts and actions are in accord with her moral judgment; if, however, the person is neexosomatic with respect to these matters, then she does what she thinks is wrong, she gets a feeling of being dead, and when she is steeped in such wrongful ways she gets the feeling of being dead all the time, and other people know she is dead, dead in spirit.[169, 170]

Originality. If a person prefers complexity and some degree of im-balance in phenomena, if he is complex psychodynamically and has great personal scope, if he is independent in his judgment, if he is self-assertive and dominant, if he rejects suppression as a mechanism for the control of impulse, if he forbids himself no thoughts, if he dislikes to police himself and others, and if he is disposed to entertain impulses and ideas that are commonly taboo, then he is exosomatic and original, his re-sources to problematical situations in the culture being uncommon to the particular group of which he is a part but adaptive to the reality of his

167 Cf. Frank Barron, *op. cit.*
168 Cf. James John Jelinek, *op. cit.*
169 Cf. Frank Barron, *op. cit.*
170 Cf. James John Jelinek, *op. cit.*

environment; if, however, there is organization with maladaptive sim-plicity, with suppression to achieve unity, with suppression of impulses and emotions to maintain semblance of stability with suppression because in the short run it *seems* to achieve unity, with suppression that inhibits development of the greater level of complexity, and thus avoids the temporary disintegration that otherwise results, then the person is neexosomaticistic and not original, his responses to problematical situa-tions in the culture being common to the particular group of which he is a part but not adaptive to the reality of his environment.[171, 172]

This, then, is an example of futurological extrapolation of inde-pendent and dependent variables inherent in a value crisis of our time— the value crisis of neexosomaticism (neergomonicism) versus exosoma-ticism (ergomonicism). As such the extrapolation attempts to lay bare certain relationships between values and education, all of which are involved in improving the human condition.

The Learning of Values in Teacher Education Programs

Thus far in our discourse on the learning of values we have pointed out among other things that the substance of operant conditioning can be stated in the form of a principle: If a trainer sets up environmental situations that force trainees to make those responses desired by her, if she reinforces the responses when they occur, if she creates an emotional response of acceptance of both herself and those competencies that are to be learned, if she presents problem-solving situations in this context of acceptance, if she extinguishes largely through nonreinforcement and partly through mildly punishing contingencies behavior that interferes with the trainees' learning the competencies she wants them to learn, if she presents situations in which the trainees know in strict behavioristic terms what they are to learn to do, if the trainees receive immediate feedback from their trainer concerning the responses they make and they compare their progress with their past performance to see if they are doing what they are supposed to do, then the trainer changes the behavior of trainees, individually and in groups, so that they behave in ways she wants them to behave and they do not behave in ways she does not want them to behave.[173]

---

171 Cf. Frank Barron, *op. cit.*

172 Cf. James John Jelinek, *op. cit.*

173 Cf. the following by B. F. Skinner: *Contingencies of Reinforcement: A Theo-retical Analysis.* New York: Appleton-Century-Crofts, 1969; *Science and Human Be-havior.* Riverside, New Jersey: The Free Press, Macmillan Publishing Co., Inc., 1965; B. F. Skinner, editor. *Cumulative Record: A Selection of Papers.* New York: Appleton-Century-Crofts, 1972; see also: M. Daniel Smith. *Theoretical Foundations of Learning and Teaching.* Waltham, Massachusetts: Xerox College Publishing, 1971.

That this principle has wide appeal in teacher education is clearly evident. The approach to the implementation of the principle is the approach of consensus cognoscenti—the process in which the elite in the profession and the society determine what behaviors shall be conditioned and built into the structures of learners.

The Associated Organizations for Teacher Education (AOTE), for example, has requested experts "to identify the competencies and behaviors of teachers desired at each level. . . . The Delphi technique," states the chairman of AOTE in his letter to me, "will be used, which will provide a rank ordering of behavior and competencies. . . . Keep in mind," he says, "such questions as, what behaviors and competencies should he or she have at the end of training, and what competencies should be stressed in in-service training?"[174] What the Associated Organizations for Teacher Education calls the Delphi technique is, of course, nothing more nor less than consensus cognoscenti, or, as the television people say, objectives by Nielson Rating.

Likewise the American Association of Colleges for Teacher Education (AACTE) through its Distinguished Achievement Awards Program and through its Executive Secretary emphasizes the desirability of and the need for "behavior-based, competency-based, performance-based systems approaches." In recent years virtually all the awards have been given to institutions for "performance-based, field-centered programs," "on-site school teacher education programs," "highly individualized, performance-based programs," and the like.[175]

In the words of Edward C. Pomeroy, Executive Director of the Association, "Performance-based teacher education . . . has the potential for restructuring the education of teachers. It bespeaks the emerging future and points the way for teacher education. A significant number of AACTE member colleges and universities have already committed their teacher education programs to performance-based goals and are now going all out to forge a new approach to preparing teachers."[176]

In Arizona, too, the State Board of Education issued its manifesto on performance-based criteria to be used by administrators in the evaluation of teachers for their recertification. The State Superintendent of Public Instruction in Arizona states, "There is no one policy which will strengthen the common and high schools more than recertification of

---

[174] Letter to the Author from Arthur G. Martin, Chairman, Associated Organizations for Teacher Education, One Dupont Circle, Washington, D.C., October 2, 1972.

[175] *Excellence in Teacher Education: Distinguished Achievement Awards of the American Association of Colleges for Teacher Education*, 1972, 1971, 1970.

[176] Edward C. Pomeroy. *Beyond the Upheaval*. Thirteenth Charles W. Hunt Lecture, American Association of Colleges for Teacher Education, Washington, D.C., 1972. 21 pp.

teachers based upon performance. To achieve a recertification procedure based on teacher performance, courses in graduate colleges in education will need to be drastically revised."[177]

The ways in which this revision occurs are many and varied, but when prior structures are evident, as of course they are with performance-based criteria and behavioristic objectives, the mode is one of conditioning. The mode prevails on all levels—elementary, secondary, and higher education.

Supervisors in Chandler, Arizona, themselves under the supervision of three university professors, offer one example of this conditioning process. They monitor their student teachers with an electronic feedback system. Using "The Instrument for the Observation of Teaching Effectiveness" (an instrument for performance rating), the supervisor, while the student teacher conditions the pupils in the class, stands in the back of the room conditioning the student teacher with various types of reenforcement, verbal feedback, in a low voice through a transistor microphone. The pupils in the class cannot hear any of the comments of the supervisor but the student teacher hears them through an earphone as he or she conducts the class and behaves in accordance with the directions of the supervisor![178]

As students of teaching, we should examine critically the relationship of ends and means, theory and practice, inherent in this emphasis in the preparation of teachers. "To place the emphasis upon the securing of proficiency in teaching and discipline," Dewey warned two-thirds of a century ago, *"puts the attention of the student teacher in the wrong place, and tends to fix it in the wrong direction. . . .* For immediate skill may be got at the cost of the power to keep on growing. The teacher who leaves the professional school with power of managing a class of children may appear to superior advantage the first day, the first week, the first month, or even the first year. But later 'progress' may with such consist only in perfecting and refining skills already possessed. Such persons seem to know how to teach, but they are not students of teaching." Unless a teacher is also a student of teaching, "he cannot grow as a teacher, an inspirer and director of soul-life." (The emphasis is in the original.) [179]

In these terms whether the growth of the student is continuous or sporadic, whether it begets more growth or disappears in arrestment, is

[177] "Performance Based Recertification Procedure Is Sought for Teachers." *Phoenix Gazette;* June 26, 1972, p. 14.

[178] "System Monitors Student Teachers." *Phoenix Gazette,* June 27, 1972, p. 14.

[179] John Dewey. "The Relation of Theory to Practice in Education." National Society for the Scientific Study of Education. *The Relation of Theory to Practice in Education.* Third Yearbook, Part I. Bloomington, Illinois: Public School Publishing Company, 1904.

utterly dependent upon whether that student is educated or trained, whether he is intrinsically motivated or extrinsically motivated, whether he is a learner or an achiever, whether he is inner directed or outer directed, whether he experiences positive disintegrationism or negative disintegrationism.[180] These alternatives merit our close scrutiny.

There are in substance two main aspects to the case against performance-based criteria for training. One is that in a world of transience no trainer can know with any degree of certainty those behaviors to build into the structure of his trainees to equip them effectively to cope with the world of tomorrow. The second is that the trained individual, conditioned as he is to invoke responses which he cannot change, is quite incapable of reconstructing his experiences in the world of transience in which he finds himself.

Toffler's concept of future shock strongly suggests that there must be balance, not merely between rates of change in various sectors of the society and its culture but between the pace of environmental change and the limited pace of human response. Future shock grows out of the increasing lag between the two.[181]

Again, by way of Toffler, we recognize that the behavioristic competencies of a bygone day are inadequate to the needs of today and the behavioristic competencies of today will be inadequate to the tasks at hand in the future. Of the 450,000 usable words now in the English language more than one-half of them would be incomprehensible to William Shakespeare. The pace of turnover in art is vision-blurring— the viewer scarcely has time to "see" a school develop, to learn its language, so to speak, before it vanishes. Ideas come and go at a frenetic rate. In science that rate is one hundred times faster than a mere century ago. The family of old is shattering only to come together again in strange and novel ways—with purchased embryos, professional parents taking on the childbearing function of others, communal arrangements, geriatric group marriages, homosexual family units, polygamy, and serial trajectory marriages. As technology becomes more sophisticated and the cost of introducing variation declines, uniformity in business is giving way to diversity, the origins of overchoice for consumers and producers. In schools and universities complex standardizing systems based upon degrees, majors, minors, cognate minors, and the like, are changing to the point at which no two students move along the same track. In the broader sense even the old ways of integrating a society, methods based

[180] James John Jelinek. "A Reconstructed Epistemology for Philosophy of Education." *Philosophy of Education: 1969*. Tempe, Arizona: Far Western Philosophy of Education Society, 1969. pp. 17-24.

[181] Alvin Toffler, *op. cit.*

on uniformity, simplicity, and permanence are no longer effective and are giving way to a new, more finely fragmented social order based on more diverse and short-lived components we have not yet learned to link together and integrate into the whole.[182] And so it goes.

As the society speeds up change in the outer world, says Toffler, the individual is compelled to relearn the environment at every moment. This, in itself, places a unique demand upon the education he or she pursues and has a profound impact upon it. The people of the past, adapting to comparatively stable environments, maintained longer-lasting ties with their own conceptions of "the-way-things-are." We, moving into a high-transience society, are forced to truncate these relationships. Just as we make and break our relationships with things, places, people, and organizations at an ever more rapid pace, so, too, do we turn over our conceptions of reality, our mental images of the world at shorter and shorter intervals.

Transience, then, the forcible abbreviation of human relationships, is not merely a condition of the external world. It is within us as well. New discoveries, new technologies, new social arrangements in the external world erupt into our lives in the form of increased turnover rates—shorter and shorter relational periods. They force a faster and faster pace of daily life. They demand a new level of effective intelligence—behavior guided by an anticipation of consequences, behavior based upon the reconstruction of experience; not behavior based upon conditioned responses built into structure by trainers engaging in acts of cognition relevant only to an obsolete or at best obsolescent environment, not behavior that sets the stage for the devastating social illness Alvin Toffler calls "future shock."[183]

Any response built into the structure of the learner, if it cannot be changed by him, is a dangerous response to acquire. The educated person, the free person, rethinks his experiences and faces subsequent situations a different person. The trained person is forever the slave of his trainer, no matter how benevolent the trainer, no matter how sophisticated the trainer in his knowledge of prior structures. The behaviorists of today who have arrogated to themselves various titles inherent in social engineering recognize, of course, no ground between behaviors they would build into the structures of students and dark, blank, hopeless uncertainty and insecurity.[184] Not until they have been reborn into the life of effective intelligence will they recognize the security inherent in methods

182 Alvin Toffler, *op. cit.*

183 Alvin Toffler, *op. cit.*

184 B. F. Skinner. *Beyond Freedom and Dignity*. New York: Alfred A. Knopf, Inc., 1971. 225 pp.

of inquiring, observing, experimenting, and hypothesizing. Thinkers do not see as disastrous the ineffectiveness or inappropriateness of a given behavior because they retain security of procedure, the process by which they reconstruct, rethink, their experiences.

Selected Readings

Frank Barron. *Creativity and Personal Freedom*. Princeton, New Jersey: Van Nostrand Reinhold Company, 1968.

John Barron. *KGB: The Secret Work of Soviet Secret Agents*. New York: Bantam Books, 1974.

Eli S. Chesen. *President Nixon's Psychiatric Profile: A Psychodynamic Genetic Interpretation*. New York: Peter H. Wyden, 1974.

Kazimierz Dabrowski. *Positive Disintegrationism*. Boston: Little, Brown and Company, 1964.

_____. *Personality-shaping Through Positive Disintegration*. Boston: Little, Brown and Company, 1967.

John Dewey. "The Relation of Theory to Practice in Education." National Society for the Scientific Study of Education. *The Relation of Theory to Practice in Education*. Third Yearbook, Part I. Bloomington, Illinois: Public School Publishing Company, 1904.

_____. *Theory of Valuation*. Chicago: University of Chicago Press, 1939.

Paulo Freire. *Pedagogy of the Oppressed*. New York: Herder & Herder, Inc., 1972.

Ivan Illich. *Deschooling Society*. New York: Harper & Row, Publishers, 1971.

James John Jelinek. *Principles and Values in School and Society*. Tempe, Arizona: Far Western Philosophy of Education Society, 1976.

_____. "The Outcomes of Training as Contrasted with Teaching." Cassette Recording. Tempe, Arizona: Far Western Philosophy of Education Society, 1976.

_____. "Competency-Based Education: Consensus Cognoscenti Versus Reconstructio Experientiae." In: James John Jelinek, editor. *Philosophy of Education: 1972-1973*. Tempe, Arizona: Far Western Philosophy of Education Society, 1973.

_____. "A Reconstructed Epistemology for Education." In: James John Jelinek, editor. *Philosophy of Education: 1969*. Tempe, Arizona: Far Western Philosophy of Education Society, 1969.

_____. "The Influence of Teaching of Certain Elementary Principles of Philosophy Upon Modification of Basic Aspects of the Concept of Self

Held by College Students." In: James John Jelinek, editor. *Philosophy of Education: 1968.* Tempe, Arizona: Far Western Philosophy of Education Society, 1968.

Stanley Milgram. *Obedience to Authority: An Experimental View.* New York: Harper & Row, Publishers, 1969.

George G. Nathan. *The New American Credo: A Contribution Toward the Interpretation of the American Mind.* New York: Alfred A. Knopf, Inc., 1927.

Milton Rokeach. *The Nature of Human Values.* New York: Free Press, 1973.

B. F. Skinner. *Beyond Freedom and Dignity.* New York: Alfred A. Knopf, Inc., 1971.

Joel Spring. *A Primer of Libertarian Education.* New York: Free Life Editions, 1975.

Claude Steiner. *Scripts People Live.* New York: Grove Press, Inc., 1974.

J. Stephens. *The Process of Schooling: A Psychological Examination.* New York: Holt, Rinehart and Winston, Inc., 1967.

8 Education for a Changing Society

Shirley H. Engle, Wilma S. Longstreet

By the year 2000, there will no longer be a need for eyes—radar will have replaced them. Fingers will be reduced to one because only one is necessary to push the button to accomplish anything that is needed. I will be a freak because I will still have eyes and five fingers.

The above is a fairly typical excerpt from a set of compositions written by a class of college freshmen who were asked to imagine what technology will mean to their lives in the year 2000. Sadness and a sense of inevitability pervaded all the compositions. Once, technological progress would have meant the hope of something better to come. Now, though vestiges of hope remain, the progress of technology seems to have become the unfolding of an inexorable human tragedy. The imminence of technological disaster oppresses us; the influence of mindless industries on the nature and quality of our lives offends us; and yet, we seem resigned and determined to indulge in an escapism that offers us, at best, some fleeting semblance of pleasure before the holocaust.

Regaining Control

We have lost control of technology and, in the process, of ourselves as well. This is the critical reality we must confront before we will again be capable of directing the future. Our loss of control has been an immensely subtle process, beginning quite slowly and sporadically at first, then growing exponentially.

The initial development of scientific research and its applications for the satisfaction of human needs was a long-term phenomenon bridging many generations. This development sometimes involved moments of creative intuition; far more frequently it involved the dogged, even plodding rational analyses of painstakingly gathered empirical data. The heart of the industrial revolution was the repeated applications of rational system to an empirically discerned world.

Even though technological progress was based on the pyramiding of scientific studies and their practical applications, the technological break-through remained, until this century, an individual effort based on the rational capacities of individuals often working in near isolation. This essential individuality of early technological progress may have made it appear logically compatible with the economic model of free enterprise. Certainly, in the centuries prior to our own, the rational, individually oriented development of technology benefited from the support that individual businessmen gave to technologists in order to meet the demands of consumers as these were interpreted by the individual (or small group of) investor(s). The maximizing of a company's profits, which remains to this day a fundamental tenet of free enterprise, encouraged increasing financial support to technological researchers and produced enormous benefits to humankind which not only meet but far supersede the survival needs of humanity.

It is at the point when the basic needs of humanity are satisfied and the demands of consumers decreasingly reflect such needs that free enterprise becomes an irrational model, the functioning of which often defies reason and any logical prediction of future direction. One manufacturer tries to sell as many guns as he can; another pushes nonreturnable bottles as a cost saving device; still another dumps PPB in a river because it is cheaper. So long as it may be assumed that consumer demand and basic human needs are closely related, the technological developments supported by business will naturally follow patterns beneficial to humankind's survival. What was perhaps not predictable as free enterprise and technological development became closely associated was that the essential needs of consumers living in the Western world would be reasonably well satisfied by the late 1800's. This meant that businesses, acting individually, would not only respond to but develop needs in consumers.

We would be hard pressed to demonstrate any real link between much of today's technological production and our survival needs. The irrational multiplication of "developed needs" from transistor radios to photocopying machines to Saturday night handguns to the genetic manipulation of genes has not only increased the complexity of our lives beyond calculation but has brought us all to the point where we feel we have lost control of technology even if we believe it to be no more than the product of our own rational powers. This sense that we cannot direct technology may well be a major source of the apathy that pervades our society today. Our rational efforts seem to turn into irrational outcomes.

In other words, while each technological accomplishment is necessarily a product of people applying their logical powers of reason to an empirically oriented question, the management of these accomplishments, taken from the perspective of their overall impact on human life, has been left to the haphazard efforts of individual businesses involved, primarily, in developing a demand for their products so that profits may be maximized.

This less-than-rational management, at least from the broad perspective, of our technological successes may account in part not only for the pervasive apathy that afflicts so many of us, but for the growing resentment among the young toward business and toward formal rational analyses. The flight to sensitivity training, though having merits in its own right, is also a partial manifestation of the sense that while we have lost control of technological-industrial society as a whole, we still have ourselves and, on our own, we can achieve some desirable qualities of life. It is a sort of "go-it-alone," hedonistic resignation to technological drift. Even the clamor for local control may be a partial reflection of this yearning to escape into ourselves. The "escape," however, is really not a choice available to us. The benefits of technology are too much a part of our survival and of the very texture of our lives.

Rather than how to escape, the question is that of how to regain control. It is, of course, a question having far-reaching implications for our future and for the political, economic, and social interests of our society. However, regaining control must first mean dealing with the nature and qualities of the rational powers of reasoning and reflection that have made possible the technology which now holds an irrational though powerful sway over the course of our lives. There is no simple way of reorganizing technological production so that the total will again be directed by human rationality. There is, however, the possibility of developing the intellect so that individuals will be interested in and better able to control the direction and influence of technology on their lives. Our educational institutions, notwithstanding some very significant changes in the functions they serve, remain the fulcrum of rational development and reflective reasoning. They cannot but be entwined in the unfolding of the future and they are a key in any effort to regain control. It is urgent that the efforts and functions of the schools come to be seen in this light.

There are significant intellectual phenomena which have arisen as a result of the accelerating pace of change, and which the schools must deal with. Nearly 50 years ago, Alfred North Whitehead recognized that technology had brought us to, "the first period of human history in which it could not be assumed that each generation will live in an environment substantially similar to that of the preceding generation."[1] Since these words were written, the acceleration of change has increased so steadily that its very acknowledgment has become prosaic. Prosaicism notwithstanding, the differences have become so immense and so hasty that they are no longer merely between generations but within the span of one generation. In other words, added to the generation gap is a new, far-reaching intellectual phenomenon, that of *intra-generational disjuncture*. The experiences of our youth, that come to be an intimate part of the way we think, of what we are, are increasingly less relevant to our adult lives. The things we grow to love and believe in as youngsters are distant from the realities of our maturity. The conceptions we hold of our own roles in society or of the proper functions of business and government or of what is acceptable technological progress, which we begin to acquire in early childhood, are largely inappropriate guidelines for our own future activities and decisions. For instance, we go on consuming gas wildly, buying cars which make no sense in the face of declining petroleum reserves. The habits and beliefs for such consumption are deeply seeded in our earliest stages of childhood development long before most of us are even in command of our abstract reasoning powers or can judge the quality of these habits and beliefs. Rational thought processes, which reach their full developmental stages somewhere between the ages of ten and twelve, have increasingly come to be at odds with our own early development. In a sense, the disjuncture is an intra-generational crisis of identity. There is an inevitable disorientation and our ability to make decisions has suffered significantly. If our rational capacities and our control over technology are to be increased, the schools must deal with intra-generational disjuncture as a problem of intellectual development.

The roots of technology have reached far into the very modalities of human thought. McLuhan long ago recognized the importance of new media upon the processing and storing of information, concluding that alphabetized knowledge was obsolete and would inevitably be replaced by a multi-dimensional patterned format, which would, in turn, influence the derivations of meanings and their human significance.[2] It may well be true that a new kind of reasoning is developing which is quite different from the hierarchical, cause-effect, either-or logic that has so long held sway over Western thought. It may also be true that since its development is somehow involved with the multitude of divergent sensations created by such technological products as television, flashing strobe lights, elec-

[1] Alfred North Whitehead. "Introduction." In: Wallace B. Denham. *Business Adrift*. New York: McGraw-Hill Book Company, 1931. pp. 18-19.

[2] Marshall McLuhan. *Understanding Media: The Extension of Man*. New York: Signet Books, 1964.

tronic synthesizers and computers, this new pattern of thought may not be useful in regaining control over the direction that technology as a whole will take. In other words, it may be a way of dealing *within* the context of variously related patterns of meaning without, however, yielding an overall view of the way technological products come together to influence the nature of our lives. The tenets of patterned thought processes are far from clear and while this does not render them less important, it does seem to recommend the continued development in the young of those rational thought processes which made our present technological advancement possible. We must, however, try to expand the range and nature of our intellectual capacities in the hope that this will contribute to our ability to confront the multifariousness of our present technological situation.

McLuhan's conclusions regarding the obsolescence of alphabetized knowledge must be taken with caution. Alphabetized knowledge is, after all, one way of organizing knowing. What is certain is that our ways of perceiving and dealing with the world, of reflecting about life and its problems are presently undergoing far-reaching changes which can be variously linked to the multiplication of new media. The fiction we used to read in long, intimate hours of reacting and exploring our reactions has been replaced by the T.V. program bringing life, love, death and the soap commercial together in a quick succession of associationistically-cast emotions. We have little time or inclination to explore the underlying meanings, the ideals, the inconsistencies of what we have watched.

Our immensely increased powers of transportation have created a similar situation. We take 11-day bus tours of Europe, passing quickly through towns full of quaint images that have turned our way of coming to know foreign lands into a series of high-interest flicks having neither beginning nor end. We get on a mass transit system and go 40 miles away to work far from our community and local allegiances. One-hundred-miles-an-hour motorcycles offer us the thrill of speed for its own sake. Coney Island roller coasters, high-speed water skiing, parachute jumps from thousands of feet out of the sky are only a few of the action-packed thrills that we have either come to know or expect in our leisure time. The hours of sitting around and talking or reading or just plain thinking are now equated with painful boredom.

It is extraordinary that in a period when there are so many things to do, boredom has become a major affliction, especially of the young. It is as though technology had offered us a set of new drugs from which to achieve highs never before experienced. We have grown to expect hours packed with high-level stimuli. When the stimuli are gone, boredom, rather than thoughtful reflection, results. The "withdrawal" symptom is painful and many of us desperately search for a new technological high, which, though not LSD or some other chemical stimulant of the subconscious, will help us fill our minds with images and reactions of great intensity. What is more, as with chemical drugs, when true addiction occurs, our need for intense stimuli increases. If the "humanized technological society" is to happen at all,[3] somehow we must come to grips with the quantity and nature of new media and their interaction with the human intellect.

Quiet reflection, when the rational analysis of what we are doing and where we are going can occur, has become progressively less possible. The growing popularity of transcendental meditation is in many ways an effort to regain those aspects of human thought that prosper in periods of quiet reflection. It is an effort to regain control at least over ourselves. Still, it is only a small movement surrounded by a continuing inundation of mindless technology. The schools, in their quest to develop human rational capacities, will need to foster periods of reflection or, in other terms, of intellectual review of what is happening, why it is happening, and whether it should happen. Our electronic computers put forth mind-boggling quantities of data, which we might use in this quest to regain control over our lives caught in technological drift if we were willing to reflect on that data, but few of us, including those who would call themselves scholars, are presently willing. We, the public, clamor for quick, simplistic solutions to our complex problems. The hours once spent by theoreticians or logicians exploring tentative conclusions may still be spent, but few, even in the professional fields, have the patience to listen to their analyses. All too frequently, they are thought to be irrelevant. Regaining the capacity and the will to engage in quiet reflection would seem to be a first necessary step to regaining control over our destinies.

On Stability and Slowing Enculturation

The schools have prepared us, and go on preparing our children, for stability, that is, for the logical continuation of what is known about the past and present. The disciplines we study, even when the emphasis is upon studying process, reiterate the stability of underlying principles and their modes of applications. Our more relevant topical studies typically deal with social concerns in the context of persistent problems that have faced humankind throughout history. Poverty and justice are frequently treated in this manner with the specific events becoming

3 Willis W. Harmin. "The Nature of Our Changing Society: Implications for Schools." In: David E. Purpel and Maurice Belanger, editors. *Curriculum and the Cultural Revolution*. Berkeley: McCutchan Publishing Corporation, 1972.

representative of these broad concepts. While such an approach is extremely helpful in developing a global perspective of social behavior, it is also a reiteration of the belief that the way humankind deals with life is essentially an unchanging way. When the broad conceptual approach to *present* problems viewed from the context of *persistent* human problems is brought together with a heavy concentration upon the disciplines, as is the case in most of our schools, the powerful, though hidden message is stability; the "nothing-is-new-under-the-sun" syndrome is imperceptibly and often unintentionally taught to youngsters whose futures are tied to continuous as well as significant technological change.

This is a message that is consistent with the traditional perceptions of the school as a primary transmitter of society's knowledge, beliefs, and traditions. It is utterly inconsistent for a society that finds itself involved in the unfolding of an intra-generational disjuncture and its inevitable intra-generational crisis of identity; it verges on the absurd to ignore new, though not clearly understood, modalities of thought and expression; it is suicidal not to recognize that the exponential increase of technological progress, accompanied by an irrational relationship between "developed" consumer demands and basic human needs, poses a set of obstacles to human survival never before experienced in history. What is more, the rational analyses and reflective reasoning, which made our initial technological progress possible, are threatened in their very essence by the continuous bombardment of high-intensity stimuli produced by our mindless technological complexes. Never before has humankind been confronted with a challenge to the nature of its intellect by the very inventions which its intellect has made possible.

The school's traditional goal of enculturating society's ways and beliefs in the young can only be based upon such values and modes as are already established. The perplexing questions of intra-generational disjuncture and of coping with change and with the decisions that an unfettered technology and an unstable future require, can be avoided and are avoided within this conception of the functions of schooling. The scholastic goal of enculturation fits the development of the mind into present reality and its ways of perceiving and dealing with events. It reinforces a view of cultural stability and interferes with the individual's capacity to participate in decisions affecting technological progress and the cultural trends of his or her own times. In other words, enculturation by schools may interfere with the survival of democratic governance.

The primary goal of the schools can no longer be to enculturate. Indeed, such a goal seems pointless and of little use to any of us. The enculturation of the individual begins practically the day he or she is born. Family, friends, religion, status symbols, and so on, are far more powerful molders of a person's way of thinking and being than the schools could ever be. Rather than being one more additional and relatively minor factor in the enculturation process experienced by the developing child, the schools ought to be straining toward *slowing down enculturation,* and helping the student to attain as much intellectual flexibility and open-mindedness as possible.

Of course, to a considerable extent, it will be impossible for the schools not to enculturate—teachers and administrators are, after all, cultural products of their own times—but the conscious effort needs to be toward increasing the intellectual range of students beyond the limits of the present and of a specific culture. The primary function of education in an era of rapid, far-reaching change, dominated by an immensely productive though irrationally organized technology, must go beyond merely developing an awareness of alternatives to developing the capacities necessary for dealing with and even creating the alternatives. If the schools are uncertain of the capacities that will be necessary, then they must develop as broad and effective a range of capacities as is latent within human intellectual potential.

In a sense, it is being suggested that the processes of enculturation and indoctrination be consciously made separate functions by the educational enterprise. The dictionary defines *enculturation* as "the process by which an individual learns the traditional content of a culture and assimilates its practices and values"[4] and *indoctrination* as the giving of, "instructions, especially in fundamentals or rudiments" and "to cause to be impressed and ultimately imbued."[5] It is not possible to teach without eventually imbuing the student with fundamentals or rudiments. It is being suggested that these fundamentals should not necessarily reflect the traditional practices and values of society—even if that society is a democracy—but should rather indoctrinate the young with the reasonable use of those intellectual skills which can be utilized in the effort to regain control over technology and the direction society is taking.

Of course, all that has just been said makes the assumption that a democratic system involving the active, significant participation of individual citizens in determining the course of society and the quality of their own lives is not only desirable but an ultimate goal of schooling in a changing society. However, to allow the simultaneous enculturation and indoctrination of specific forms of democracy to dominate the essence of schooling is tantamount to enclosing the minds of the young within

[4] *Webster's Third New International Dictionary.* (Unabridged.) Springfield, Massachusetts: G. & C. Merriam Co., 1971.

[5] *Ibid.*

a stability of governance, albeit democratic in form, which may be completely inappropriate to the nature of their future lives.

We must realize that if a democratic governance, regardless of its specific form, is to survive, the mounting quantities of information that are now feeding the irrational growth of technological production must be brought under control of individual citizens. Without information, and without skills for rationally and flexibly dealing with that information, it is doubtful a democratically oriented control of technology can be attained. Allowing the future to become merely the inexorable results of present realities, or a series of chance occurrences, or the product of decisions by a handful of elite in control of modern technology, or even some odd mixture of these is undesirable and would eventually lead to the annihilation of any form of democratic participation. If we believe that democracy of some kind ought to survive into the future, then we must find ways in the present to develop and protect the active, informed participation of individuals in the decisions of their society. The schools cannot accomplish this alone; but they can help.

The Functions of Schooling in a Changing Society

Whenever the functions of schooling are discussed, there seems to be a finality in the discussion as though the educational institution could blind itself to the circumstances of the times and determine in some abstract land of knowledge what it ought to do and be for now and for all times. This is really a misinterpretation of the nature of the institution. It is, at all times, an institution intended to prepare people for something (or a set of somethings). What that something shall be specifically and the kind of preparation that will be offered must necessarily be determined by the historical circumstances within which the schools find themselves. This is true, even if some basic premises about human beings and society are taken to be absolutes. For instance, democracy may be taken as a given and the effective participation of citizens in the governance of society as a persistent goal of the schools. Nevertheless, the functions of schooling may have to change considerably, depending on actual circumstances. Once, regaining societal control of technology would not have been the overriding function of schooling. Indeed, in a sparsely settled America, when specific skills were essential to survival, apprenticeship-type training might have significantly contributed to the continuation of a democratic form of governance.

This chapter has taken the position that the present historical circumstances of accelerating change, multiplying information, and runaway technological production have escaped the control of our democratically oriented society, threatening its survival, and that regaining control via the systematic use of logical analyses, reflective reasoning, and an increased independence from enculturating processes must take precedence over all other possible functions of schooling. There are, admittedly, other functions which schooling might take on that could be justifiable even within the context of the position taken by this paper. For instance, if the individual is central to the democratic decision-making process, should not one's personal development and one's coming to understand how one's well-being within society is best served, be a major function of schooling? How can one's participation be adequate if one is not adequately in touch with oneself? The questions are valid and the answers must hedge—must admit that the response is qne of prioritizing the limited resources available to America's public schools today.

The emphasis on *individual* control of information and rational processes must necessarily take into account individual intellectual abilities as well as the personal reactions and experiences that students have with technology, governance, and so forth. However, that personal development which is emphasized in sensitivity training, that investigation of the human being's sense of isolation and alienation, taken not as a general sociological phenomenon but as a very personal, psychological development, has been excluded from the functions of schooling in this paper. The exclusion is not for all times but for our present circumstances. While Carl Rogers' perception that when "the individual's survival needs are satisfied," he is for the first time "freed to become aware of his isolation, aware of his alienation,"[6] is reasonably accurate, it overlooks the questions of runaway technological progress and its significant threat to the survival of democracy. Obviously, if Rogers is fully aware of these threats, his priorities are quite different from those established in this paper: For the schools to spend significant time helping us to work out our own psychological "ids," while the totality of our lives is being dragged in ways and in directions that we would not go if we were fully cognizant of the conditions around us, would be, under present historical circumstances, a misuse of educational resources. Indeed, it is somewhat questionable whether the school, as a group-oriented, public institution, would be capable of dealing with the intimate psychic development of each of its millions of youngsters. However, that the schools might become capable and that in a person-centered, democratically oriented society, the function of schooling as personal development might become a priority is admitted and even held out as a hope.

Another function of schooling that is often given major importance,

[6] Carl R. Rogers. "Interpersonal Relationships: U.S.A. 2000." *The Journal of Applied Behavioral Science* 4 (3) :266; 1968.

especially in the context of a changing society, but which this chapter has omitted from the functions of schooling is that of career preparation. Obviously, in proposing the development of a wide range of intellectual powers fostering reflective thought and rational analyses, careers of all kinds would benefit from schooling. However, while it can be expected in our free enterprise organization that businesses will take over the specific training of their employees, it is inconceivable that they would contribute importantly to a function of education that would posit regaining rational control over the free enterprise development of technology. Furthermore, in this period when nothing is changing more quickly than the careers developed by technology, any training offered by the public schools, at best a secondhand interpreter of the needs of a multitude of diverse industries, would have obsolescence built into its very nature. Certainly when such training had a longer life span and when technological production was still responding to basic human needs, career preparation, which took on various forms of apprenticeship, was a defensible function of schooling, and it may someday become defensible again.

While the function of socialization via its direct relationship to enculturation has been specifically rejected in this paper, the Deweyian belief that what the young study must be related to the significant problems and decisions of the society has been fully embraced. The position supported in this paper, which assumes that individual people, engaged in democratic processes, can plan and participate in a better life, both as individuals and as members of society, is Dewey's position. Despite the acknowledgment of significant changes in historical circumstances since Dewey opened his experimental school in 1896, the functions he would have attributed to school closely resemble those presented in this paper. We can, however, no longer count on the experience of our youth to support the conclusions of our adulthood; and the nature of our thought processes has expanded beyond the Deweyian "felt-needs" model of intellectual development. Notwithstanding, Dewey's faith in the democratic application of rational processes reflects a view of the functions of schooling similar to those of this paper but removed to a new set of historical circumstances.

Other functions of schooling have developed in recent times which are not only fundamentally inappropriate to the nature of schooling, but a reinforcement of our present technological-industrial irrationality. The public school has become a repository for the unemployed young. This "internment" cannot reasonably be related to their preparation. Indeed, with great frequency, the conditions with which they are held in school make it impossible to fulfill any kind of "preparation" function. When

30 to 40 youngsters are placed together in a class led by a teacher who may have 150 students a term, the function of school can only be that of keeping the young off the streets.

Interestingly, the recent rise of the alternative school conception can be related to this view of the schools as "holding" centers for the excess in employment population. The alternative school conception posits that any possible function of the school which might suit a group of students' needs is acceptable and should be supported by the public. Rather than being a societally oriented instrument of preparation, schooling is perceived to be a center for meeting the personal interests of the young, whatever these may be, *so that they will stay in school.*

Adult schooling, presently going under the nomenclature of "lifelong learning," often reflects this same potpourri of the functions of schooling and has, in a sense, become the new "holding center" for the elderly.[7] Vocational training and hobby-like leisure courses fill most adult school calendars. Increasingly, it is a place for the elderly to go to fill their time with interesting things to do. This function is perhaps the least objectionable of all—and even so, it must be asked whether the limited resources of education ought to be spent in such undirected, haphazard ways. As we stand at the precipice of technological disaster, can we really afford such flippancy in what we expect from the schools? As the multiplication of data threatens our very capacity to continue the democratic participation of citizens, can we allow ourselves the pleasure of ambling around wherever our pleasure may be? Obviously, the position of this paper is that the functions of schooling must be prioritized in the light of circumstances, and a plan must be developed to best meet those circumstances.

Structuring an Open Curriculum for a Changing Society

The Future-Oriented Curriculum. If the schools are to help us regain control over irrational technological development, if they are to help us cope with the disorientations of an ever-increasing intra-generational disjuncture and the rise of new modalities of thought, if they are to contribute to the survival of democratic participation in the decisions of society, then what we plan to happen in the schools must change significantly. *We must bring the future into what we do in the schools.* We must bring the future consequences of technological progress under the careful, rational scrutiny of the young. "Who am I?" cannot continue to

[7] In September 1976, the Fromm Institute for Life Long Learning, a college in the University of San Francisco, began offering academic courses to local residents 50 years of age or older. The New School for Social Research in New York City also has a special school for older students, and the movement promises to broaden.

be perceived only in terms of immediately relevant responses. Identity, which is derived from the people and events around us as well as from what we are individually, extends across the span of a lifetime. It is as much a future concern as a present one. We cannot continue to allow our youngsters to face the confusion and insecurity of a predictable intra-generational crisis of identity without adequate preparation. To look at our changing society, as Willis Harmin would, "as a society in process of choice—choice among alternative futures, choice among alternative belief-and-value systems, choice between ennobling versus debasing images of man, choice of how some sense of coherent authority will be restored,"[8] is of little significance unless we bring future consequences into the personal awareness of the young and help them to develop the reflective, rational skills for engaging in cogent decisions that go beyond the material gratifications of a free enterprise technology.

To bring the future into the school's curriculum must not, however, come to mean future-oriented, educational indoctrination of a specific kind of future. To take a set of future events, institutions, roles, etc., regardless of their desirability, and present them to the young as the proper future (or even the inevitable future) implies capacities for future forecasting well beyond our present means. It also implies that we, who have planned rather poorly for ourselves, could do vastly better for future generations.

More important, however, the future incorporated as a specific kind of future in the school's curriculum poses an ethical question: Do the members of the present society have the right to formulate the life-styles of generations to come? It is one thing to say that the future develops from the present, and quite another to say the future shall be shaped by the present. The former statement recognizes the influence of present realities on the future but does not take away from the future the right to decide what ways and means shall be used to cope with its own times. The latter assumes that the present society can decide better than the future society what the most desirable alternatives for future life-styles will be. In a sense, the present would undertake a form of vocational training for future living while simultaneously denying democratic processes to the future. At stake is each person's right and each generation's right to participate as decision-making agents in the solutions of their problems and in the establishment of their ideals.

The curriculum must not close in the future. So long as bringing the future into the curriculum is translated educationally into a series of open-ended processes and broad generalizations, the use of which promises to lead toward a greater individual ability to cope with a changing world,

8 Harmin, *op. cit.,* p. 58.

it is supportive of a future conceived in democracy and free choice. If, instead, it becomes a series of closed models supporting a particular concept of the ideal world, it becomes an invasion of basic human rights and an exercise of little intellectual use in the quest to regain control over the mindless meanderings of technological production. To deal with the future, the school's curriculum must have as a major goal the development of rational skills and the study of content that would help the individual view the phenomena of his/her culture with increased objectivity and from an increased range of alternatives. Central to such an effort is the availability and use of the most up-to-date information regarding present and future possibilities, and the continuous analyses and revision of established models for personal and societal living, and a constant impetus to modify and/or develop new models whenever these would seem suited to a more desirable quality of life. The student must be in command of these modifications; he must be an active participant in both leadership and followership; he must be a fulcrum from which the rational unfolding of the curriculum occurs.

The Open Curriculum. The curriculum is perceived to be more than the simple arrangement of content (s) to be transmitted to students; it is the planned interception of students' experiences both inside and outside of school and the interface of those experiences with the intentionally developed experiences of schooling. Students bring with them to school knowledge about the world and models about how things operate in the world, which may or may not be very accurate or consistent, but which need to be accepted by the schools as points of departure. In the "open curricular design" that will be proposed in this paper, this acceptance (or interception) is to lead from the students' models of the world to more powerful, accurate models not only of the students' present world but of their own possible futures; it is to yield fuller control of the data base underlying their world and continuing technological progress; it is to develop in them greater intellectual skills in logical and other thought modalities and, hopefully, encourage their increased participation in the significant decisions of their times.

Curricular design is always no more than an approximation of the real curriculum which can only be finalized as it happens day to day. This is true even when the disciplines undergird the design. However, the personal experience and knowledge of youngsters cannot be consistently incorporated into a closed curricular design based on disciplines because what youngsters know and believe is of such a disparate and diffused nature that dealing with it would be a real hindrance while trying to acquire an understanding of the efficiently organized structures of specialized disciplines. Disciplines for the most part hold that all else remains unchanged while they undertake to explore a specific area of concern. They posit objectivity and ignore the subjective involvement and concerns which lead to significant value conflicts whenever society as a whole must make important decisions. Deciding on such questions as limiting strip mining may involve knowledge derived from the geologic disciplines but it also involves, importantly, the effects of the visual devastation of the countryside on the everyday lives of people inhabiting the area.

The structure of an open curricular design is inherently different from the traditional organization of the American school, especially that of the comprehensive high school which treats each course, even if interdisciplinary or problem-centered in nature, as a discrete, self-contained unit. The open curricular design systematically plans certain kinds of interceptions and certain ways of developing the interfacings of students' experiences with those of schooling without, however, detailing the specific data or events to be studied. While the outcomes of schooling may be expressed in terms of broadly conceived goals, *the specific results cannot be predicted in advance*. The student is always at least partially in command of what happens.

The distinction between an open and closed curricular design has tended to be confused in the past by emotionally placing an unstructured school experience in opposition to traditional curricular designs which are seen as inhumanely ignoring personal development. Of course, the unstructured school experience is seen as allowing for individual differences and personal growth. Regardless of how true such generalizations may be in the real world of the public schools, they are not dealing with the structural attributes that distinguish the closed curricular design, now dominant in the schools, from an open curricular design. Some exploration of distinguishing attributes is relevant to the planning of an open curricular design incorporating the future and will therefore be undertaken in the next few paragraphs.

A discipline is a specialized system of investigation, which limits its activities to certain kinds of ideas and/or empiricals, studying these via a set of suitable instruments, processes,* and procedures* in order to achieve progressively more powerful concepts, generalizations, and theories about how whatever is being studied works and can be predicted and/or controlled. Diagrammatically, a discipline may be represented as an isosceles triangle with the three equally important apexes representing the three major components:

---

* "Procedures," as used here, are seen as a specific, sequentially ordered set of activities which offer one means for the more generalized "process" to be put into practice. More than one procedure may be used for each process.

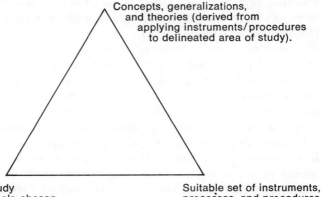

Concepts, generalizations,
and theories (derived from
applying instruments/procedures
to delineated area of study).

Delineated area of study
(ideas and/or empiricals chosen
for study).

Suitable set of instruments,
processes, and procedures.

Figure 1.

Physics is an example of a discipline. Its area of study is the operation of the physical empiricals of the universe. "Momentum" is, for instance, one of a number of concepts, developed by physics, which has
been utilized in achieving important generalizations and theories about
how the physical world functions. A volt-ammeter is one of many measuring instruments used, and controlled experimentation is one of its
major processes (having, of course, more than one procedure). The
school subject of physics is a reduction and simplification of the discipline
for pedagogical purposes. In the process of making a discipline into a
school subject, the dynamic search for new knowledge, which is always
present out in the field and which benefits greatly from the specialized
structure of the discipline, is often lost. This "freezing" of disciplinary
knowledge in the schools turns the efficiency of the disciplinary structure
into a way of shutting the minds of students to new perceptions and new
structures in a field.

Grammar is an example of another type of discipline. Oral language
and its written representation is the area delineated for study. Recording
spoken conversation and analyzing for similarities and differences in
sentence structures are among the major procedures in the process of
describing the language. Such concepts as "word," "sentence," and "subject" are used to achieve generalizations which can, in turn, be used to
predict an infinite number of future expressions. What these two very
different disciplines have in common is their stable, efficiently structured
interactions between the delineated area of study, the instruments,
processes and procedures used for the study and the development of

concepts, generalizations, and theories, the success of which will probably serve to modify the delineated area of study as well as the set of suitable instruments and procedures. In sum, there is an ongoing interaction of the isosceles apexes, which yields considerable intellectual though quite specialized power, and which has little leeway for dealing with the multifarious models of youngsters' ways of knowing and dealing with their world. Disciplines are very resistant to models which do not fit their patterns and often reject the reality of youngsters merely on that basis. For example, classic economic models which are a macro view of financial activities, rarely coincide with what youngsters experience, as individuals, in the everyday economy. In this sense, the discipline is a fragmented and unreal view of everyday experience. School study filled with such fragments is of little use to the individual trying to regain control over the direction of society.

Within the context of the above description of a discipline, the school subject of English is not a reflection of a specific discipline but rather a bringing together of various kinds of concerns which, in one way or the other, have the English language in common. Literary creativity is variously studied from the perspective of English history, personal creative capacities, and more modern forms of expression; reading and writing abilities are developed on the basis of a smattering of grammar, a great deal of practice in writing compositions, and even the daily reading of a newspaper. Nevertheless, in the closed curriculum of the public schools, so heavily influenced by the disciplines, English is treated as though it were a discipline. Its syllabi usually list what plays of Shakespeare shall be studied and at what grade level—as though it were necessary to read Julius Caesar before reading William Faulkner's works. In essence, the subject of English has had the structure of disciplines inconsistently imposed upon it. The disciplines, often distorted as they are translated into school subjects, have pervaded formal education for so long that even those subjects which are not based on disciplines have come to be treated as though they were, in fact, based on disciplines. What is studied, how it is studied, and the order in which it is studied are predetermined and not easily modified within the curricular sequence.

For the first half of this century, opening the curriculum has meant, via the comprehensive high school, increasing the number of school subjects available to the student for selection. A student could choose, for instance, between algebra and trigonometry or between biology, chemistry, and physics. However, once a discipline was selected, the student was essentially locked into its format. He had to deal with the discipline's delineated area of study, its instruments, processes and procedures, its concepts, generalizations and theories. Otherwise, he really was not studying physics or trigonometry or whatever but some takeoff of a part of the discipline's content that in some way was related to another interest. Any determination on the part of the student of what he would study had to happen before the course was taken. Diagrammatically, the curricular design of the comprehensive high school might be represented as in Figure 2.

What needs to be understood about this kind of choice is that the disciplines, even while continuously modifying themselves, are closed systems for looking at reality. The theoretical models around which disciplines are built may even be retained long after their ability to reflect reality has been widely and importantly questioned. For example, the Ptolemaic view of the earth's movements was generally sustained even though known facts had undermined its validity. The inability of classical economics to explain inflation linked with unemployment in the 1970's has not prevented its continued use as a guide in making important economic decisions. In other words, the disciplines are liable to lock in a future-oriented curriculum with fixed and unyielding models even if the translations into school subjects are accomplished with more sensitivity to the research orientation of disciplines out in the field.

Furthermore, the disciplines, by their very nature, fragment reality, distorting any holistic view of reality as it exists in the lives of people. The method of study, which concentrates on one aspect of reality and assumes that all other aspects remain constant, while necessary to the advancement of a discipline, is so distant from the individual's experiences that it cannot be readily used by her in making decisions about life and its directions. The transfer of the methods of investigation and analysis from school to daily living, linked as they are to the disciplines, is not a likely outcome of present-day schooling.

John Dewey, in fostering a topical approach to education, was essen-

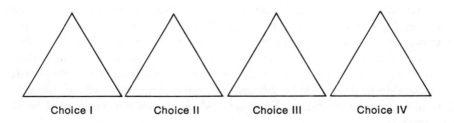

"Students May Choose From the Above"

Figure 2.

244 IMPROVING THE HUMAN CONDITION

tially involved in opening up the closed curricular structure imposed by the dominance of the disciplines. The use of topics makes it possible for the apexes of the disciplines to be unlinked from each other so that one of the apexes may be emphasized and even carefully described by the curricular design while the other apexes remain unspecified and open to the input of students and teachers. A topic may be a delineated area of study, or a concept, or a process. Topically, one may start from any one of the apexes, and develop an organized study guide. For example, "city slums" may be designated as the delineated area of study and students could be asked to develop generalizations, etc., via instruments and processes of their own choice. On the other hand, the curricular guide could call for the study of such concepts as: (a) the population, composition and distribution in a city, (b) the extent and distribution of wealth, (c) the quantity and quality of employment opportunities, and (d) the quantity and quality of community facilities. These concepts would offer the framework for the empiricals which students would be asked to find. They might use the statistical data available in the latest census for their investigation, or they might collect their own data. On the basis of their data, students might then develop a series of general- izations about the concept of "power in a city slum," or they might even engage in achieving a conceptual distinction between a slum and a non- slum. The curriculum guide could, similarly, outline the processes of literary analyses to be studied while allowing students to choose their own readings and undertake at least the effort to produce a viable literary theory of their own. Each apex, taken alone, offers a mode for achieving a structured but open curricular design, as in Figure 3.

Furthermore, as each of the apexes is freed from the restraints of the other apexes, restraints quite important to the power of a discipline, the nature of the apexes becomes more flexible and more capable of respond- ing to the complex milieu of a changing society. For instance, processes can be broadened so as to include general questioning techniques or logi- cal criteria to be followed for developing categories. Students may be asked to develop classification systems based on what they believe to be the major conceptual components, say, of a changing society. Via the collec- tion of data describing this changing society and processes of empirical verification, they may be asked to reconsider their categories. While it is impossible to determine in advance what the categories will be, the cur- riculum can, nevertheless, be structured to ensure a certain quality of preparation.

Dewey did not actually consider the "opening up" of curriculum from a structural perspective, being far more concerned with the social relevance of what was studied and the personal involvement of young-

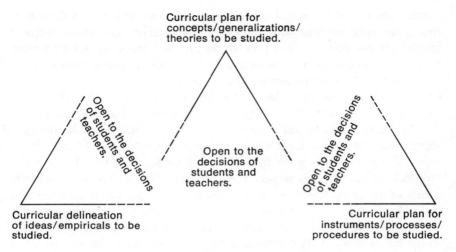

Figure 3.

sters in the resolution of social problems. That the schools' curriculum can be structured for openness has been widely overlooked. In the past several decades the schools have incorporated numerous topical courses in the selections made available to students. For the most part, however, these courses have tended to be a series of haphazardly related studies which, when taken together, offer little of the intellectual power accompanying the disciplines. Of course, given the tremendous increase in data, even the school study of disciplines can no longer be a thorough memorization of the three apexes. In the late fifties and sixties, understanding the basic concepts, generalizations, and theories of a discipline or knowing how to use the basic processes and procedures of a discipline began to take precedence over the discipline as a whole, although the essential nature of the discipline being studied was always present and much of its intellectual power was retained. However, when topics like "Wars" or "The Role of Protest" or "The Control of Technology" were to be studied, their curricular design became completely disorganized if not simply a collection of the teacher's opinions or a new organization for factual memorization.

Opening up the curricular structure can be an intellectually powerful process of viewing a topic first from one and then another of the major apexes, that is, from the perspective of a clearly delineated set of empiricals and/or ideas, from the perspective of an organized group of concepts, generalizations, and theories, and from the perspective of instruments, processes, and procedures. From each perspective, the open curriculum would allow and encourage students to explore, via their own input, the relationships with the other perspectives. Of course, neither empiricals, nor concepts, nor procedures can be learned in isolation from each other. The important objective is that students become fully aware of the interrelationships among the three as well as the control which each makes possible over the others. Diagrammatically, the study of a topic in an open curricular design may be represented as in Figure 4.

Major concerns of our present technological society can be brought together in the overall structure of the curriculum as sets of interrelated topics. Such curricular groupings of related topics shall be referred to as "topical strands" in this paper. Topical strands, conceived as major elements of an open, future-oriented curricular design, would include: the technology strand, the symbolic systems strand, the present realities strand, and the values strand. Each of these strands is seen as a response to the needs of a swiftly changing society that somehow lost control over the technology it has created. The *real* curriculum is seen as a series of transactions between carefully developed study guides for each topical strand and the experiences, knowledge, and capacities of students. The active, knowledgeable, and rational participation of free citizens in determining the direction of technology and of society as a whole is the fundamental goal of this open curriculum.

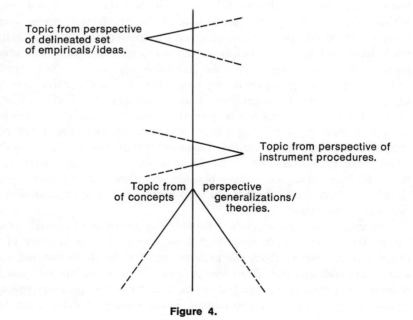

Figure 4.

A Curriculum for Tomorrow

The Technology Strand. The topical strands of a curricular design incorporating the future would naturally reflect what have been presented in this paper as society's major concerns if a democratic form of governance is to survive. The present state of technology, the prospects for its progress, the techniques of future forecasting with its exploration of possible alternatives and the processes of decision making available to us as we engage in studying the future would comprise the core of a curricular strand on technology. The perspectives would be alternately used to explore the various aspects of the strand. For example, on the basis of knowledge which the students of a class have about the present state of technology, they could be asked to devise a classification system under which all technological advances might be categorized.[9] The students could be asked to compare their own individually developed classification systems with those of other students and determine the rational origins of the differences (that is, the underlying generalizations or assumptions), the quality of each system, and which of the systems is preferable. Once the classification system has been established, it could offer the structure for collecting more accurate, researched data of the present state of technology. As the quantity of such data would quickly become unmanageable, students could be asked to make use of different kinds of data retrieval instruments, adapting their instruments to their classification systems or *vice versa*. They might then be presented with the following generalization: The structure of a data retrieval instrument affects the way data are perceived and used. Their task would be to prove, disprove, or indicate uncertainty about the validity of the generalization. Subsequently, they could be shown a set of future forecasts by one or another well-known forecaster, such as Herman Kahn or Wayne Boucher, and be asked to determine whether the set of predictions is supported by the data available to them. The segment of the curricular strand on technology described above can be represented as in Figure 5.

It should be noted that while the technological strand would make planned use of the three major perspectives, the strand itself, because of its nature, would emphasize the acquisition and use of empirical data and the predictions possible given the data. While rational and other kinds of skills would be developed in this strand, the strand itself is informationally oriented. The strand as a whole confronts such questions

[9] There are already many such systems available and students could refer to these. Theodore J. Gordon used such a system in his 1964 Rand paper, *Report on a Long-Range Forecasting Study*. He used six categories: Scientific Breakthrough, Population Growth, Automation, Space Progress, Probability and Prevention of War, and Future Weapons Systems.

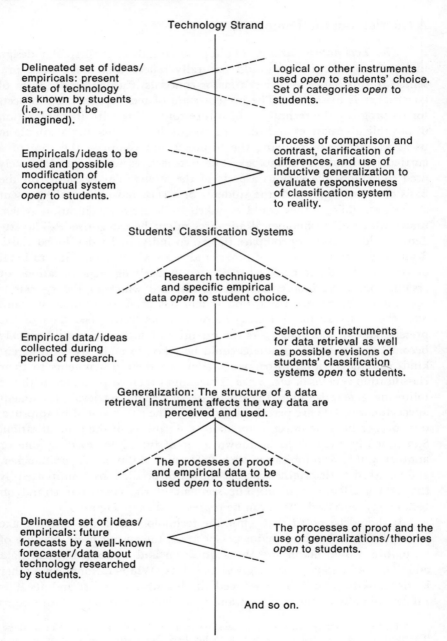

Figure 5.

as: What specifically is happening technologically? What might be the consequence of present technological developments? How can data about technological development be arranged differently for different uses?

The Symbolic Systems Strand. Another curricular strand, Symbolic Systems, would emphasize the development of diverse kinds of intellectual processes even while making planned use of the three major perspectives. This strand would have as its goal the literal increase in the range of rational, symbolic, and other kinds of intellectual systems which might be made available to the individual. Though the present state of knowledge is less than adequate to fulfill this goal satisfactorily, a start in its direction by the schools is necessary to ensure the knowledgeable, cogent participation of citizens in the decisions of society.

While there is a growing awareness that new modes of intellectual operations are holding increasing influence over the directions taken by society, the schools have done little to modify their basic approach to the development of linguistic and other symbolic systems. English is a haphazard conglomeration of literary heritage, an inordinate emphasis on one graphemic system, reading, a bit of practical and creative writing and, perhaps, some debates, often taken as an opportunity for youngsters to say whatever comes off the top of their heads. The awareness of, say, the bimodal nature of computer programs, and the inconsistency of this bimodality with the complexities encountered in a swiftly developing technological society are not even considered let alone studied as fundamental inconsistencies between a major symbolic system in use by society and societal realities.

The study of such inconsistencies arising from diverse symbolic systems would have to be open-ended and incomplete. Nevertheless, the awareness itself would be beneficial to students' intellectual development. It is not necessary, educationally, to have a complete grasp of new kinds of symbolic systems for the schools to include these profitably in the curriculum. If such were not the case, efforts to develop art and music appreciation in the young, often undertaken by the schools, even though no one is certain of what "appreciation" means, would be totally useless. Developing an awareness has often proved profitable to the future of humankind even when what one was becoming aware of escaped *precise* human definition.

Besides the beneficial aspects of developing symbolic awareness, there is also the consideration of how youngsters mature intellectually. Again, not much is known with certainty. However, Wilder Penfield, whose neurological studies undertaken during surgery have made history, came to the conclusion that children are able to develop new neurological circuits for each new language learned prior to the age of ten or so.[10] After this age, circuits already established have to be adapted to the learning of a new language. This would seem to support the fact that after a certain age, a new language is never learned as if it were a native tongue.

Language, of course, is one of several symbolic systems available to modern technological society. If what is true for spoken tongues is true for other symbolic systems, and the extension of the generalization seems reasonable though based on retroductive insight, we must cease to emphasize the learning of reading in the elementary grades and undertake to broaden what potential for learning diverse symbolic systems is available to the young. If McLuhan's position, discussed earlier in this paper, has any validity, it further supports the development of a symbolic systems strand in place of the present language arts/English approach.

Although there is a continuing debate regarding how language is related to thought, there is general agreement that increased power in language corresponds to increased power in thought. The child's capacity to process grammatical patterns may depend upon innate syntactical abilities existing prior to the influence of a particular language,[11] or it may be acquired through a process of internalizing the instrument(s) of communication.[12] In either case, the development of language corresponds to increased intellectual potential that is poorly understood but widely acknowledged. Again, the extension of th   bolic systems in general is a retroductive hypothesis. I   on of new media and new systems of arranging data   a reality, the concern with teaching reading and writing, which is often based on simpler levels of language than those of which children are capable when they first enter school, might still be a defensible scholastic enterprise. The crisis that now confronts us warrants curricular plans based on new hypotheses.

A symbolic systems strand might include the following components:[13]

10 Lee J. Cronbach. *Educational Psychology*. New York: Harc   Jovanovich, Inc., 1963. p. 101.

11 This position is sustained in the following works: Susan Ervin. In: Eric Lenneberg, editor. *New Directions in the Study of Language*. Cambridge, Massachusetts: M.I.T. Press, 1966. pp. 163-90; Jerome S. Bruner. *Toward a Theory of Instruction.* Cambridge, Massachusetts: Belknap Press, 1955. pp. 104-105; Roger Brown and Ursula Bellugi. "Three Processes in the Child's Acquisition of Syntax." *Harvard Educational Review* 34:131-51; Spring 1964.

12 This position is sustained in the following works: L. S. Vygotsky. In: Eugenia Hartman and Gertrude Vakar, editors. *Thought and Language*. Cambridge, Massachusetts: M.I.T. Press, 1960; Willard Van Orman Quine. *Word and Object*. Cambridge, Massachusetts: M.I.T. Press, 1960.

13 A similar symbolic systems strand has been proposed by Wilma S. Longstreet in her article, "The Demise of English," in: *Educational Horizons* 53 (4) :167-68; Summer 1975.

1. The Exploration of Images as Symbolic Systems: Free graphic (the encouragement not only of drawing but of graphic manipulation as, for instance, in the children's toy, the Spirograph) ; Diagrammatic and other model construction, e.g., constructing a model of school organization, making and using maps, diagramming an electric circuit, etc.; Projective geometry; Associationistic placement of filmed events; Two- and three-dimensional collages.

2. Mechanical Languages (restrained by the characteristics of a machine) : Computer programming (including the exploration of its bimodal premises) ; Computer language such as FORTRAN, COBOL, and SNOBOL; Transistor and other forms of communicating information to machines.

3. Precision Languages (free from the mechanical restrictions of machinery) : Mathematics (including diverse number bases), algebra, calculus, etc.; Statistics and its diverse applications; Scientific systems of research; Symbolic logic, set theory, information theory, etc.; Systematic representations of chemical interactions (possible as an elective development) .

4. Exploration of Music as Symbolic Systems: Various means of musical notations; Diverse systems underlying musical composition across cultures and historic periods; The meanings of non cursive sound; Active participation/reflective exploration of meanings and feelings derived from such participation.

5. Nonverbal Forms of Communication: Diverse systems of body movements (kinesics) ; Systematic spatial arrangements (proxemics) ; Meanings derived from touching (haptics) ; Diverse dance patterns across cultures and historic periods; Abstract forms and motions/reflection on how and what these communicate; Associationistic use of odors, colors, etc.; Reflection on how and what these communicate.

6. C   Language: Structural analysis of English and, possibly, one or more foreign languages; Reading/writing; Diverse literary forms and uses of English across cultures and historic periods; Comparison of diverse English dialects; Other graphemic systems based on oral language such as the international phonetic alphabet and Sir James Pitman's I/T/A.

These components are only an initial effort to expand the number of rational and other-than-rational symbolic systems dealt with in the school curriculum. There is every reason to believe that an improved set of components can be developed. While art, dance, music, and literary appreciation would not comprise a separate curricular core, some familiarity with these areas of expression are seen as an integral part of the symbolic systems strand. The broadening of the student's range of command over symbolic systems must mean dealing with these areas not merely for appreciation but for a fuller understanding of how they carry meaning and the qualitative differences of such meanings. The major purpose of the present, admittedly tentative outline of the symbolic strand is to demonstrate the feasibility of such a strand and to show its possible uses in an open curricular structure. Under free graphics, for example, a series of collages produced by famous modern artists could be presented to students as the delineated set of empiricals. They could be asked to find for each collage a concept or generalization best depicting the collage, offering their underlying reasoning or, at least, the impressions leading to their selection of concepts. Subsequently, a single concept such as "Power" could be the basis of free drawings by students. A comparison of drawings and an effort to determine similarities and differences in their free graphic representation of "power" would lead, hopefully, to the kind of reflective activity so often lacking while the image-packed experiences of television are occurring. With television in mind, a short excerpt from a T.V. show covering, say, ten minutes, and including a dramatic event of life, coupled with a commercial, but not including either the beginning or the end of the story, could be shown to students who would be asked to develop a series of questions about the excerpt. The nature of the questions and ways to vary their quality would become part of the next phase. This very brief curricular example is represented in Figure 6.

The development of Mechanical and Precisions languages, vital to the curricular design being proposed, could occur in their own right and as part of the instruments, processes, and procedures perspective, which is structured into all of the curricular strands. In their own right, not only would the necessary skills for their use be developed but a conceptual view of how each system influences and even modifies information would be emphasized. Experimental methods using controls would, for instance, be compared with statistical models that might be used to deal with the same information. Conceptual grasp of various symbolic systems is a major goal.

The Present Reality Strand. If youngsters are to achieve objectivity over their present circumstances, they must have objective knowledge of what those circumstances are. In part, the technology strand deals with these circumstances. However, the dominant forms of governance, the traditions and social institutions, the economic conditions and the state of international relations would be only indirectly dealt with under the technology strand. These must, of course, be squarely faced. A citizen who is to be an active participant in society must understand the intended

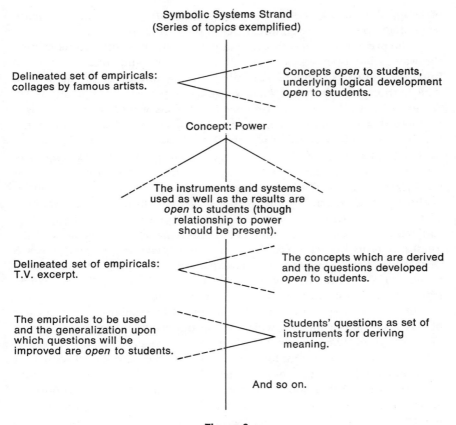

Figure 6.

and actual forms of his or her governance. He or she must also be aware of the phenomena, traditional and otherwise, molding the cultural milieu.

Although information about the structures of society would be a major thrust of the present reality strand, the effort to slow down enculturation, that is, to acquire the necessary distance from one's own cultural influences, would also be an important aspect of the strand. In this context, the achievement of concepts able to bridge different cultures and different historical periods would be the essential function of the strand.

While a conceptual approach to society has been used in schools before, often creating in youngsters the impression that human society has changed very little, the meshing of this strand with the technological and symbolic systems strands would change its results, hopefully, from a possibly apathetic complacency of "nothing-will-change-anyway" to one of being able to take stock of what is the reality, and what influence technology will bear on social realities in the future.

The presentation and subsequent development of concepts describing the way society operates and the effects of society and social interaction upon each of us as individuals would comprise one phase of this strand. The authors of this paper have suggested elsewhere that a set of six "action concepts" and their associated questions would be a useful way of organizing information about present realities. The "action concepts," which are equally applicable to describing broadly social and intimately personal situations, include: (a) conflict, (b) power, (c) valuing, (d) interaction, (e) change, and (f) adjustment.[14] Each concept is seen as the origin of a series of investigative questions that may be used in dealing with all possible topics of the present realities strand. Examples of the investigative questions are: How is power functioning? What conflicts are present? What changes are occurring, etc.? Refinement of the questions is to be achieved via continual exploration of the concepts themselves. For instance, power is explicated through authority and a number of different kinds of authority can be discerned. Power evolves from wealth as well as intellectual capacities, and so forth.

Other sets of concepts could be developed by students based on their research, say, about lobbies, which are so important in our present form of governance. The concept of influence and its place in a democratic society might be such a development if students were presented with a set of documents describing, among others, Nader's Raiders and the nationally organized Milk Lobby and requested to analyze the operations of governance from the point of view of a member of congress. On the other hand, students might be presented with a series of questions about governmental agencies. Their task would be to use the questions while researching several agencies with which they or their family have had personal experience. On the basis of the data collected, students would extend and revise the questions. As in the other strands, even though conceptual development would be emphasized, all three of the major apexes or perspectives would serve as alternating fulcrums for curricular organization.

The Bi-level Scenario: The Values Strand. In all of the strands, there would be not only a continual use of various kinds of analyses, but a repeated returning to questions of valuing. "Are there better ways?" and "Why are they better?" are questions that implicitly flow from every aspect of this curricular design. Technological advancements or modifica-

[14] Shirley H. Engle and Wilma S. Longstreet. *A Design for Social Education in the Open Curriculum.* New York: Harper & Row, Publishers, 1972.

tions in governance and/or traditions inevitably change our quality of life in general as well as our own personal way of living. However, for students to deal with such changes in ways meaningful to them, some mechanism for internalizing change as a real phenomenon having significance at the personal level is probably necessary. Collecting—analyzing —conceptualizing—even valuing technological data or structures of governance can be very distant and very unmeaningful to young people[15] unless there is an interception and an interfacing of what they are studying with their own daily life-styles. This is necessary if rational systems of valuing are to be experienced in their proper light of urgency. This strand is meant to achieve cogent but deeply felt ways of valuing in the young.

The employment of the bi-level scenario might help to give this otherwise distant study a sense of personal reality. The bi-level scenario would employ, in its first phase, the rational development of scenarios based on well-documented data, such as might be collected in a review of technological advances in weaponry systems. Students would be asked to forecast the future of society on the bases of the data and by use of statistics and other symbolic systems. Once these scenarios have been developed, and their probability of actually happening estimated, students would be asked to redevelop the scenarios in terms of their own lives. In other words, first students would explore the question, "What might the world be like?" and then the question of how that kind of world would change their own personal ways of living. In sum: "What might this mean for my life, for what I cherish, for what I hope to be?" etc. Subsequently, value questions, applied societally and personally, to the changes predicted would be explored by students.

A brief example of a bi-level scenario follows:

The Computer: A Prediction of Its Future Role in Society

The computer will be involved in most daily activities. A small computer will be available for installation in all kinds of vehicles. Trips made regularly, such as driving back and forth to work, will be programmed and computer-guided to their destinations. It is possible that autonomous driving will become obsolete.

The Computer: A Prediction of Its Future Role in My Life

I like to drive. The computer has interfered not only with my driving but with the places I can go to. I can't afford one of the more advanced computers so that I can't program a trip into the country. It seems every-

15 Alvin Toffler, author of *Future Shock,* came to this conclusion after numerous encounters with groups of young people and often refers to this in his various presentations.

thing I want to do has to fit a computer program. I wish I could work hard, taste sweat, feel the sun burn my cheeks. The computer says I am obsolete.

There are a series of value conflicts at both the societal and personal levels arising with the continued expansion of computer technology. Using processes derived from the symbolic systems strand, students could be asked to clarify their personal value systems. They could then be asked to research the value systems functioning at the societal level. A comparison of these might then lead to each student developing a set of generalizations about the relationship of his or her values to those held by the society at large. The bi-level scenario would be returned to frequently in an effort not only to explore what is valued personally or societally, but what priorities ought to be set for different kinds of values.

The mechanism of the scenario could further be used to achieve the alternating emphasis on the different apexes or perspectives underlying the structure of this open curriculum. In one phase, for example, students would have the data presented to them in a scenario and the learning experiences planned would involve the use of instruments and/or processes to achieve a set of generalizations about values; in another, the generalizations about values might be presented and students would be requested to modify technological progress so that the values expressed in the generalizations can be sustained, and so forth. To explore one's own concepts of what is desirable, important, and necessary, in light of information and in command of the most efficient instruments and processes available, is the major function of the values strand.

A Summary and Prologue. An essentially different kind of curricular structure has been proposed which would systematically plan studies alternating around one of three perspectives: a delineated set of empiricals/ideas, a set of concepts/generalizations/theories, and a set of suitable instruments/processes/procedures. Within each curricular phase, students would have open to them the determination of how the two perspectives not being used as foci are to be used in undertaking the curricular task. In this fashion, it is hoped to achieve the interfacing of curricular plans with the personal knowledge and experiences of students.

Four curricular strands have been proposed to act as major areas of curricular planning. The strands are seen as responses to the needs of a society in technological disarray and of a people in serious danger of losing all opportunity to participate effectively in the future directions of their society as well as of their own personal lives. Information and the control of information are seen as vital to the survival of a democratic form of governance and are fostered throughout the curriculum, but especially by the technological strand. The present realities strand also emphasizes knowing about the present state of governmental, institutional, and traditional societal structure. It is important to note, however, that the present realities strand places its major emphasis on the development of objective, conceptual ways of viewing one's own societal milieu in an effort to slow down enculturation. The symbolic systems strand, with its effort to expand into new areas of thought, is also believed to support a slowing of the enculturation process. The retention of rational skills along with the expansion into new symbolic systems are, however, the primary functions of the symbolic systems strand. Without an increase in individual intellectual skills and an accompanying willingness to make active use of these skills, the regaining of control over technological progress by individual citizens is seen as highly unlikely. The values strand with its bi-level scenario mechanism is an effort to increase personal willingness to participate in the significant decisions of society. In particular, personal and societal forms of valuing what is a desirable quality of life are intertwined and alternated in the hope that individual students will come to internalize what is happening in society as something happening to their own personal lives. The prioritization of values for individuals, for society, and for individuals in society is central to the strand's function.

The open curricular structure proposed here would involve not only a logical flow from one phase to the other along a curricular strand but also a continual interaction between strands so that the activities of one strand are overlapping and supportive of the other strands. What is more, positing student knowledge, experience, and choice as an essential ingredient of each strand is likely to make the interaction between strands, given the same group of students, even more consistent than the curriculum could achieve via a closed plan. Figure 7 is an overview of the proposed curriculum and should be compared with Figure 2 representing the traditional school curriculum.

The proposed curriculum does depart in significant ways from traditional curricula. The sciences *as disciplines* would not be studied until major aspects of the four proposed strands had been accomplished. Neither the arts nor history would be studied as separate subjects until the strands had been fairly well explored. Of course, implicit in the plans of the four strands are studies in the sciences and arts. The symbolic systems strand conceives of the methods of the sciences, the methods of logic, the methods of the arts, etc., as fundamental parts of human intellectual development over which more control or new kinds of control need to be attained. As such, there is active participation in all of the arts and considerable use of scientific systems as well. However, the study

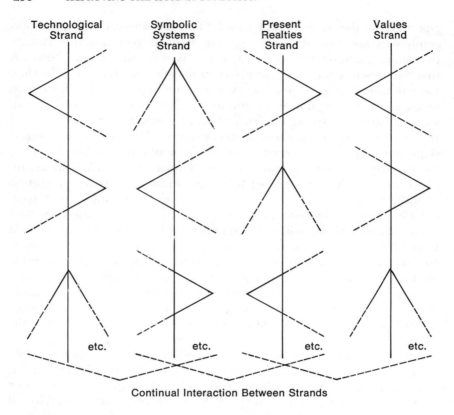

Continual Interaction Between Strands

Figure 7.

of these areas, for their own sakes and for the unique contributions that each makes to human knowledge, would be delayed until the last two or three years of schooling (as it is now organized).

The disciplines and discipline-like subjects are areas of specialization which should not be allowed to come between individual citizens regaining control of their destinies and the school curriculum. Presently, the intellectual isolation implicit in each discipline has been allowed to fill the function of intellectual preparation held by the schools. What this has meant, in practice, is the creation of a chasm between what people study in the schools and the way people participate in the major decisions of society. The open curricular structure proposed, with its active incorporation of the future, is an effort to bridge the chasm. When this has been done, the study of disciplines and even the search for one's own inner meanings are proper concerns for the schools.

One final note: The development of the open curricular design does not assure the accomplishment of an open education system. The instructional methodologies adopted by teachers and the bureaucratic organization of the schools are of fundamental importance to the success of the enterprise proposed here. If administrators insist on lists of specific objectives, standardized testing and the purchase of textbooks to be utilized for a minimum five-year period, the results of schooling are not likely to reflect the open curricular design; and if teachers persist in students knowing the right answers or awaiting directions before any investigative study is undertaken, the curriculum may seem different but the results will be as per usual. Truly open education can foster the unpredictable development of complex human systems for dealing with complex social life. It is a way of opening the intellect to its own potential.

Selected Readings

Jerome S. Bruner. *Toward a Theory of Instruction*. Cambridge, Massachusetts: Belknap Press, 1955.

Lee J. Cronbach. *Educational Psychology*. New York: Harcourt Brace Jovanovich, Inc., 1963.

Shirley H. Engle and Wilma S. Longstreet. *A Design for Social Education in the Open Curriculum*. New York: Harper & Row, Publishers, 1972.

Susan Ervin. *New Directions in the Study of Language*. Eric Lenneberg, editor. Cambridge, Massachusetts: M.I.T. Press, 1966.

John I. Goodlad. "Schooling and Education." Unpublished paper. 1969.

Willis W. Harmin. "The Nature of Our Changing Society: Implications for Schools." In: David E. Purpel and Maurice Belanger, editors. *Curriculum and the Cultural Revolution*. Berkeley: McCutchan Publishing Corporation, 1972.

Wilma S. Longstreet. "The Demise of English." *Educational Horizons* 53: 167-68; Summer 1975.

Marshall McLuhan. *Understanding Media: The Extension of Man*. New York: Signet Books, 1964.

Willard Van Orman Quine. *Word and Object*. Cambridge, Massachusetts: M.I.T. Press, 1960.

Carl R. Rogers. "Interpersonal Relationships: U.S.A. 2000." *The Journal of Applied Behavioral Science* 4 (3) ; 1968.

Alvin Toffler. *Future Shock*. New York: Bantam Books, Inc., 1970.

L. S. Vygotsky. *Thought and Language*. Eugenia Hartman and Gertrude Vakar, editors. Cambridge, Massachusetts: M.I.T. Press, 1960.

Alfred North Whitehead. "Introduction." In: Wallace B. Dunham, editor. *Business Adrift*. New York: McGraw-Hill Book Company, 1931.

ASCD 1978 Yearbook
Committee Members

James John Jelinek, *Chairperson and Editor,* Emeritus Professor, Arizona State University, Tempe

James B. Boyer, Professor of Curriculum and Instruction, College of Education, Kansas State University, Manhattan

Paul F-Brandwein, Editor in Chief, Harcourt Brace Jovanovich, Inc., New York, New York

Shirley H. Engle, Professor Emeritus of Education, Indiana University, Bloomington

Pauline Gratz, Professor of Human Ecology, School of Nursing, Duke University, Durham, North Carolina

Arthur Hoppe, Professor of Education, Northern Illinois University, DeKalb

Wilma S. Longstreet, Professor of Education, The University of Michigan, Flint

Jerry C. McGee, Associate Professor of Education, Tennessee State University, Nashville

Stephen Viederman, Head, Social and Demographic Research Technical Unit, United Nations Fund for Population Activities, United Nations, New York.

The Authors

NORMAN ABRAMOWITZ is an Associate in Foreign Area Studies at the Center for International Programs and Comparative Studies, New York State Education Department. He received his bachelor of arts degree, Phi Beta Kappa, from the City College of New York and his master of arts degree in history from the University of Tennessee. He has served as a researcher and reviewer of New York State social studies syllabi in area studies and is the author of articles on teaching international studies. He is the co-author, with William A. Nesbitt, of a teacher's guide to *Teaching Youth About Conflict and War,* published by the National Council for the Social Studies, 1973.

JAMES B. BOYER is Professor of Curriculum and Instruction and former Director of the Institute on Cultural Understanding at Kansas State University. He attended Bethune-Cookman College, Colorado State University, Florida A&M University, and completed his Ph.D. degree in curriculum and instruction at Ohio State University. Dr. Boyer is a member of the Association for Childhood Education International and the Association for Study of Afro-American Life and History. He is recipient of the Martin Luther King Award for Contribution to Higher Education. His recent books include *Curriculum and Instruction After Desegregation* and *Curriculum Desegregation in Public Schools: An Action Manual.*

PAUL F-BRANDWEIN is Senior Vice President, Harcourt Brace Jovanovich, Inc., and Head, School Curriculum and Instruction Group. He is also Vice Chairman for the International Center for Educational Advancement in Florence, Italy; Adjunct Professor, University of Pittsburgh, and member of the National Humanities Faculty. He is primarily interested in developing a coordinated curriculum in the elementary school, and toward this end he has been curricular designer and senior author of three programs of instruction and learning in the elementary schools: *Concepts in Science; The Social Sciences: Concepts and Values;* and *Self Expression and Conduct: The Humanities.* He

262

is author and co-author of 55 books and numerous research articles in science and education.

SHIRLEY H. ENGLE is Professor Emeritus of Education at Indiana University where he taught for 31 years. Prior to earning his doctorate in education at the University of Illinois, he taught for 14 years in the public schools. His writings include over 20 articles, the co-authorship of two books, the editorship of one NCSS Yearbook and the authorship of numerous chapters in the yearbooks of NCSS and ASCD. His best-known writing is an article "Decision Making: The Heart of Social Studies Instruction" published in *Social Education* (November 1960) which was widely quoted and reprinted. More recently, Dr. Engle co-authored, with Wilma Longstreet, a book, *A Design for Social Education in the Open Curriculum,* published by Harper & Row in 1972 which addresses the topic of this yearbook.

GERALD V. FLANNERY is a Professor of Mass Communication and head of the broadcast journalism area at Middle Tennessee State University. His professional background includes work in nearly every aspect of mass media, notably as a writer and critic. He holds a B.A. in journalism, an M.A. in communications, and a Ph.D. in speech with emphasis in television/radio/film. He has developed and taught large section mass media courses for general education students as well as mass communication majors at several universities. He writes television documentaries and publishes articles in journals and magazines.

PAULINE GRATZ is Professor of Human Ecology in Nursing at Duke University Medical Center, Durham, North Carolina. She is a graduate of Hunter College of the City University of New York with an M.A. and Ed.D. from Teachers College, Columbia University. Prior to joining the faculty at Duke University, she was an Associate Professor of Natural Sciences at Teachers College, Columbia University and taught in the area of human ecological problems. She has published extensively in the area of environmental problems and interdisciplinary teaching. Professor Gratz is author of *Integrated Science—An Interdisciplinary Approach* and a forthcoming book in Human Ecology.

FREDERICK M. HARRIS is a doctoral student in education at Kansas State University, Manhattan, Kansas. He assisted Dr. James Boyer and Dr. Rudolph E. Waters in the writing of Chapter 6 in this volume, "Justice, Society, and the Individual."

RALPH E. HILLMAN is an Assistant Professor of Speech at Middle Tennessee State University. He has taught in the elementary and secondary schools of Illinois and Hawaii and served on the faculty in the university systems in Pennsylvania, Wisconsin, and Ohio. He has taught Speech Methods for secondary teachers, placed and supervised student teachers, and trained graduate student instructors. He has published several articles in the area of communication.

ARTHUR HOPPE is Professor of Education at Northern Illinois University. His persistent interests have been the application of democracy to school affairs and the humanizing of education. But his first interest has been teaching, mostly in curriculum and instruction, at William and Mary, George Washington, Indiana, Temple, and NIU. He has been a long-time member of the Curriculum Professors and of ASCD, having served as Chairman of the Core/General Education Commission, as editor of the columns on Curriculum Bulletins and Curriculum Development in *Educational Leadership,* and as State President of ASCD in Indiana.

JAMES JOHN JELINEK, Chairperson of the ASCD 1978 Yearbook Committee and Editor of the Yearbook, is Emeritus Professor at Arizona State University, Tempe, Arizona. He is a former high school teacher, department chairman, college dean, newspaper and literary critic, professor of humanities and social sciences, member of the ASCD Board of Directors, Factotum of the Professors of Curriculum, and member of the Executive Committee of The John Dewey Society. He has written 48 books, some of which are *Principles and Values in School and Society, The Professional Education of Teachers in American Democracy, The General Education of Teachers in America,* and *The High School in Sociological and Philosophical Perspective.* At present he serves as editor of the Far Western Philosophy of Education Society.

ANDREW J. LEIGHTON has earned a bachelor's degree in economics from Hartwick College (Oneonta, New York) and a master's degree in sociology and education with special emphasis in population education from Teachers College, Columbia University. While co-authoring Chapter 5 in this volume, he was a research assistant in the Demographic Division of the Population Council in New York City. Presently he is employed as a consultant in the Textbook Evaluation Program of the Population Institute in Washington, D.C.

WILMA S. LONGSTREET is a Professor of Education at the University of Michigan-Flint. She received her Ph.D. in curriculum from Indiana University. Her publications include, among others, *A Design for Social Education in the Open Curriculum* (with Shirley H. Engle), *Beyond Jencks: The Myth of Equal Schooling* (ASCD, 1973) and a chapter in the 1973 NSSE Yearbook. Areas of her present research deal with the effects of ethnic diversity in public school teaching, and the exploration of "decision making" as a fulcrum of social studies curriculum development.

JERRY CANTRELL MCGEE is an Associate Professor of Education at Tennessee State University, Nashville. He has been a school teacher, supervisor, assistant superintendent, and college dean. He has published over 35 articles and monographs. He has served for the past five years as editor of the *Tennessee Association for Supervision and Curriculum Development Journal.* He is a past president of the Tennessee ASCD.

WILLIAM L. RIVERS is the Paul C. Edwards Professor of Communication at Stanford University. He has written and researched widely in the communication field, most notably in mass media, and his publications number in the hundreds. Several of his widely used books are *The Mass Media, The Mass Media and Modern Society, The Adversaries,* and *The Opinionmakers.*

RENEE RODGERS, doctoral student at Arizona State University, served as an Intern for Dr. Jelinek in the editing of this book.

STEPHEN VIEDERMAN is Head, Social and Demographic Research Technical Unit, United Nations Fund for Population Activities. Trained as a historian, he has been involved in a variety of projects relating to the social sciences and education in the U.S. and overseas during the past 20 years. He co-authored *The Behaviorial and Social Sciences: Outlook and Needs* and a major UNESCO report on the conceptualization of population education published in 1977. In addition, he has authored more than 30 articles. His main interests are ethical issues in education, and educational planning and change.

RUDOLPH E. WATERS is Vice President of Alcorn State University, Alcorn, Mississippi.

266

Board Members Elected at Large

James A. Banks, University of Washington, Seattle (1980)

Gwyn Brownlee, Education Service Center, Region 10, Richardson, Texas (1979)

Reba Burnham, University of Georgia, Athens (1981)

Virgie Chattergy, University of Hawaii, Honolulu, Hawaii (1981)

Theodore Czajkowski, Public Schools, Madison, Wisconsin (1980)

Ivan J. K. Dahl, University of North Dakota, Grand Forks (1979)

Lawrence S. Finkel, Chester Township Public Schools, Chester, New Jersey (1979)

Ben M. Harris, University of Texas, Austin (1980)

Lucille G. Jordan, Public Schools, Atlanta, Georgia (1978)

Chon LaBrier, Dulce Independent School, New Mexico (1978)

Ardelle Llewellyn, San Francisco State University, San Francisco, California (1981)

Norman V. Overly, Indiana University, Bloomington (1978)

Marshall C. Perritt, Shelby County Schools, Memphis, Tennessee (1980)

James A. Raths, University of Illinois, Urbana (1978)

Mary-Margaret Scobey, Educational Consultant, Eugene, Oregon (1979)

Dolores Silva, Temple University, Philadelphia, Pennsylvania (1978)

Ronald Stodghill, Public Schools, St. Louis, Missouri (1981)

Bob Taylor, University of Colorado, Boulder (1981)

Georgia Williams, Unified School District, Berkeley, California (1980)

Mary J. Wood, Public Schools, Las Cruces, New Mexico (1979)

Unit Representatives to the Board of Directors

(Each Unit's President is listed first; others follow in alphabetical order.)

Alabama: J. V. Sailors, Morgan County Public Schools, Decatur; Alvis Harthern, University of Montevallo, Montevallo; Dorthea Grace Rockarts, University of Alabama, University.

Arizona: Mary Belle McCorkle, Public Schools, Tucson; Mary Rill, Public Schools, Phoenix; Ben Furlong, Kyrene School District, Tempe.

Arkansas: Philip Besonen, University of Arkansas, Fayetteville; James C. Williams, Geyer Springs Baptist Church, Little Rock.

California (liaison): William Georgiades, University of Southern California, Los Angeles; Leonard Herbst, Moreland School District, San Jose; Jessie Kobayashi, Whisman Elementary School District, Mountain View; David Martin, Mill Valley School District, Mill Valley.

Colorado: Dale F. Graham, Adams School District #14, Commerce City; Alex Reuter, Northglenn-Thornton School District 12, Denver; P. L. Schmelzer, Poudre School District R-1, Fort Collins.

Connecticut: Joan D. Kerelejza, West Hartford Public Schools; Philmore Wass, University of Connecticut, Storrs.

Delaware: Donald H. H. Wachter, Delaware Department of Public Instruction, Dover; William J. Bailey, University of Delaware, Newark.

District of Columbia: Jacqueline T. Robertson, Public Schools, Washington; Andrea J. Irby, Public Schools, Washington; Phyllis J. Hobson, Public Schools, Washington.

Florida: Patrick F. Mooney, Public Schools, Miami; Charles Godwin, Palm Beach County Schools, West Palm Beach; Richard Stewart, Lee County Schools, Ft. Myers; Charlotte Eden Umholtz, Hillsborough County Schools, Tampa.

Georgia: Iris Goolsby, DeKalb County Schools, Decatur; George W. Stansbury, Georgia State University, Atlanta; Martha Sue Jordan, University of Georgia, Athens.

Hawaii: Albert Tamaribuchi, Kailua Intermediate School, Honolulu; Elmer S. Dunsky, Chaminade College, Honolulu.

Idaho: Caroline Hulse, Nampa School District 131, Nampa; David A. Carroll, Public Schools, Boise.

Illinois: Luceille Werner, Southern Will County Public Schools, Peotone; Leone Bergfield, Public Schools, Litchfield; R. Kim Driggers, Public Schools, Centralia; Chester Dugger, Public Schools, Peoria; Raymond E. Hendee, Public Schools, Park Ridge; Blanche Martin, Public Schools, Rockford; Donald W. Nylin, Public Schools, Aurora.

Indiana: Charles E. Kline, Purdue University, West Lafayette; Clive C. Beattie, Public Schools, Portage; Donna Delph, Purdue University, Hammond; Imogene Jones, Public Schools, Portage.

Iowa: Robert Pittman, Public Schools, Clinton; Joe Lamberti, University of Northern Iowa, Cedar Falls; Robert Wrider, Public Schools, Waterloo.

Kansas: Weldon Zenger, Fort Hayes State University, Hayes; Walter L. Davies, Public Schools, Kansas City; Paul Koehn, Public Schools, Concordia.

Kentucky: J. R. Ogletree, University of Kentucky, Lexington; William Bolton, Clark County Public Schools, Winchester; Ernest H. Garner, Public Schools, Bowling Green.

Louisiana: E. Patsy Maloney, Public Schools, New Orleans; Darryl W. Boudreaux, St. Mary Parish Schools, Morgan City; Julianna Boudreaux, Public Schools, New Orleans; Edwin H. Friedrich, (retired) Public Schools, New Orleans.

Maine: Phillip A. Gonyar, Public Schools, Bangor; Kenneth E. Marks, Public Schools, Farmington.

Maryland: Ruth Burkins, Harford County Board of Education, Bel Air; Louise M. Berman, University of Maryland, College Park; Benjamin P. Ebersole, Baltimore County Board of Education, Towson; Janice Wickless, Maryland State Department of Education, Baltimore.

Massachusetts: Paul V. Congdon, Springfield College, Springfield; Gilbert Bulley, Public Schools, Lynnfield; C. Louis Cedrone, Public Schools, Westwood; Carolyn Teixeira, Public Schools, Wellesley Hills.

Michigan: David Newbury, Public Schools, Hazel Park; William Cansfield, Public Schools, Mt. Clemens; LaBarbara Gragg, Wayne County Intermediate School District, Wayne; James L. Leary, Public Schools, Walled Lake; Stuart Rankin, Public Schools, Detroit; Virginia Sorenson, Western Michigan University, Grand Rapids.

Minnesota: Arnold W. Ness, Independent School District 256, Red Wing; Richard Kimpston, University of Minnesota, Minneapolis; Marjorie Neihart, Public Schools, St. Paul.

Mississippi: Robert J. Cagle, Public Schools, Greenwood; Norvel Burkett, Mississippi State University, State College.

Missouri: Harold E. Turner, University of Missouri, St. Louis; William Anthony, Public

Schools, Jefferson City; Frank Morley, Ladue School District, St. Louis; Patricia Rocklage, Normandy School District, St. Louis.

Montana: Henry Worrest, Montana State University, Bozeman; Donald R. Waldron, Public Schools, Libby.

Nebraska: Marlin Nelson, Public Schools, Ralston; Ron Brandt, Public Schools, Lincoln; Dorothy Hall, Public Schools, Omaha.

Nevada: Edward Howard, Nevada Department of Education, Carson City; Melvin Kirchner, Washoe County School District, Reno.

New England: Philmore Wass, University of Connecticut, Storrs; Jeanne M. Gardner, Rhode Island Department of Education, Providence.

New Jersey: William R. Kievit, Public Schools, Morristown; Mary Jane Diehl, Monmouth College, Witong Branch; Jean L. Green, Public Schools, Morristown; Frank Jaggard, Public Schools, Cinnaminson; Nicholas J. Sferrazza, Gloucester Township Public Schools, Blackwood; Arnold D. Tversky, Public Schools, Dover.

New Mexico: Chon LaBrier, Public Schools, Dulce; Patricia Christman, Public Schools, Albuquerque.

New York: James A. Beane, St. Bonaventure University, St. Bonaventure; Robert S. Brellis, Public Schools, Ronkonkoma; Thomas E. Curtis, State University of New York, Albany; Frank Dunn, State University of New York College, Potsdam; Albert J. Eichel, Lawrence Public Schools, Cedarhurst; Helen Gerhardt, Public Schools, Rochester; Marcia Knoll, Public Schools, Forest Hills; Conrad Toepfer, Jr., State University of New York, Buffalo.

North Carolina: Donald T. Lassiter, Nash County Schools, Nashville; Lucille Bazemore, Bertie County Schools, Windsor; Robert C. Hanes, Chapel Hill/Carrboro City Schools, Chapel Hill; Marcus C. Smith, Public Schools, Salisbury.

North Dakota: Quinn Brunson, The University of North Dakota, Grand Forks.

Ohio: M. Herman Sims, Ohio Department of Education, Columbus; Michael Barnhart, Public Schools, Troy; John Cunningham, Public Schools, Mansfield; Carolyn Sue Hughes, Public Schools, Parma; Charles A. Loparo, Public Schools, Brecksville; James K. Uphoff, Wright State University, Celina.

Oklahoma: Nelda Tebow, Public Schools, Oklahoma City; Russell B. Dobson, Oklahoma State University, Stillwater.

Oregon: Vera Larson (retired), Public Schools, Portland; Max L. Brunton, Public Schools, Portland; Trostel Werth, Public Schools, Gresham.

Pennsylvania: John R. Reitz, Wilson School District, Reading; Bertha Boyd, Pennsylvania State Department of Education, Harrisburg; Kenneth R. Chuska, Peters Township School District, McMurray; Gladys E. Creagmile, Philadelphia School District 8; Joseph H. Kane, Methacton School District, Fairview Village; Edgar L. Lawton, Clarion Manor Intermediate Unit, Shippensville.

Puerto Rico: Gladys Davila de Fuente, University of Puerto Rico, Rio Piedras; Ilia Del Toro, University of Puerto Rico, Rio Piedras.

Rhode Island: Guy N. DiBiasio, Public Schools, Cranston; Sidney Rollins, Rhode Island College, Providence.

South Carolina: Joe Bonds, Public Schools, Florence; Elmer Knight, South Carolina Department of Education, Columbia; John L. Sprawls, Public Schools, Columbia.

South Dakota: Maizie R. Solem, Public Schools, Sioux Falls; A. Joyce Levin, South Dakota State Department of Education, Pierre.

Tennessee: Aubrey Moseley, Middle Tennessee State University, Murfreesboro; Barbara G. Burch, Memphis State University, Memphis; Jack Roberts, Tennessee State Department of Education, Knoxville.

Texas: Vance K. Bearden, Public Schools, Greenville; M. George Bowden, Public Schools, Austin; R. C. Bradley, North Texas State University, Denton; Rita Bryant,

Texas Eastern University, Tyler; Dwane Russell, Stephen F. Austin State University, Nacogdoches; James L. Williamson, Pan American University, Edinburg.

Utah: Florence C. Chandler, Public Schools, Salt Lake City; Florence Barton, Weber State College, Ogden.

Vermont: Philip Dwyer, Public Schools, Castleton; Robert Kellogg, Vermont State Department of Education, Montpelier.

Virginia: Lois Jones, Public Schools, Richmond; Gennette Nygard, Arlington Public Schools; Bob Sigmon, Public Schools, Richmond; Russell L. Watson, Campbell County Schools, Rustburg.

Washington: Ted Knutsen, Public Schools, Oak Harbor; Roy Duncan, Public Schools, Pasco; Donald Hair, Washington State Office of Public Instruction, Olympia.

West Virginia: Mary Lou Fluharty, Monongalia County Schools; Betty Livengood, Mineral County Schools, Keyser.

Wisconsin: James Ticknor, Public Schools, Rio; Russell Mosely, Wisconsin Department of Public Instruction, Madison; Ronald Sime, Public Schools, Plattville.

Wyoming: Cameron Kent Allen, University of Wyoming, Laramie; Leo Breeden, Public Schools, Cheyenne.

ASCD
Review Council

271

ASCD
Headquarters Staff

Executive Director: Gordon Cawelti

Associate Director; Editor, ASCD Publications: Robert R. Leeper

Associate Director: Ruth T. Long

Associate Director: Roosevelt Ratliff

Governmental Relations Coordinator: Steven Hallmark

Business Manager: John H. Bralove

Administrative Assistant: Virginia O. Berthy

Staff Assistants: Elsa Angell, Sarah Arlington, Joan Brandt, Clara M. Burleigh, Barbara Collins, Patricia M. Connors, Anita Fitzpatrick, Teola T. Jones, Anne Loucks, Frances Mindel, Nancy Olson, Ruth Peterson, Charlene Rothkopf, Carolyn Shell, Barbara J. Sims, Larry Sims, Christine Smith, Myra K. Taub, Doris K. Wilkerson, Colette A. Williams, Linda Wysocki

Acknowledgments

Final editing of the manuscript and publication of this booklet were the responsibility of Robert R. Leeper, Associate Director and Editor, ASCD publications. Additional editorial and production services were provided by Elsa Angell, with the assistance of Production Manager Nancy Olson, Myra K. Taub, Teola T. Jones, Patsy Connors, and Charlene Rothkopf. The cover and design of this volume are by Linda S. Sherman.

ASCD Publications, Spring 1978

Yearbooks

Education for an Open Society (610-74012)	$8.00
Education for Peace: Focus on Mankind (610-17946)	$7.50
Evaluation as Feedback and Guide (610-17700)	$6.50
Feeling, Valuing, and the Art of Growing: Insights into the Affective (610-77104)	$9.75
Freedom, Bureaucracy, & Schooling (610-17508)	$6.50
Improving the Human Condition: A Curricular Response to Critical Realities (610-78132)	$9.75
Learning and Mental Health in the School (610-17674)	$5.00
Life Skills in School and Society (610-17786)	$5.50
A New Look at Progressive Education (610-17812)	$8.00
Perspectives on Curriculum Development 1776-1976 (610-76078)	$9.50
Schools in Search of Meaning (610-75044)	$8.50
Perceiving, Behaving, Becoming: A New Focus for Education (610-17278)	$5.00
To Nurture Humaneness: Commitment for the '70's (610-17810)	$6.00

Books and Booklets

About Learning Materials (611-78134)	$4.50
Action Learning: Student Community Service Projects (611-74018)	$2.50
Adventuring, Mastering, Associating: New Strategies for Teaching Children (611-76080)	$5.00
Beyond Jencks: The Myth of Equal Schooling (611-17928)	$2.00
The Changing Curriculum: Mathematics (611-17724)	$2.00
Criteria for Theories of Instruction (611-17756)	$2.00
Curricular Concerns in a Revolutionary Era (611-17852)	$6.00
Curriculum Leaders: Improving Their Influence (611-76084)	$4.00
Curriculum Theory (611-77112)	$7.00
Degrading the Grading Myths: A Primer of Alternatives to Grades and Marks (611-76082)	$6.00
Differentiated Staffing (611-17924)	$3.50
Discipline for Today's Children and Youth (611-17314)	$1.50
Educational Accountability: Beyond Behavioral Objectives (611-17856)	$2.50
Elementary School Mathematics: A Guide to Current Research (611-75056)	$5.00
Elementary School Science: A Guide to Current Research (611-17726)	$2.25
Eliminating Ethnic Bias in Instructional Materials: Comment and Bibliography (611-74020)	$3.25

Emerging Moral Dimensions in Society: Implications for Schooling (611-75052)	$3.75
Ethnic Modification of Curriculum (611-17832)	$1.00
Global Studies: Problems and Promises for Elementary Teachers (611-76086)	$4.50
The Humanities and the Curriculum (611-17708)	$2.00
Impact of Decentralization on Curriculum: Selected Viewpoints (611-75050)	$3.75
Improving Educational Assessment & An Inventory of Measures of Affective Behavior (611-17804)	$4.50
International Dimension of Education (611-17816)	$2.25
Interpreting Language Arts Research for the Teacher (611-17846)	$4.00
Learning More About Learning (611-17310)	$2.00
Linguistics and the Classroom Teacher (611-17720)	$2.75
A Man for Tomorrow's World (611-17838)	$2.25
Middle School in the Making (611-74024)	$5.00
The Middle School We Need (611-75060)	$2.50
Multicultural Education: Commitments, Issues, and Applications (611-77108)	$7.00
Needs Assessment: A Focus for Curriculum Development (611-75048)	$4.00
Observational Methods in the Classroom (611-17948)	$3.50
Open Education: Critique and Assessment (611-75054)	$4.75
Open Schools for Children (611-17916)	$3.75
Professional Supervision for Professional Teachers (611-75046)	$4.50
Removing Barriers to Humaneness in the High School (611-17848)	$2.50
Reschooling Society: A Conceptual Model (611-17950)	$2.00
The School of the Future—NOW (611-17920)	$3.75
Schools Become Accountable: A PACT Approach (611-74016)	$3.50
The School's Role as Moral Authority (611-77110)	$4.50
Social Studies for the Evolving Individual (611-17952)	$3.00
Staff Development: Staff Liberation (611-77106)	$6.50
Supervision: Emerging Profession (611-17796)	$5.00
Supervision in a New Key (611-17926)	$2.50
Supervision: Perspectives and Propositions (611-17732)	$2.00
What Are the Sources of the Curriculum? (611-17522)	$1.50
Vitalizing the High School (611-74026)	$3.50
Developmental Characteristics of Children and Youth (wall chart) (611-75058)	$2.00

Discounts on quantity orders of same title to single address: 10-49 copies, 10%; 50 or more copies, 15%. Make checks or money orders payable to ASCD. Orders totaling $10.00 or less must be prepaid. Orders from institutions and businesses must be on official purchase order form. Shipping and handling charges will be added to billed purchase orders. **Please be sure to list the stock number of each publication, shown in parentheses.**

Subscription to **Educational Leadership**—$10.00 a year. ASCD Membership dues: Regular (subscription and yearbook)—$25.00 a year; Comprehensive (includes subscription and yearbook plus other books and booklets distributed during period of membership)—$35.00 a year.

Order from: **Association for Supervision and Curriculum Development**
Suite 1100, 1701 K Street, N.W., Washington, D.C. 20006